"Cornets & Pickaxes is rich, rare, illuminating, and triumphant fanfare to the remarkable musical communities of "ordinary" Finnish Americans, painstakingly yet exuberantly created from interviews, photographs, newspaper accounts, sheet music, reminiscences, and other mostly ephemeral sources that would have eluded a less dedicated and able researcher."

--James P. Leary
Birgit Baldwin Professor of Scandinavian Studies
Director, Center for the Study of Upper Midwestern Cultures
University of Wisconsin-Madison

" I am one of the newer Finnish musicians in Minnesota. But we can look back more than a century to when hundreds of them came here to play in brass bands in the mining and lumbering communities "up north." Paul Niemisto's new book "Cornets & Pickaxes" is the first written history of that era of music making and these pages make a convincing case that the Finns made a great contribution to Minnesota culture. It is also a good overview of the band music history in Finland and a summary of contemporary musical life among Finnish Americans."

--Osmo Vänskä, Music Director and Conductor
Minnesota Orchestra

"It is with pleasure that I recommend important work on Finnish and Finnish American bands by Paul Niemisto particularly as he shows their role as a part of American culture. "Cornets & Pickaxes" includes exhaustive detail on the subject. In fact the book is encyclopedic in its coverage of those instrumental groups in both the old country and the US. Thus the work is a scholarly contribution to colleagues in the field as well as a stimulus to students interested in the subject. In that regard it is a model for others with its lengthy bibliography and its prolific original visuals."

--Victor Greene, Emeritus Professor of History
University of Wisconsin - Milwaukee
Author of "Passion for Polka"- Old Time Ethnic Music in America

"A town without its brass band is as much in need of sympathy as a church without a choir. The spirit of a place is recognized in its band." So wrote William H. Dana, in his 1878 Practical Guide. *When there were very few orchestras, the presence of a band was a status symbol; it was estimated that by 1889 there were more than 10,000 bands active in the United States. Those same years saw a large Finnish emigration, and it should not be surprising that they brought their brass bands with them as part of their cultural heritage. Paul Niemisto, in his* Cornets and Pickaxes, *has exhaustively researched these Finnish bands, with special emphasis on the Iron Range region of northern Minesota. While quickly assimilating American brass band tradition, the Finns also retained a special brass combination, the 7-piece* Amerikan poijat, *both types of ensembles flourishing in the many small communities. Niemisto's book, while thoroughly scholarly, provides an accessible, readable and enjoyable historical narrative."*

--Raoul F. Camus
Professor Emeritus of Music, The City University of New York.
Historian, The American Bandmasters Association

Cornets & Pickaxes

Finnish Brass on the Iron Range

by

Paul Niemisto

Cornets & Pickaxes

Finnish Brass on the Iron Range

Published by

APMusic

Finnish American Musical Research, Performance, and Publication

608 Zanmiller Dr W

Northfield, Minnesota 55057

www.ameriikanpoijat.org

Ameriikan poijat is a non-profit organiation.

affiliated with the Finlandia Foundation Twin Cities Chapter

Printed by Book Concern Printers

Book Publisher to Finnish America since 1888

129 E. Franklin St. P.O. Box 330 Hancock, Michigan 49930

www.bookconcernprinters.com

Niemisto, Paul

Cornets & Pickaxes: Finnish Brass on the Iron Range /

Niemisto, Paul p. cm.

ISBN 978-1-4675-7527-0

1. Finns>Minnesota>History. 2. Finnish American Musicians. 3.Finnish Americans. 4. Minnesota Musical Tradition. 5. Brass Bands> United States> History. 6. Music and Socialism. . 7. Minnesota> Emigration and Immigration> History.

HF0000.A0 A00 2010

299.000 00–dc22 2010999999

First Edition

14 13 12 11 10 / 10 9 8 7 6 5 4 3 2 1

DEDICATION

This book is dedicated to the memory of those first researchers who defined the study of Finnish American culture: Minnesotans Mike Karni, Timo Riippa, Matti Kaups, Carl Ross, and even though I never met him, Doug Ollila. They led me on the path to the Iron Range and into the spirits of the Finnish immigrant musicians. Finally, this book honors Simo "Holmi" Westerholm, Kaustinen ethnomusicologist and tenor horn player in the Kaustinen Seitsikko, who took great interest in this research and was my Finnish "guru" until the very end. I really wish I could put a copy of the book in his hands.

FOREWORD

Under the North Star, the first book in Vaino Linna's North Star Trilogy on the Finnish Civil War, begins with a classic literary comment, "In the beginning there were the marsh, the hoe – and Jussi."

Americans who have read the trilogy are instantly caught up in the hardships our ancestors faced no matter where they were living before coming to America. By the time readers get into Linna's second book, The Uprising, people from Minnesota, Wisconsin and the Upper Peninsula of Michigan have to wonder how we kept the Finnish Civil War (1918) from spilling over into our own towns, countryside and city streets.

This extends far beyond the Finns. Minneapolis schools report 9,200 students are from homes where languages other than English are spoken. Approximately 90 different languages make English the second language for these families. Ethnic and national origin data from the 2010 Census are still forthcoming, but the U.S. Census Bureau used 94 different origin categories from 2000 to profile Minnesotans in 2004.

To a remarkable degree, we have kept the Balkan wars and ethnic strife from playing out on the Minnesota Iron Range and other communities. We hold the Somali Civil War at arms lengths from the streets of Minneapolis, Rochester and other cities in the Midwest. Hmong, Cambodians, Laotians, Vietnamese and other refugees from Asian conflicts are integrating into the fabric of St. Paul and Wisconsin cities. Like in Linna's third book of his trilogy, Reconciliation, we should recognize Upper Midwest states and all of America have religious leaders, community leaders, school officials, union leaders, nonprofit organizations and even community band leaders and musicians to thank for keeping the peace, bonding community, and moving society forward.

Paul Niemisto's Cornets & Pickaxes offers an anthropological and sociological glimpse at how music makers bring harmony to our communities. The role of culture in creating community cohesion enriches us, doesn't divide us, and remains under-appreciated in our land of immigrants and refugees. Let this be the first of multi-disciplinary looks at ethnic and national origin cultural contributions to making a new America, and let Niemisto's Finns shine a light for newer Americans to follow.

Lee Egerstrom is an economic development fellow at Minnesota 2020, a public policy think tank in St. Paul, MN. He has been a journalist and writer on economic development and rural history.

FRONTISPIECE

Figure 1: Rice River Finnish Band, Rice River, Minnesota, Eero Matara, bandmaster. Date unkown.

Picture from the Iron Range Research Library, Chisholm, Minnesota

TABLE OF CONTENTS

ILLUSTRATIONS

Cover: The cover photograph was taken by Mark McGee with items collected by the author: a silver cornet borrowed from the Baraga High School (Michigan) band room, a band cap borrowed from Minnesota music historian and collector Paul Mayberry, a pick axe from Risto's Hardware in Hancock (Michigan), and a miner's helmet with carbide lamp from Quincy's Bar in Dollar Bay (Michigan). The backdrop is the paving stones outside the Finnish American Heritage Center, Finlandia University, Hancock (Michigan).

Inside Cover: a panoramic photograph of the Northern Minnesota Band League Festival, held in Virginia, Minnesota, 1915. Photo courtesy the Virginia Historical Society.

INTRODUCTION

Severus Ruuhela poses with his cornet, and puts down his cigar for the Bovey Finnish Miner's Band Midsummer photograph. Seen in Figure 1 in a hayfield near the edge of town after the parade, these well dressed boys were among the thousands of Finnish immigrants who settled on the Minnesota Iron Range around 1900, many amateur brass players came with high hopes of forming bands in the new iron mining communities. Brass-band playing had become an integral part of community culture among the working class in Finland since about 1880. The musicians hoped for an easy continuation of this tradition in North America, but were often surprised by the challenges presented.

Figure 2. The Bovey, Minnesota, Finnish Workers Band, 1906
Photo courtesy IRHC

Some of the names of those pictured in this photograph are Matti Koski, Oscar Ahola, Victor Möttönen and, in front and center, the boutonniered Severus. With hats tipped back, gazing into the horizon, they showed swagger and pride in their status as bandsmen. Especially festive are the smoldering cigars and the boutonnières of wildflowers. Such Finnish immigrants filled the great need for workers in Northern Minnesota's rapidly expanding iron-mining industry. Because military and village brass bands were common in Finland, a number of the Finns who came to Minnesota's Iron Range were already experienced brass players when they arrived. The more experienced musicians often taught others who wanted to join them, especially younger players. As I studied this photograph and many other documents, trying to understand how these immigrant bands functioned in the rough and remote environment of Iron Range Minnesota, I asked myself a number of questions: how was it possible for brass bands to develop and survive in the rugged living conditions of remote mining settlements? What motivated the musicians? How did the Finns and the wider community receive their band music? What were the gains and losses as this ethnic culture integrated into the American mainstream? Much documentation has been lost in the passage of a century, so many of the questions will remain unanswered. Yet, important information was discovered while researching for this book, often by simply correlating available facts from diverse sources. It became my mission to collect and preserve information about Finnish brass bands that would otherwise be lost, to measure the value and influence that these Finnish bands had in the cultural life of the early twentieth century Iron Range, and to present the medium of the old Finnish brass band as distinct and worthy, with its own repertoire, sound, and tradition.

This research journey did not begin for me in Minnesota, but in Finland. Seventy five years after the Bovey band photograph was taken, I was sitting at a lakeshore pavilion listening to a similar Finnish group of cornets, alto and tenor horns, euphoniums and tubas playing polkas, schottisches, waltzes, and other old dance music. These were veteran Finnish brass players attending a newly formed brass festival in Lieksa, near the Russian border. One of the men got up for a break and handed me his tenor horn, signaling me to sit down and take his place. The waltz just kept going as someone pointed to the sheet of music, indicating where I should continue. I was looking at a folio of handwritten notes, written generations ago, smudged, water stained, and hard to read. Erkki Karjalainen, Olavi (Ankka) Lampinen, and Holger Fransmann, the old pioneers, invited me to this first experience with the old bands as they had existed in Finland over a century ago. My being a part of living history spurred an interest in its origins.

During subsequent visits to the Lieksa Brass Week, I heard several groups from many regions of Finland who were striving to keep the tradition alive, and I learned about the "*seitsikko,*" the Finnish brass septet comprised of an E-flat soprano cornet, two B-flat soprano cornets, an E-flat alto horn, a B-flat tenor horn, a B-Flat euphonium, and a tuba (either E-flat or BB-flat.). Figure 2 shows the modern Stoolin Brass Septet playing outdoors at the Lieksa Brass Week in August 1982. The euphonium player commonly sits in the center, perhaps because his part is in the center of the scoring, and possibly the group leader. The instruments played here are original models, some very old. The tuba, in particular, is clearly nineteenth century. Many such septets were formed or revived in the 1980s.

In 1987 Sakari Lamberg, a colleague from the Ostrobothnian city of Kokkola moved things forward for me by presenting a complete set of duplicate parts taken from very old original septet books, hoping I might try to read through them with friends back in Minnesota. Three years later I organized a reading session, inviting Midwestern brass players who also expressed an interest the material. By 1990, after a few reading sessions, we established an ensemble that would dedicate itself to performance of Finnish septet repertoire on a permanent basis, calling ourselves "*Ameriikan Poijat*" (Boys of America). The title in Finnish uses an archaic Ostrobothnian spelling meant to evoke the ensemble's century-old beginnings. Ostrobothnia (*Pohjanmaa, in* Finnish) is the westernmost province of Finland and the birthplace of the largest proportion of emigrants who came to America. *Ameriikan poijat* continues today, after more than a decade of concert touring and recording, and is both a genesis and living laboratory for my research. (See figure 3)

Figure 3. Stoolin Brass Septet, Lieksa Brass Week, August 1982.
P. Niemisto photograph.

The story of the Finnish American brass bands has provided a unique window for a study of the regional culture of the time, when Iron Range communities were heavily influenced by many elements of Finnish immigration. This study considers three general periods of Finnish American band activity beginning with the development in the 1880s of brass bands in Finland, then the arrival of immigrant Finnish brass players to the United States and their activities here, and, finally, the integration of the Finnish brass band players into regional Iron Range culture. The distinct history of the Finn Bands was directly influenced by the rapidly and constantly evolving conditions of life on the Iron Range.

Figure 4. Boys of America (Ameriikan poijat) brass band, October 2002 in Superior, Wisconsin. Left to right: Marko Foss-Bb cornet, Eric Peterson-tuba, Brian Borovsky-alto horn, Paul Niemisto-euphonium, Tracey Gibbens-tenor horn, Denise Pesola-Bb cornet, Russell Pesola-Eb soprano cornet, and Don Hakala- Bb cornet.

Chapter One
BANDS IN FINLAND

Finnish National Identity

Many of the cultural characteristics found among Finnish emigrants arriving in America, including brass bands, had developed in Finland during the last decades of the nineteenth century. Much of Finnish culture, such as language, folk songs, dances, forest and agrarian traditions, have rather ancient roots. Yet, more modern elements such as a political identity, a distinctly Finnish art culture, economic independence and a recognized literary language were just then emerging as indicators of a nation seeking independence.

Finland's political history most closely parallels the history of those European national groups that were under political domination during the 1800s. Through the centuries of Gustavian Swedish control of Finland, from Medieval times to 1809, the Finnish-speaking population was primarily of the peasant class, with the land owners and merchants being primarily Swedish-speaking. The Swedish era ended during the Napoleonic wars when Finland was ceded to Russia in 1809 and became a Grand Duchy with a degree of autonomy under the Czar.

Finland's geographical and political identity was a relatively remote region throughout its history prior to 1900. An obscure language, Finnish was unlettered until the Reformation. Mikael Agricola (1510-57) was the Finnish-born bishop of Turku who introduced Lutheranism to Finland. His basic language textbook of 1538 is the first known book to be written in Finnish, and his translation of the New Testament (1548) marks the beginning of Finnish as a literary language. He is thus considered the "Father of Finnish Literature." Using German spelling, Agricola adapted the rich, spoken language of the Finnish countryside into a literary form for the first time. Finnish literature slowly evolved over the next few centuries, although literacy in Finland was first cultivated by the Swedish-speaking elite, motivated initially by Christian evangelism. Those who spoke Finnish as a mother-tongue began to learn to read the language in Lutheran church confirmation classes. The national epic, the *Kalevala* (collected oral poetry published in 1835) formed the basis for the great Finnish cultural awakening, which eventually inspired musical contributions. The publication of the *Kalevala* can be said to have aroused the first awareness of the Finnish nation both internally and abroad, starting a movement toward a Finnish political entity and independence. The Finnish language finally gained official acceptance in the Grand Duchy of Finland in 1863, 28 years after the first publication of the *Kalevala*. This was a significant milestone in the ultimate evolution toward nationhood. Unfortunately, this crystallization of the Finnish political and cultural dream coincided with an increasingly unsympathetic relationship with each succeeding czar in St. Petersburg. Finland's nationalistic momentum was eventually thought of as a threat. In response, the last Czar, Nicholas II, announced new edicts regarding Finland including the disbanding of indigenous Finnish military regiments, Finnish military conscription into the Russian Army, and the political repression of the Finns. The February 1898 Manifesto precipitated yet another greatly increased and sudden emigration abroad, as well as a groundswell of independence activity. It is from this migration that America saw the largest influx of new, and well-trained, Finnish bands musicians.

Unlike its larger, more powerful neighbors in Sweden and Russia, the native Finnish-speakers never had a nobility or military establishment that maintained musicians. In the eighteenth century some chamber music was performed by military musicians, but this was essentially music by foreigners for foreign listeners who happened to be in Finland on assignment. It was not until the late nineteenth century that any art music performances began to be available to the general public; this occurred primarily through the church and military centers of Turku and Helsinki.

"The Society for Culture and Education" (*Kansanvalistusseura*, or KVS) was founded in 1874 and was the first cultural organization formed by and for Finland's common people. Intended primarily for the Finnish-speaking population, the KVS mission was to practice and study native arts and culture with a goal of awakening Finns to their own heritage. The first KVS music festival was held in the central city of Jyväskylä in 1881, following a format inspired by earlier Estonian song festival models, with grand massed choir-singing in an outdoor pavilion.[i]

This first amateur music festival was a great success, and the number of choirs in Finland grew rapidly thereafter. The festivals also inspired brass bands, as the instruments and musical leadership became more available across the country. The earliest published festival music for brass bands was issued in 1880, in anticipation of the Jyväskylä event. This first publication was an album of six scores for brass band, mostly patriotic songs or folk music arrangements. It was intended that individual village bands would copy their own parts. Notational errors in the Finnish hand-written amateur brass band books are a common hazard in any modern rendition. Written errors may have been corrected mentally during the performance process, although never corrected by the musicians on the printed page. The summer music festival tradition in Finland is still strong today, having evolved into an expanded summer music calendar going far beyond what any small country would normally offer in sophistication and variety. This format of the summer song festival became a model for Finnish musical organizations that immigrated to America.

Important events were happening in Helsinki that would influence the Finnish musical culture of the day. The year 1882 was particularly significant in the history of Finnish musical art with the establishment of The Helsinki

University Chorus (*Ylioppilanlaulajat*), the first Finnish-language choir. Most performing arts activity in Finland had been oriented to the Swedish or Russian languages; a vocal group that performed in the Finnish language was unprecedented. In that same year, Robert Kajanus (1856-1933) formed the Helsinki Orchestral Society, today the Helsinki Philharmonic Orchestra, and teacher/conductor Martin Wegelius (1846-1906) founded the Helsinki Music Institute, today the Sibelius Academy. Several Finnish-born musicians studied abroad in the late 1800s, going mostly to Leipzig, Germany. When they returned, they modeled Finnish musical activities according to German systems, rather than drawing influences from the more proximate St. Petersburg or Stockholm. Germany also became Finland's ally in its quest for independence from Russia, politically, culturally, and militarily.

The decline of Russian society under Nicholas II coincided with a rising Finnish nationalism, creating both an opportunity for independence and also a very risky scenario. The new political winds reached outside the Finnish cities to rural areas. As social organizations increased in popularity, musical life among amateur groups blossomed. Choirs and bands were founded in almost every village to support industries or to celebrate political and social causes. Community and leftist workers' halls of many varieties were built, and regular entertainment schedules organized. With the help of the many newly trained bandmasters and choir directors coming from the military or newly established music academies, singers and bandsmen found themselves busy.

Figure 5 shows a festival setting with elaborate decorations of fresh wreaths that were common pavilion adornments for the Finnish midsummer festivals. Such festival stages were usually temporary structures, built only for the event and then later dismantled. The Finnish patriotic emblem in the center of the pavilion underscores the public movement toward national identity from that time, still thirty years before independence. The small island to the back and the right of the stage was likely the site of the traditional midsummer bonfire. The graphic is a bit obscure, but the image in the background of the pavilion stage shows choral risers for a massed choir performance. The massed brass band would often be on the ground, just in front of the stage. Modern midsummer festivals in Finland still have newly cut birch festoons around the festival site.

Finland declared independence from a newly formed Soviet Russia in 1917. The national self-awareness movement that led toward independence had been initiated only eighty-two years before, starting with the *Kalevala*, and is still relatively recent history. These strong national feelings surrounding independence and its antecedent movement are still felt by contemporary Finns. Finland experienced a bitter civil war shortly after its independence from Russia. This civil war (January to May, 1918) was one of political philosophy, pitting the left-leaning "Red" Finns against the more traditional "Whites." The Russian revolution was waged in miniature in Finland: the civil strife was fueled, in part, by a continuing close affiliation of leftist Finns with new political movements in Russia at the turn of the century. The "Whites," a Finnish political group representing landowners, business, and the state church, prevailed in the civil conflict. The defeated Finnish "Reds" were primarily the working class and young intellectuals. The political movements associated with this strife became platforms for political discourse in Finland for the entire twentieth century. Though defeated, Finnish leftists have still maintained a strong presence in the Finnish Parliament and in all political affairs. Today the party in power, the Finnish Social Democratic Party, though far to the right of communism, is still partially a derivative of the leftist philosophies of 1917. The political movements that developed in Finland in the late 1800s influenced those who left for America to seek better economic opportunity.

Figure 5. The performance pavilion of the Kansanvalistusseura Song Festival in Tampere in 1888.[ii]

Every significant national society that fostered musical activity, such as *Suomen Työväen Musiikkiliito* (Finnish Workers' Music Society, STM), *Kansanvalistusseura* (The Society for Culture and Education, KVS), *Nuorisoliitto* (Finnish Youth League, SNL), *Raittiusseura* (Temperance Society), *Suomen Laulajen ja Soittien Liitto* (Finnish Choral and Instrumental Music Society, SULASOL), and *Vapaapaehtopalokuntaa* (Volunteer Fire Brigades, WPK), was identified with one side or the other in the civil controversy at the time of independence. Each of the social organizations mentioned above continues to function today, many still sponsoring band activities. The emigrants who had brass band experience in Finland became the leaders in developing bands in the Finnish-American communities.

The Earliest Finnish Bands

The earliest records of military music in Finland mention the Swedish bands of woodwinds that occasionally performed in Turku as early as the 1500s. Turku (Åbo in Swedish) is a coastal city that was a government and religious center in the western region of Finland for centuries. It was Finland's largest city during the era of Swedish rule. Current research points to the late 1700s as a time when a more permanent wind band activity can be verified. Kari Laitinen and Päivi Liisa Hannikainen's articles published in 1994 and 1995 summarize the earliest wind band activity from that time, including the Turku Infantry Regimental Band, the Turku Music Society circa 1790, and the Savo Jäger Regiment Band in Kuopio after 1800. "The instrumentation resembled the wind octet, with clarinets replacing oboes, and a second horn replaced by natural trumpet," *i.e.*, four clarinets, a horn, a trumpet, and two bassoons.[iii] Laitinen points out that this specific instrumentation is but one isolated example, and instrumentation varied greatly in both make-up and numbers, occasionally even including violin and serpent.[iv] He refers to some historical research done on this subject in the early twentieth century by Heikki Klemetti, but notes that many of Klemetti's research reports are lost.

Hannikainen's recent research reports the arrival of a military Harmoniemusik ensemble from Pomerania to Finland. In the 1700s, the Vasa Swedish Empire extended to the southern coast of the Baltic Sea: Pomerania, the Baltic States, and the Lappish regions of northern Sweden and Norway and into Estonia where dialects of Finnish were spoken. Hannikainen relates how a regimental band came from Pomerania on a tour of the Finnish region, introducing wind music to many communities. Many of these musicians, trained also as church organists and choirmasters, ultimately settled in Finnish towns, becoming community music leaders. Their contribution to the history of wind playing and music in general, has not yet been fully evaluated. Many Finnish bandmasters from later generations were also trained to play the organ as a part of their general military music education, perhaps as a continuation of these Pomeranian models.

The Helsinki University Library has a set of original part books for a Harmoniemusik ensemble as described above. They were discovered in Heinola, a village near Helsinki with a long military history. These rare books, now called the "Heinola Books" by Finnish scholars, have been the subject of musical discussion and speculation for many decades. They appear to have been compiled for two functions: half the repertoire for social dancing and listening, and the other half for marching and ceremonial purposes. Other Finnish band folios from the nineteenth century were organized in a similar fashion. The technical demands of the musicians in this material were of a high level. For example, the waldhorn book included technical exercises as difficult as anything in a modern horn tutor. While they have been associated with Heinola, the history of these books and their source is not clear. Notes and memoranda in the margins of the music refer to the coastal city of Porvoo suggesting that the band that used this music resided there. The fact that the material was found in Heinola may also suggest that the books traveled among various military installations, possibly even used by more than one ensemble. The time frame for writing the Heinola Books could be from the late 1700s to the first decades of 1800, making it likely that this music was played by a band (or bands) under the Swedish flag, and then after 1809, by the same musicians under the Russian flag. Both national sources of the repertoire are present, implying that the books were compiled over several years.

The Imperial Russian Band Tradition Comes to Finland

After 1812, military bands in Finland were reorganized with a goal toward a larger instrumentation, with Russian military marches added to the repertoire. The model for this new band in Finland was the Helsinki Guards Band, founded in 1819. A particularly interesting document relating to the military band reformation is a published conductor's score of marches composed and arranged by Dörfeldt, now found in the University of Helsinki Library.

The instrumentation follows the model that Czar Alexander I, an amateur musician himself, had requested for the imperial bands. From the dedicatory note in the score, it is obvious that Finnish bands also used this material. It is based on an essentially Prussian military band model, since Dörfeldt was brought from Prussia to develop the innovations. Alexander's comradeship with King Frederick William I of Prussia, prompted many exchanges, including military music innovations and fashions. This expanded Harmoniemusik ensemble illustrated in the Dörfeldt St. Petersburg scores predates the arrival of valved brass to Russia and Finland. Yet, the number of lines in the scores (15-17) foretells the larger brass instrumentation that Russian bands would adopt some decades later. The penned inscription on the score, *Lif Gardets finska skarpskytte bataljons Musik Kor, År 1827* [The Czar's Life Guards Finnish Rifle Battalion Music Corps, 1827] confirms that it was used by the Helsinki Guards Band. Brass band books of the Guards Band from later decades include many of the same pieces, the brass players being expected to execute the same musical techniques previously assigned to woodwinds. No other part books directly connected with Dörfeldt's St. Petersburg score have been found in either the Helsinki archives or elsewhere in Finland. The Heinola Books may have been copied from this score, but it is not certain. There were several regimental bands in Finland at that time, and thus other military bands probably had copies available of this important published source.

In 1809, at the age of 28, Dörfeldt traveled as a young military musician from Bohemia to St. Petersburg. He had come as the new Imperial Russian Director of Music at the School of Military Music, as well as the conductor of the Czar's Life Guards Band in the city. He composed new marches as part of his duties and also arranged some others, including Austrian and Prussian works. Compiled into the" Imperial Russian Army March Collection," this repertoire by 1815 contained about 70 slow and 70 quick marches.[v] The marches discussed here are from the same collection as the published score in Figure 6. This Bohemian bandmaster and composer living in St Petersburg not only influenced Finnish band music, but also influenced the band culture of the German-speaking world at that time. The Bohemian musicians living in St. Petersburg had other significant influences on wind music history.

The Kuopio City Historical Museum in eastern Finland has a collection of remarkable and very old valved brass instruments, apparently used by the Kuopio 4th Sharpshooters Battalion Brass Band during the decade 1820-1830. This unusual collection of instruments made by in St Petersburg prior to 1830 (the year of the dissolution of the band) makes it apparent that innovations in brass instruments were not only happening in German speaking countries, but also in Russia. The Anderst valve system, an early experiment preceding more successful rotary and piston valves, involves a fairly simple system of a butterfly valve encased in a brass housing. These instruments are unusually light and delicate in construction, and in remarkably fine condition. The valves are still functional, and the instruments have remained untouched in storage for 175 years (see Figure 7).

Langwill's Index lists twenty-three instrument makers of Germanic heritage working in St. Petersburg during the nineteenth century. Bandmaster Dörfeldt is also included on this list, but most likely as a woodwind maker.[vi] The activity of Bohemian instrument-makers in St. Petersburg goes back much further. Ferdinand Kölbel, a Bohemian living in St. Petersburg, designed and made a chromatic horn as early as 1766, fifty years before Stöltzel and Blühmel.[vii] It may be that some of the very earliest experiments in valved brass design took place in St. Petersburg and not in the German speaking countries.

Little detail is available about these early years of brass playing in Russia and Finland, but the first instance of such activity was apparently initiated by Dmitri Lvovich Narishkin, (1758-1838) who is attributed to be the "Founder of St.

Petersburg's first brass band." This information is from the records of his burial site in the Alexander Nevsky Monastery in St. Petersburg. No further information about him has been found, but he probably was involved in the "Russian Hornkappele" tradition, a unique ensemble of single-tone horns.

The conventional Russian brass band score of the late 1800s had about fifteen parts with transpositions only into Eb, Bb, and F. Earlier scoring experiments had a much wider range of keys and instruments. It is notable that

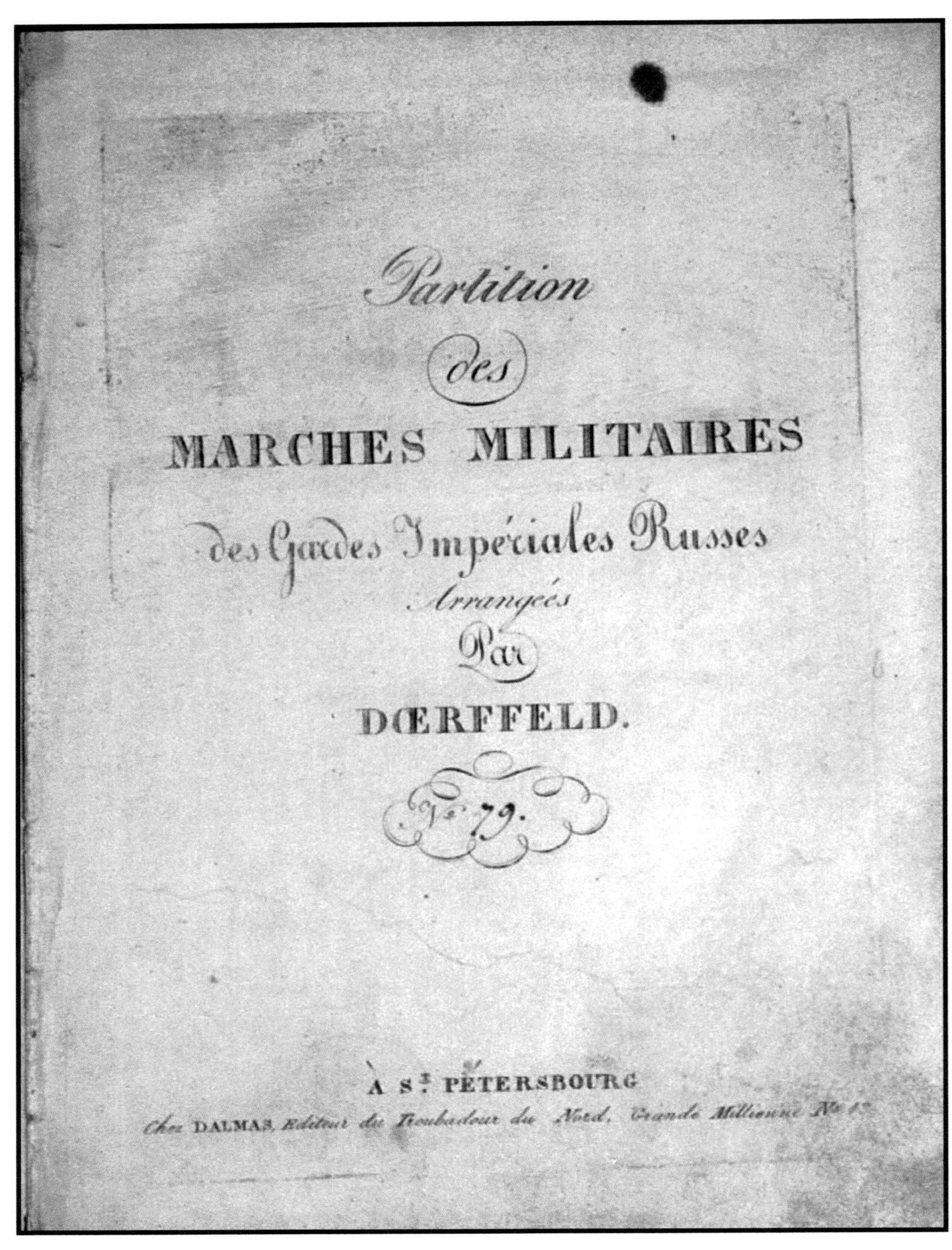
Partition
des
MARCHES MILITAIRES
des Gardes Impériales Russes
Arrangées
Par
DŒRFFELD.
N° 79.
À S.t PÉTERSBOURG
Chez DALMAS, Editeur du Troubadour du Nord, Grande Millionne N° 1.

Figure 6. "Partition des Marches Militaires des Gardes Imperiales Russes arranges par Doerffeld, Petersbourg." Photo by Author.

there are trumpets and horns in F, the only older instruments added to the new Saxhorn-style band. The valved F trumpets played a low range and functioned as accompaniment instruments in the alto range. The F horns were the natural, unvalved horns common in wind bands and orchestras of the time. Transcriptions of operatic and orchestral literature created the primary concert repertoire for Russian and Finnish bands. The new valved-brass instruments were expected to produce technically what the woodwinds had done previously, but with more sonorous power. This new repertoire of highly demanding music written for valved brass bands was to be a continuation of the Harmoniemusik tradition into the valved brass era. Performances of this florid music must have been demonstrations of amazing technical facility.

Figure 7. Four instruments by J. F. Anderst, St. Petersburg. Photo by Author.

Following the invention of valved brass instruments by Heinrich David Stöltzel (Berlin, 1777-1844) and Freidrich Blühmel (Kraslice, d. 1845), they were quickly embraced by bands throughout Europe and beyond. Herbert Heyde charts the very earliest valve inventions as Stöltzel's first valve (*stopferventil*) in 1814 and Blühmel's first (*kastenventil*), also in 1814. In 1818, Stöltzel created the first full family of brass instruments with the *stopferventil* valves.

The noted Finno-Swedish clarinetist Bernhard Henrik Crusell mentions in his diaries that he met Stöltzel in Berlin in 1821, when an example of the valved cornet was first demonstrated to him.[viii] This could be the first time valved brass was introduced to any Nordic musician. These new instruments were first introduced to Stockholm in 1836, and to the czar's army bands in St. Petersburg shortly afterwards. By 1840, Adolphe Sax had refined the instruments into a family of conical bore saxhorns, from soprano to contrabass. Prussian military bandmaster Wilhelm Wieprecht adopted Adolph Sax's brass-instrument design in 1860, at about the same time as it was accepted in Stockholm and St. Petersburg. Two original instrument collections in Finland, Moisio and Hämäläinen (see Bibliography) contain many nineteenth-century instruments from makers in Germany, St. Petersburg, and Stockholm used in the military bands.

The Russian military reorganized its bands from the traditional Harmoniemusik ensembles into all valved-brass bands by the 1850s with the Finnish military bands soon adopting these new fashions in band instrumentation. The Anderst instruments found in Kuopio suggest that some of the Russian military bands were adopting new valved brass instruments earlier than anywhere in Europe. The Helsinki Guards Band was converted to a brass band by 1853, probably because of the the arrival of the Prussian-born Kappellmeister Ernst Wilhelm Flössel to Helsinki. This period also saw a large increase in the availability of mass-produced brass instruments all over Europe. For instance, by 1847, the city of Kraslice, Bohemia, had 46 active instrument-makers and 78 apprentices.[ix]

Flössel was appointed conductor of the Helsinki Guards Band presumably to help bring about the transition to an all brass band configuration. Many scores in Flössel's own hand survive in the Helsinki University Library, with instrumentations varying from 15 to 21 parts. Flössel experimented for several years, until a 15-17 line score (including percussion) became most common in the 1880s. His instrumentation is now called *normaalivanha* (old-normal) scoring by current Finnish military music historians and imitates the scores of the Russian brass bands. These scores include transcriptions of many popular opera medleys and orchestra repertoire played by the Guards Band in its concerts at the Esplanade bandshell by the harbor in Helsinki.

The Finnish brass septet (*torviseitsikko*) soon appeared as a solution for smaller Finnish villages to meet the need for a band with minimal instrumentation, as Finns began to adapt the military brass band to community needs of the day. The *torviseitsikko*, still a popular ensemble today, includes an E-flat soprano cornet, two B-flat cornets, and E-flat alto horn, a B-flat tenor horn, a B-flat baritone horn, and a tuba (BB flat or E-flat). While Finnish brass players take pride in the septet score as a uniquely native instrumentation, it must be noted that at least two examples of Prussian cavalry bands and the Moravian brass bands in America are very similar to the Finnish model. It seems, though, that this basic septet scoring concept is discernable as the basis for all traditional Finnish band music that followed. When instrumentation was expanded beyond seven players, the septet root was somehow still preserved: the extra alto, tenor, tuba and trumpet or horn parts were almost always cross-cued in the basic septet instrumentation. The additional voices merely supported the basic seven, providing either some additional depth or relief for difficult lines. Even when twentieth-century Finnish bands began to follow the international trends toward the Janissary or American mixed and expanded instrumentation, the music often could still be reduced to the seven lines of the *torviseitsikko*, with some instrumental doublings.

Finnish Bands Develop Their Own Traditions

After Russia's occupation of Finland in 1812, most Finnish affairs, including musical life, saw a decline in Swedish influence. However, Finland remained a primarily Swedish-speaking society in the most important circles. The bandmasters in various Finnish regiments of the late 1800s, for instance, were almost exclusively Finns of Swedish extraction, such as Forsman, Hedman, Kock, Leander, Liljeström, Lindfors, Lindholm, Lundelin, Mannerström, Palin, Sandström, Sjöblom, Wallenius, Wasenius and Willgren. The only bandmasters with Finnish names in those decades were Hämäläinen, Kahra, and Ahonen.[x] The Swedes continued to maintain contact with military musicians in Stockholm, and Swedish military bands had a parallel though separate evolution toward the adoption of valved brass instruments. A sextet of Eb cornet, Bb cornet, alto horn, two tenor valve trombones, and a tuba is discussed by Ann-Marie Nilsson as being a typical small military brass band, and was established following the mixed woodwind/brass *kavaliermusik* ensembles of the mid-1800s.[xi] The Stockholm brass instrument-makers Åhlborg & Olssohn were manufacturing brass instruments already in the 1850s, including a uniquely shaped rotary-valved cornet with a conical flügelhorn-style bell, known as a "Swedish cornet." The Finnish bands regularly played pieces of military music, folk dances, and concert pieces from Swedish sources. The instruments found in a typical Finnish brass band were manufactured in Kraslice, St. Petersburg, and Stockholm.

Flössel, the Prussian, was succeeded in 1875 by Finnish-born Adolph Leander Jr. (1833-1899) as conductor of the Helsinki Guards Band. Leander further refined the brass-band instrumentation, adding greatly to the repertoire available to the Guards Band with his own compositions and arrangements. His influence ultimately extended to all military and village brass bands in Finland. His father was a player in the Guards Band from about 1830 on, and so Adolph Jr. witnessed the period of conversion from the eighteenth-century Harmoniemusik to the valved brass band. To Finnish brass band history, Leander contributed a large volume of published repertoire, and a method book for technique and ensembles. That method book, the first published in Finland, had a widespread impact on how amateur brass players were trained. The completion of a new Finnish railway system between Helsinki, Turku, and Hämeenlinna precipitated an era of easy commuting in southern Finland. Newspaper articles chronicle many brass band performances by the Helsinki Guards musicians from 1875 and afterwards. With train travel both easy and available, a Guards band in the form of a septet made appearances outside Helsinki for the first time. The seeds of a national brass-band movement were thus sown. Leander's influence on Finnish brass players and conductors, including those who left for America in the 1890s, was certainly direct.

Leander's pioneering brass-method book, published in 1885, was another element in his important influence on the brass-band movement in Finland. This comprehensive text begins with advice to the brass player:

Rules for the brass pupil

- The mouthpiece is placed on the embouchure in such a way that there is only light pressure on the lips and teeth, but with perhaps more of an anchor on the lower lip.
- Air pressure pushes forth the sound.
- When inhaling one should feel the chest rise.
- The left hand should hold the instrument in such a way that (not too tightly-or press too hard) it does not prevent resonance.
- Right hand fingers should be placed directly over the top of the valves, and push down accurately, with only light pressure.
- The player is permitted to practice at the most for an hour, continuously; if after that, he is tired, he should take a rest.
- Scales and other exercises should always be started slowly. After that, they can be sped up.
- Take in and use as much air as possible, but not so as to overstrain the lungs.
- A final consideration to mention is that, in order to play a brass instrument well one needs, first of all, to have the following: a good ear, strong lips, straight teeth, flexibility, patience and a sustaining enthusiasm.12

Each element of these instructions remains valid today, and shows that brass pedagogy was already sophisticated in the 1880s, partly having evolved with the valved instruments and also having been based on centuries-old brass-playing concepts.

In the preface to this *School of Brass Playing*, Leander refers to an earlier Russian trumpet method by Vassily Würm, a German-born brass teacher and player who was a pioneer in the Russian school of brass playing. Published in St Petersburg, Würm's method and etudes were commonly used by the czar's bands during their transition to valved brass instrumentation.[xii]

Figure 8 is a page from Leander's method book. It shows the multilingual milieu of the early Finnish brass player, having text in three languages. Although based on Leander's work with the Finnish Guards Band, this book was published by *Kansanvalistusseura* (KVS), an amateur music society. It was the common method used to assist amateur brass bands then forming in communities all over Finland. Although no copies of this book have as yet been found in the United States, it is still fairly certain that many emigrant bandsmen were trained with this method. There were no alternatives in the Finnish language at that time.

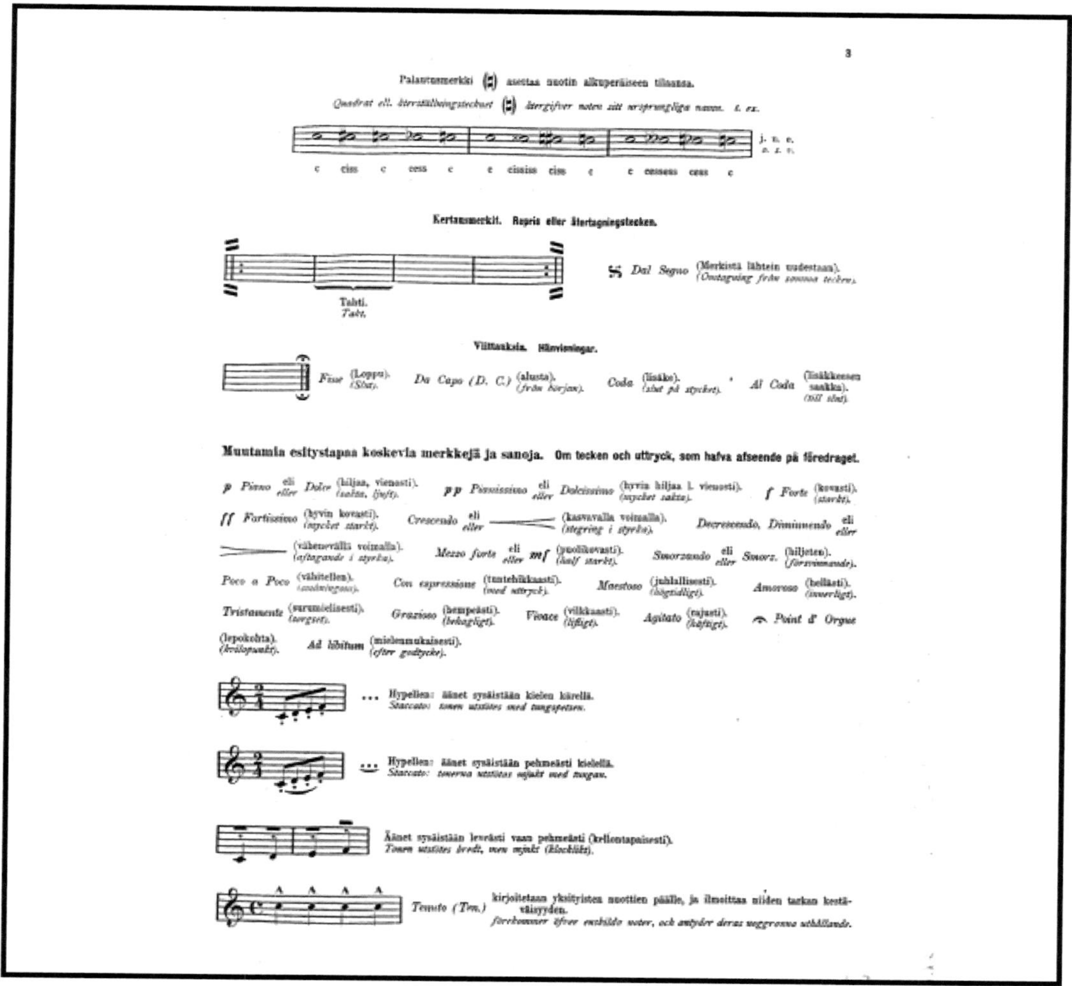

Figure 8. Adolph Leander, School of Brass Playing, Page 3. (Torvisoitannon oppikirja).

Brass bands could be heard in most Finnish villages by the 1880s. They played at concerts, funerals, music festivals, dance halls, and social events. These brass bands became a part of Finnish folk- and social-dance traditions, with cross influences from country fiddlers and accordion players, some of whom took the brass music melodies and adapted the tunes for their own use.[xiii] The brass septet also borrowed Finnish folk songs, arranging them for its use.

The first village brass bands in Finland were influenced by the same mixture of German, Russian, and Swedish traditions that were found in the military bands. The newly formed village bands at first had no other music available. Through the efforts of individual bandmasters, composers, and festivals, the village septets eventually had music especially written for their needs. This growth in brass band activity was international, with mass production of valved brass instruments also taking place in the United States, England, and other centers where music for the industrial worker was becoming popular.

The brass band from the village of Mänttä was formed in 1882 making it one of the oldest village bands in Finland. Later, Antti Ahonen (1845-1915) retired from the Helsinki Guards Band and became the bandmaster in Mänttä. His signature appears on many brass band arrangements in the Guards music archives, and he continued as an arranger, teacher, and conductor for many years after leaving Helsinki. The Mänttä Band in Figure 9, with Antti Ahonen as leader (with waistcoat and baton) shows instruments of the older style, with conical saxhorn bores in the euphonium, tenor horn and the bass helicons. All instruments appear to be rotary-valved except the Eb cornet, which is piston-valved.

Figure 9. The Mänttä Paper Facory/Fire Brigade Brass Band, 1890s (Photograph courtesy Kaustinen Folk Music Institute.)

A century later, during the 1980s and 1990s, almost every Finnish village observed a musical centennial that brought early firemens' bands and workers' choirs back to public attention. This popular revival of local interest in old

Finnish bands has fueled current study in Finnish band history by providing many published histories, as well as reviving the performance of the old music. The following is a tally of bands sponsored by civic organizations, municipalities, and industries formed in Finland at the end of the 1800s. The founding year is followed by the number of brass bands formed: 1876-1, 1877-5, 1878-4, 1879-3, 1880-5, 1881-5, 1882-16, 1883-10, 1884-18, 1885-11, 1886-7, 1887-21, 1888-10, 1889-6, 1890-10, 1891-11, 1892-8, 1893-9, 1894- 13, 1895-6, 1896-9, 1897-10, 1898-29, 1899-13, 1900-13.[xiv]

Possible participation in a music festival was often the incentive for starting a new band. The four years with the largest growth in new Finnish bands are: 1882 with 16, 1884 with 18, 1887 with 21, and 1898 with 29. The reason for such growth differs somewhat from year to year. 1883, 1884, and 1887 fall during the decade when the large KVS music festivals spurred the development of community ensembles. Of the 55 bands formed in those three years, seven were fire brigade bands, with a smaller number sponsored by factories. Other bands came from communities across Finland, sponsored mostly by local KVS affiliates. The largest growth year, 1898, included newly identified bands almost entirely associated with *Nuorisoseura* (Society of Youth). *Nuorisoseura* was organized at the same time as many other social and political organizations in the late 1800s; it had activities and meeting halls for young people and sponsored many of the early brass bands. These bands were supported by the talents of hundreds of newly available military bandsmen who had just been released from active duty as a result of Czar Nicholas II's edict disbanding indigenous Finnish army units. Westerholm suggests that many bands first listed in 1898 were probably formed earlier, but were officially listed following the formation of a national organization of the youth societies, *Suomen nuorisoliitto* (SNL) in 1897. He added "The instruments were expensive, there was a lack of competent conductors, and if a fire brigade or workers' society already had a brass band, you didn't necessarily found a brass band of your own. In 1890s the political differences weren't so fixed yet."[xv]

Finnish musicologists do not yet recognize that the amateur choral and brass-band traditions made important contributions to Finland's musical culture during her drive for independence, even though these groups rendered, by far, the most commonly performed music. That they were amateur in status, hastily trained, and affiliated with social or political societies may have made them seem countrified to an urban population and its critics in a society that was striving for an international cultural recognition. In the early 1900s, prominent Finnish composers would occasionally write music for the amateur groups, but the music was often more functional in nature, such as festival fanfares or processionals, and did not necessarily show the composer at his creative best. A cadre of composers, usually affiliated with these musical societies, wrote a large volume of music for the amateur ensembles to perform. Some of this repertoire continues to be played and sung today as Finland's patriotic and nostalgic music.

With the industrialization of Finland and the many new factories there came a need for both fire brigades and labor unions, two institutions that sponsored many brass bands. Many companies also sponsored bands as community service gestures. One can consider the brass instruments themselves as mass produced art objects of a new mechanized society. While some Finnish amateur bands were connected with factories, many others were sponsored by institutions developing along political lines, in addition to some who espoused traditional agrarian village culture. The parallel formation of fire brigade bands and workers' bands of the 1890s symbolized a societal division that would emerge more strongly in the next decade. As Finland became more industrialized, society was becoming more urbanized, but Karjalainen notes "On the other side, the inception of the public education system and the ideologies of educational and workers' organizations also have been influential in establishing brass septets. Partly it seems to be evidenced that brass playing belonged to the national aims to dispose of all social and educational differences between the classes."[xvi] There was clearly a division between social classes in nineteenth-century Finland, most easily identified by language. Swedish speakers, for centuries, were the clerics, landowners, and professionals. Finnish speakers usually came from the working-class sector. Karjalainen's comment suggests that Finnish-language speakers were most enthusiastic participants in these efforts to dispose of social and educational differences. Through most of the 1800s, Russia supported the efforts of Finnish speakers to gain influence, with the assumption that any effort by Sweden and its allies to retake Finland would be made more difficult with a strong Fennoman political presence. "Fennoman" was the name of a political party formed in the 1860s but was also a general term for the movement to raise the culture of Finnish speakers. That support faded during the reign of Nicholas II, as it became clear that Finns were aiming for complete independence.

Today, many of the social and musical societies formed a century ago still exist but have been transformed into service groups for the wider population, often with an emphasis on music for youth and community. However, Finland places tradition in very high regard, and an historical nostalgia for these old societies apparently will maintain an identification with the original roots into the future. The Finnish Workers' Music Society and The Society for Culture and Education are still very proud and active organizing forces in Finnish musical life and education today, with negligible political agendas compared to their founding years.

A summary of the most common instrumentations found during the rise of the village brass band in the 1880s and 1890s is included in Karjalainen's book.[xvii] Players who came as immigrants to America had played in such combinations.

---

i Kerstin Smeds and Timo Mäkinen, *Kaiu Kaiu, lauluni,* (Keuruu: Otava Publishing, 1984), 10.

ii *Kansanvalistusseura* (Society for Culture and Education) calendar, 1890.

iii Paivi Liisa Hannikainen, "Pommerista Pohjanmaalle—Saksalaissotilassoittaja ja urkurit suomessa 1700 Jualipuiskolla" ("From Pomerania to Ostrobothnia—German Military Bandsmen and Organists in Finland in the 18th Century"), *Tabulatura* [Sibelius Academy Church Music Department Journal] (1995): 66.

iv Kari Laitinen, "Harmoniemusik in Finland: On Military Music in 18th Century Savo," *Balticum–A Coherent Musical Landscape in the 16th and 18th Centuries. Studia Musicologica,* (1994): 106.

v Joachim Toeche-Mittler, *The German Army March Collection,* vol. 2:3, http://www.worldmilitarybands.com/germarch.htm. See also Achim Hofer, *Die "Koeniglich Preussische Armeemarschsammlung" 1817-1839* (IGEB Reprints und Manuskripte Materialien zur Blasmusikforschung,, Vienna: Johann Kliment, 2007).

vi William Waterhouse, *The New Langwill Index : A Dictionary of Musical Wind Instrument Makers and Inventors.* (London: Tony Bingham, 1993), 479.

vii A. L. Porfir'yeva, and A. A. Stepanov, *Musical St.Petersburg, a Musical-Encyclopedic Dictionary* (St. Petersburg, 1998), 2: 55.

viii Bernhard Henrik Crusell, "Diaries," ed. by Fabian Dahlström (Stockholm: Royal Music Academy Studies, 1977), 21: 141.

ix Herbert Heyde, *Das Ventilblasinstrument* (Leipzig, 1987), 11.

x Paavo Talvio, *Kenttämusiikkia varuskuntasoittokuntiin* (*A History of Finnish Military Music*) (Helsinki: Topograffikunnan Kirjapaino, 1980), 14-17.

xi Ann-Marie Nilsson, "What is Swedish about a Swedish Wind Octet?" *Kongressbericht Northfield / Minnesota, USA 2006, Alta Musica* (2007), 26: 319-337.

xii For details on Wassily Würm, see Anatoly Selianin, "The Peculiarities of Trumpet Method Development in Russia," *International Trumpet Guild Journal,* 8/1 (1983), 40-45.

xiii Conversation with Simo Westerholm, July 1992. Westerholm is a noted Finnish ethnomusicologist from the Kaustinen Folk Music Institute who has done extensive research on Finnish brass history.

xiv Data collected by Simo Westerholm and published in articles written during 1995 in *Kansanmusiikkilehti,* a folk-music journal published in Kaustinen (volumes 5/1 and 6/1).

xv Westerholm, e-mail correspondence, June 5, and October 10, 2003.

xvi Kauko Karjalainen, *Suomalainen Torviseitsikko–Historia ja perinteen jatkuminen* (*The Finnish Brass Septet—History and Living Tradition*) (Tampere, Finland: Tampere University Press, 1995), 62.

xvii Ibid, 17-18.

Chapter Two
FINNISH BANDSMEN IMMIGRATE TO AMERICA

The Reasons for Immigration

During the late nineteenth century, Finland experienced the same population explosion that was the primary motivation behind the great European migration to America. Between 1811 and 1900 Finland's population more than doubled, from 1,053,000 to 2,700,000, outrunning the capacity of its agricultural production and emerging industrial sector. Before 1810, the Swedish crown retained large amounts of land, with the subdivision of individual farms among numerous owners and tenants resulting in impractically small parcels for tillage and cattle. Russian rule in the early 1800s continued this system of small farms, which were still incapable of providing sustenance for either owners or tenants. Between 1815 and 1875, tenant populations exploded in size, with the number of landless, itinerant workers growing even faster. Eventually, as the economy further deteriorated, large numbers of tenant farmers were obliged to become migrant workers. Some of these first Finns to seek new possibilities abroad moved to Sweden, where they found employment opportunities in forestry and in farming. Others went to Helsinki, or began to look to travel further abroad.

In the mid-1860s northern Finland endured a series of famines that drove many Finns to migrate to the mining and fishing regions of Arctic Norway, where a Finnish community had been founded as early as the mid-sixteenth century in Finnmark. In the late nineteenth century, the tar-distilling industry declined in Finland, as world demand was greatly reduced due to changes in ship-building and other technologies. For decades, the tar industry provided much employment, though it also retarded the development of the other possible wood industries in Finland. This depression in the tar market also added to the roster of émigrés.

Before 1883, no official emigration records were kept in Finland, although some personal data were collected via passport applications and steamship passenger manifests. Church parishes kept records of birth, marriage, and death. [1]In 1883 and 1884, the areas of heaviest population loss due to emigration were the two northwestern provinces of Oulu and Vaasa, which by then had begun keeping better records. However, population statistics for the entire country were officially available only after 1893. These records have occasionally been of some value for tracing biographical information about Finnish bandsmen. The quality of information has been affected by the fact that passports were not issued to minors, and that surname changes were common both in Finland and upon arrival in the new land.

Estimates of Finnish emigration in the early years between 1865 and 1882 range from 7,000 to 15,000 people. Between 1883 and 1892, approximately 40,000 Finns emigrated. The "Great Migration" accounted for 250,000 to 265,000 departures, largely of unskilled, Finnish-speaking laborers. Pre-1899 emigrants were primarily drawn from the rural northern and western provinces, which suffered the harshest agrarian crisis. Most of those who left during the later period after 1900 departed from the cities and from the farms of southern Finland. In 1873, farmers and the children of farmers constituted 53.6% of Finnish emigrants; in 1893, the figure was down to 34.3%, and by 1913 it was only 28.4%. It is easy to see a connection between the rise in the proportion of urban industrial Finns immigrating to the United States and the rise in leftist political activity within Finnish-American communities.

A noted Finnish statesman Oskari Tokoi (1873-1963) came to America from Ostrobothnia as a boy in 1883, an early date for Finnish miners in the United States. He returned to Finland in 1900, was active in Finland's drive for independence, and became the new country's first prime minister. Later in life he wrote an autobiography that included stories of immigrant life in America. His explanation about the destinations in America of his home region's emigrants is probably typical of many experiences:

> No one has ever been able to explain what lured the first immigrants from the forests of northern Finland to the mines of America. None of them had ever seen a mine in their own country. Yet, those who had come to America by way of northern Norway settled in the upper peninsula of Michigan to work in the copper mines. Those who came later followed their example, some going even farther, to work in the gold mines of Dakota's Black Hills.
>
> I can explain the mystery as far as it concerns the Central Ostrobothnians. In our region of Finland we remembered that one of us—a man named Lehtimäki —went to Wyoming in 1867 where, as a laborer, he had helped to build the Union Pacific. He happened to be in Carbon when the railroad was completed, and so he went to work in Carbon's newly opened coal mine. He wrote, of course, to friends and relatives back home. Some followed him to Wyoming, and they in turn wrote to relatives and friends. At one time it looked as if all the men of Central Ostrobothnia intended to work in the mines of Wyoming. I merely followed that tradition, in which my father and uncle had preceded me. I knew I would have friends in Carbon, and William's father and older brother were already working there. [2]

Tokoi travelled widely in America as a miner and a lumberman, and also played in several Finnish miners' brass bands in the Western states. His autobiography does not mention the instruments he played. Arriving in America at the age of ten, he learned to play by sitting next to the veteran players in the miners' bands, using the apprenticeship system that was normal for training young recruits. It is not likely that he continued playing after he returned to Finland.

The First Finnish Bands in America

Amateur music groups were established rapidly and profusely as the Finnish immigrants settled in North America during the 1880s and 1890s. The working class in Finland had formed many such organizations in pursuit of social, political and religious, as well as musical goals. Here in America, the bands helped preserve cultural identity in a society where that identity was somewhat threatened. At the same time, music provided an important connection for the Finns into American society, where bands were already popular nationwide

The Finnish bands in America were usually affiliated with one of two main social movements: temperance and socialism. Music-making to the many ethnic groups that arrived in the United States was both a source of nostalgia as well as a gateway into the greater American cultural milieu:

> Therefore, the European immigrant, once established in the new world, was able to fulfill any of his innate needs and desires. Egalitarianism and libertarianism removed the old-world restrictions and allowed him to delve in the fine arts, without fear of recrimination, embarrassment or restrictions. Their basic love of music was one avenue of expression that saw fulfillment in the singing societies and the community instrumental groups. Considering the latter, the immigrant masses turned not to the intimacies of the chamber groups or to the intricacies of the symphony orchestra but to the music and media they knew best, that of the wind band. Included in the realm of beneficiaries of American Democracy were the non-performing audiences. This polyglot of humanity with its egalitarian freedom was limited to the social and cultural activities only by its wills and desires, or the possible restrictions of financial disparity.[3]

According to Emil Saastamoinen, an early chronicler of Finnish-American life, the first Finnish immigrant bands were formed as early as 1877 in Astoria, Oregon, and in Michigan's Upper Peninsula. There is no other evidence of Finnish immigrant bands formed as early as 1877, but if true, that would be earlier than the founding date of most brass bands in Finland. Some of the oldest known bands included the Finnish Band of Copper Falls, Michigan (1886), the Finnish Band of Ishpeming, Michigan (1886), the Central Comet Band of Hancock-Houghton, Michigan (1887), the Finnish Band of Calumet, Michigan (1889), and the Finnish Band of Ely, Minnesota (1889). These early bands were all affiliated with temperance societies.

Among the bands later formed with socialist clubs were the Imatra Band from Maynard, Massachusetts (1899), the Detroit Finnish Workers Band, the Finnish Band of Warren, Ohio, established in the early 1920s, and several Minnesota bands discussed in Chapter 4. One example is the Rockland, California Finnish Miners Band affiliated with the local workers' hall illustrated in Figure 10. The drummer on the left does not appear to be a Finnish immigrant, but his presence in the picture gives evidence about the social dynamics of the American west at that time. He may have been the only person at the mining location who played the snare drum, and so he played for all regional bands. These bands represent a very incomplete list and are not meant to give a true picture of the number of Finnish bands in America from coast to coast. No comprehensive list has ever been made of Finnish-American bands nationally, although it is assumed to be about seventy. There were many from Washington State, Oregon, California, Montana, Wisconsin, Ohio, Pennsylvania, Illinois, Massachusetts, West Virginia, and New York.

Figure 10. Finnish Miners Band, Rockland, California.
From Amerikan albuumi *1906*[4]

In 1921, Saastamoinen wrote "the establishing of bands became a matter of fashion. Every mining town with even a few Finns simply had to have its own band, no matter what sacrifices this entailed. By 1917, the town of Calumet, Michigan, for example, was responsible for the existence of no less than ten Finnish bands, and, by 1921, there were almost 100 Finnish-American bands in existence."[5] This last statistic ignores the scores of Finnish bands with short lives in America. Many did not survive until 1921, including some Minnesota bands discussed in this study.

The stories told about Finnish bands in America usually mention struggles with finding sponsorship, leadership, and players, with these elements rising and falling in urgency from season to season. Yet the important role of the early bands in community life is often reaffirmed in personal histories and newspaper articles. While the Finns were proud of their own bands, they often took them for granted when it came to financial support.

Figure 11. Heinola brass sextet, taken in Detroit, Michigan in 1914. Photograph courtesy of Kauko Karjalainen.

Being a member of a Finnish band was something to be proud of and a means of achieving social status. In a humorous article, a former bandsman notes that belonging to a band was as much a necessity as 'the decoration of one's home with Catholic pictures of the Savior and with merchant's calendars'...The highest aspiration of a healthy, honorable, patriotic young man was to become a member of a band. Young ladies considered it a great honor to be escorted by a young man attired in a red uniform with gold braid. The pride in being a bandsman is reflected by the fact that among the few pictures taken of family members, there was sure to be a photograph of a husband or son in a band uniform, holding his instrument.[6]

Many Finns coming to America were leaving Finnish communities where they had active musical lives. For instance, in the western province of Ostrobothnia, the source of most Finnish emigration, the number of brass players going to America to seek their fortune had a measurable effect on the bands who lost these players. In the small farming village of Kaustinen "three horn blowers left for *Amerika* to get rich."[7] That would be enough for the Kaustinen band to fold until they found or trained replacements. As the number of Finnish brass players leaving for America increased, the recently formed bands back home felt their absence. If the E^b-cornet player, for example, left for America, the band was in trouble. The entire brass band from the Finnish village of Heinola left for America as a group and later was photographed in Detroit, Michigan, still playing together (see figure 11). The instruments all appear to be of American manufacture (having piston valves), and with a mellophone instead of an alto horn. Compare these instruments to those in the photograph of the Mänttä Band in Figure 9 (in chapter 2), all of which are European-made. The sextet instrumentation may imply that the group is from a Swedish-speaking community of Finns, but that is not certain.[8]

Members of another band from the village of Nivala left for North America at the same time, but these members spread out to seek their fortunes in separate destinations in the United States and Canada. According to an article in the Nivala newspaper, between 1904 and 1908 six of them came back to Nivala from their American adventures, and resumed playing in the band back home upon their return. Their story has additional episodes including that two of the players made the round trip journey to America twice![9] Return trips were apparently quite common among young Finnish men, and were part of the reason that many band musicians may be initially mentioned on a roster or in a history in America, but then seem to disappear from the records.

A National Finnish-American Band Movement

Rosters and photographs show the earliest Finnish-American brass bands to be in the model of the Finnish bands from which many of the players had come, with seven to ten bandsmen playing brass instruments, and the possibility of an occasional clarinet. Larger Finnish bands like the Sampo Band of Ely quickly adopted the American band model, made widely popular by the touring bands of Patrick Gilmore and John Philip Sousa, with expanded woodwind sections and percussion. The more successful larger Finnish bands were in Monessen, Pennsylvania (Louhi), Worchester, Massachusetts (National Band), Ashtabula, Ohio (Humina Band), and Red Lodge, Montana (Red Lodge Military Band). Eventually all had expanded instrumentation, with woodwinds, horns, and percussion added to the Finnish brass septet. The Finnish bands initiated the training of new players through the co-operative efforts of a national organization, the Sibelius Club of Monessen, Pennsylvania. The Sibelius Club published music, sponsored festivals, and published periodicals to help Finnish bandsmen and choristers in America.

Directors and players were usually paid small stipends for their band participation by sponsoring organizations. While having its own band was a great asset for any Finnish club, the stipends, the uniforms, and the instruments made that sponsorship more costly than most other sponsored activities. In some instances, the director received an adequate salary, but rarely was there any director who didn't also have another source of income, and also rarely did he conduct only one group. In Minnesota, every known Finnish bandmaster was listed in Polk Community Directories as having an additional profession. The burden of band sponsorship may also have caused many organizations to reconsider their sponsorships, especially after city bands became more established and could be hired for the occasional festival without having to underwrite year-round support.

Financial support for these bands was a tenuous matter, and usually involved the issue of the director's salary as the main point of discussion. There are numerous instances where bands went without trained conductors and had to make do by having players rotate as rehearsal and concert leaders. In most cases, even when a competent leader was found, it was difficult to retain him for the long-term. Typical band histories had long lists of Finnish-American bandmasters, each of whom directed a band for relatively short periods. Among Iron Range communities, that list of bandmasters included several musicians who seemed to have been in rotation, succeeding each other. Pakkala relates one telling instance from the minutes of a Michigan Finnish temperance brass band in Crystal Falls (1901), where its director, a Mr. M. A. Laitinen, was offered $20 a month for conducting the group. Two weeks later, it also notes that director Laitinen "withdrew as director because his wage was too small."[10] Opportunities for better financial support were part of the reason bandmasters were so often moving to new communities. Among the seasoned bandmasters, inflated expectations of what America had to offer had already developed earlier in Finland, where new village brass bands provided a trained bandmaster a livelihood. As the discharged military musicians came to America, where the reputation for easy wealth was greatly inflated, many an aspiring brass player or bandmaster was very disappointed when a secure playing or conducting position wasn't awaiting his arrival, and couldn't easily be found or created.

The histories of two Finnish bands in the eastern United States have been more carefully documented than most. The Louhi Band of Monessen,

Pennsylvania, was one of the most widely traveled and celebrated of the Finnish-American bands. Established in 1900 as a part of the Finnish Temperance Society in Monessen, its founding conductor was Akseli Ruuti, who was planning to develop a mixed instrument, American-style band when he began. However, his initial roster included only brass players in the old *seitsikko* tradition: one trumpet, four cornets, one trombone, six baritones, and drums. That first band in 1900 consisted of veterans of Finnish military bands or village musicians who came to Monessen to work in the steel plants. In later years, Ruuti achieved his goal of mixed instrumentation, and by then the band was also joined by non-Finnish players and was essentially a Monessen municipal band. It is not clear if Ruuti's primary goal was to Americanize the Finnish players or to celebrate Finnish band music within the Pennsylvania mining region. It seems that the Louhi Band achieved both. By 1917, the band's membership had grown to 44, and its music library expanded until it contained some 1500 compositions, the bulk of which was standard American band music. The list of conductors who were guests with the Louhi Band includes most of the prominent Finnish bandmasters in America at that time, including both Charles Kleemola (Ely, Minnesota) and George Wahlstrom, (see Figure 12). Typically Finnish bands changed directors as well as players on a regular basis, and Ruuti was one of the few who stayed with one band for more than a decade.

312. Louhi Band of Monessen Pennsylvania, George Wahlström , Director, 1918. Photograph from Wahlström family

The Red Lodge Montana Finnish "Military" Band was widely known among Finnish communities through appearing in many summer festivals and usually earning the first prize trophies. The band was also an attraction for many Finnish bandmasters and brass players who traveled to Montana to participate, if only for a few weeks during the concert season. Started in 1890 by the active and well-traveled Oskar Suojanen, it has been one of the longest-lived Finnish bands, with a version of it still playing today. The players in the 1910 photograph (see Figure 13) were mostly Montana Finnish coal miners. Charles Kleemola, who came from Ely, Minnesota, is also in this picture (second row, second from left.) The conductor is George Wahlström (first row center), who was also active in Ashtabula, Ohio and Northern Michigan. The Finnish bandsmen traveled to wherever there were playing opportunities. Suojanen also formed an all-girls' Finnish brass band while in Red Lodge. Such a group was probably unique in America in the late 1800s.[11]

Figure 13. The Red Lodge, Montana, Finnish "Military Band," 1910. Photograph from Kleemola family.

At its most active period (around 1920), the Louhi Band's performance history mentions that it participated in local school concerts, at Finnish festivals in Pennsylvania, Ohio and West Virginia, and at Finnish funerals, and it also marched in local parades. In 1918, the band took part in the All-Nations Parade in New York City, and while there they recorded *Maamme*, the Finnish national anthem, for the Victor Phonograph Company. In the summer of 1920, the band toured Finland, giving 30 concerts during their three-month stay. Composer Jean Sibelius expressed surprise at the musical quality of its playing.[12]

At the time that the Louhi Band made the Victor recordings, the conductor was Louis (Lauri) Koski, a very active personality in Finnish-American bands, who was also a composer and had some contact with American bandmasters Arthur Pryor and John Philip Sousa. Both Sousa and Pryor had included Koski's marches in their programs. These recordings are some of the earliest Finnish-American recordings made.

Another Finnish community band with a longer and more successful history was the Humina Band of Ashtabula Harbor in northern Ohio, established by John Ronberg in 1894. Rehearsals were held two or three times a week, and under the direction of such capable bandsmen as J. F. Jacobson, who directed from 1897 to 1917, the band grew into a balanced ensemble of 50 to 60 players.[13]

The 's membership followed a pattern, often repeated in other Finnish-American musical groups: original band members were mainly working men who had an amateur interest in music. As the band developed and grew and as replacements were gradually needed for older, retiring members, younger musicians trained in American school bands were added. Many of these musicians had received early training from the bandmaster himself. J. F. Jacobson succeeded Ronberg and was one of the first Finnish directors to organize a program in Ohio schools for beginning class instruction in band instruments for children from 12 to 16 years of age. Some other directors of the Humina Band included Louis Koski (previously mentioned), George Wahlström, and Kaarlo Mackey. Humina was also unique in that Jacobson and Wahlström led the band for many decades. Like the Louhi Band, the Humina Band made many concert tours to other Finnish-American and non-Finnish communities, and also, of course, to Finland. These tours included: Minnesota and Michigan (1908), New York City (1924), Detroit, Michigan (1925), New York City again (1926), Finland and Sweden (1927), and the Tercentenary Celebration of the first Finnish settlers in America at Chester, Pennsylvania (1938). At this last celebration, both the US Army and the US Navy Bands were present, in addition to the Humina Band.

Finnish bandmasters who worked in Ohio, Pennsylvania, and Massachusetts rarely came to the Iron Range of Minnesota. However, their biographies are similar enough to the Minnesota pioneers to warrant comparison. Jacobson and Wahlström were the most influential of the Ohio Finnish bandmasters. John F. Jacobson, the director of the Humina Band for twenty years, was born in 1872 in Alajärvi in Ostrobothnia. He received his early musical training as a cornetist in the Häme Battalion Military Band and later served for two years in the Navy Band in Turku (1893-1895). After emigrating to America in 1895, he directed Finnish bands in at least six different communities, including groups in New England and in the copper country of northern Michigan.

George Wahlström was one of the prominent Finnish-American bandmasters of the early twentieth century. He was born in Helsinki in 1883, and received his musical training in the Uusimaa Battalion Military Band (southern Finland). After coming to the US in 1902, he first organized a band in Maynard, Massachusetts, and later directed the Louhi Band in Pennsylvania in 1905. The record is not clear about where he fit into the Louhi Band's list of conductors, but he apparently did not stay there long. He later conducted bands in Ohio, Michigan, and Montana. He settled in northern Ohio for most of his career, where he also became a well-known school band director in Ashtabula.

Temperance societies contributed to the promotion of music in Finnish America by sponsoring the first regional and national Finnish festivals. These multi-day events began in 1898 and have continued in some form into the present. The programs, fashioned after the *Kansanvalistusseura* (KVS) festivals in Finland, included concerts and contests for musical groups. The winning bands and choirs received cash prizes. The annual temperance yearbooks indicate that the Humu Band and the Sulo Band, both from Fairport Harbor, Ohio, received first prizes in 1899. The *Vapaudenkaipuu* Band from Ely, Minnesota, and the Hibbing Finnish Band won in 1903 with the latter winning again in 1905. *Vapaudenkaipuu,* a rather poetic name meaning "Yearning for Freedom," is not found again in other sources, and most likely refers to the established Ely Finnish Temperance Band. In 1908, the Louhi Band of Monessen, Pennsylvania won. The first such temperance festival held in Minnesota took place in Eveleth in 1904.

Finns were often members of bands outside the Finnish community. In the Hancock-Houghton area of Northern Michigan, Finnish players were members of the Calumet and Hecla miners' band. The Lake Superior Mining Company of Hibbing sponsored a Finnish immigrant band calling itself the Lake Superior Cornet Band. Finnish bandmasters were often called upon to direct non-Finnish groups as well, as in the case of one conductor who took over leadership of five bands at the same time.[15] A seasonal calendar of travel apparently developed for those Finnish-American bandleaders who were in demand, being in one community for some weeks, presenting a concert, and then moving on.

Of the bands established after 1910 almost all were associated with the newly forceful socialist movement that emerged prior to World War I and spawned a new generation of Finnish-American bands. Some started as balanced ensembles with a full complement of instruments, unlike most of the traditional Finnish bands of the earlier period. Members of the later bands had better musical training, with access to school and other community band programs outside of Finnish circles. However, some later Minnesota examples were socialist-sponsored bands that endeavored to revive the old traditional *seitsikko* (septet) ensemble.

Figure 14. Program from the second annual American Finnish Music Association Festival, Ironwood, Michigan; August 3-5, 1913. From IHRC Finnish Collection

An early effort to organize a nationwide Finnish amateur music society was the Finnish-American Music Association (*Amerika-Suomi Musiikkiyhdistys*), founded in 1911. The Association had as its mission "to unite all Finnish singers and players, regardless of political beliefs, to make known Finnish music, to follow the development of the art of composition in the former homeland, and to arrange for lectures, concerts and music festivals."[16] During the few years it existed, the organization sponsored some significant festivals, but its organizational difficulty lay in a board of directors from too widely dispersed locations, making planning and meetings impossible. An elegant festival program cover is shown in Figure 14. Its date is just prior to the founding of the Sibelius Club, a group with a similar mission, but more geographically focused on Finnish communities in Pennsylvania and Ohio with chapters in Monessen,

Cleveland, Brooklyn (NY), Weirton (WV), and DeKalb (IL). Of course, each community had an active Finnish band. For several years the two organizations shared board members. The Sibelius Club, founded in Monessen, Pennsylvania, in 1914, became the successor. A letter of birthday greeting from the Sibelius Club of Monessen to Finnish conductor Robert Kajanus, dated November 14, 1916, is in the archives at the Sibelius Museum at the University of Turku. Fabian Dahlstrom, emeritus professor at the Museum in an article in the Swedish language periodical *Norden* (Oct 26, 1989) also refers to the Monessen Sibelius Club and its founder, Yrjö Sjöblom.

The Sibelius Club shared the goals of the *Amerika-Suomi Musiikkiyhdistys*, and successfully started a publishing house, a periodical, sponsored festivals, helped organize concert tours, and appeared to have assisted in the formation and instruction of new bands and choirs.

It is not exactly known when the Sibelius Club discontinued, but it was still active in the early 1920s. Examples of music that the Sibelius Club published can still be found in several band music libraries and collections, such as a folder of music from the Hibbing Socialist Workers' Band,[17] in the Berkeley (California) Socialist Workers' Band,[18] and in the music library of the Hibbing City Band. The Hibbing City Band, although not ethnically Finnish in its later years, did have Finnish conductors (notably William Ahola and Victor Taipale (discussed in Chapter 4), and was first formed with many members from the local Finnish band. The old Hibbing City Band library is typical for the city bands on the Iron Range, with a full range of published American band music of the time as well as the Sibelius Club materials and some arrangements of Finnish band music published by Carl Fischer and H. N White.

Clear evidence of support for music education among Finnish-Americans is an item published in the Sibelius Club magazine *Airut*, a list of guidelines for the aspiring music teacher. It is not clear whether the Club was in any further way involved in teacher training, but the concepts here probably reflect values of the Finnish bandmasters who were active at that time. By 1921, most Finnish-American bands had been formed (and many had already disappeared), so these anonymous guidelines may have addressed a new generation of bandmasters, anticipating future growth.

Instructions to Young Music Teachers

> *First impressions*
> Prepare for the first lessons so pupils will have a positive impression of you.
>
> *Be mindful of your own work*
> Your first responsibility as a teacher is to your own pupils, and this ultimately measures your value in the profession. This meaning also presumes that if you are openly critical of another teacher's work and you see yourself as blameless, you may have a distorted view of reality.

Do not promise too much
You are, from the beginning, incapable of guessing the potential of a new pupil. Therefore, do not beforehand boast about what might be possible. One man may be able to guide a horse to the trough, but even ten men cannot force the horse to drink.

Don't program too-difficult music, or lead too-hard rehearsals
Start out the year with a rehearsal of less difficult music, and, for however long as necessary, keep at a level that is not too difficult for the learners. Too challenging rehearsal are frequently "eternal" and "loathsome", and "hopeless" to pupils.

Endeavor to Understand Your Pupils
Paying attention to pupils' moods, attitudes, and feelings, giving a sympathetic response to their efforts, believing that their hard work will bring positive results, are a teacher's most important attitudes.

Study your pupils' facial features
Your pupils' facial features show their interest, their comprehension, their delight, or their reluctance and rebellion-like a barometer. Develop in yourself sensitivity to your pupils' moods.

Always be honest
Pupils want to become knowledgeable, and so if you speak it should always be factual. Showering them with flattery may seem to be a way to get children to like you. However, do not always be praising a pupil's playing if it is not truthfully well done.

Teach the basics
Do not ever miss the opportunity to teach within the rehearsal, or present something new. However, before beginning to conduct a rehearsal of pupils, give them a complete explanation of what is new, and how it is to be understood. Then you can expect the pupils to be interested. Also, avoid using the negative term *do not*. For example, if a pupil plays too loudly, say, "Play it softer, more quietly", and avoid saying: "Don't play it so loudly". Always, your speaking manner should be clear and conscientious, or at least only vaguely critical.

Always maintain an animated demeanor
Always remember to give your best effort when you teach and conduct. One slack, sleepy rehearsal is a mode that will be hard to break in the future.

Create and maintain a friendly atmosphere
The teacher tries to earn the pupils' and parents' confidence and gain some popularity with them. The fortunate situation is when this is truly earned through good teaching and functioning in the

classroom. One simple word on this: a single deliberate though well-meant insult, for some selfish reason, will be a costly mistake lasting a very long time. A music teacher will be excellent when, for only every other pitfall, he takes a spill! A person must try to help himself merely by helping others. The "theft" of another person's reputation may seem cheaper than the value of his money and property. If you plan to be a music teacher in the future, there will come to you also the need to care about a colleague's misfortune."[19]

The Sibelius Club did not survive beyond the end of the 1920s, when many Finnish immigrant cultural institutions either changed emphasis or discontinued, due to world conditions or the Depression. In its most active years, the club had a lively correspondence with Finnish composers, invited guest conductors like veteran Finnish bandmaster A. A. Lumme to America, and supported the only significant band music publishing effort ever to occur among Finns in America.

Finnish Bands and American Traditions

Finnish immigrant bandsmen operated with relative familiarity in America because of an already well-established community-band tradition. The American band "juggernaut" was in full force when the Finns arrived after the 1880s and the newcomers quickly adapted to American ways of doing things: easy acquisition of instruments and music, the multiple functions of the band in the community, and a process of recruiting and training new players from among the young and willing. This growing band culture in America in the late 1800s made the immigrant bandsmen feel welcome upon arrival. The Finnish bands were often called upon to provide music for civic occasions, and the Finnish players filled the ranks of the early community bands. The American band movement also eventually absorbed the Finnish bands, drawing many players away from their traditional function in the ethnic community.

The earliest history of the amateur and community band movement in America coincided with the publication of several brass-band method books prior to the War Between the States. Dodworth's *Brass Band School* (1853) was the earliest of these. The mass production of inexpensive instruments soon followed. Manufacturers also assisted newly formed bands with discounts, term payments, and trade-ins, all in anticipation of modern music merchandizing practices. Records show that the successful bandmaster of such an ensemble would have to be an effective teacher, because many recruits would enter into membership with little or no training. Thus, instrumental music education of a certain sort was very common in America in the 1800s, but not in the schools and apparently not always with glorious results. In 1885, the *Salem Leader* editorialized that the "band of mercy" was the brass band "that didn't practise (sic) evenings."[20] The line drawn between amateur and professional bandsman of the time is rather fuzzy: many "professional" players, often civil war veterans, would actually be engaged in a profession outside of music. The quality of the amateur brass player could often rival the professional who sat next to him. This is a situation similar to modern times in the musical life in most cities, where professional players are often performing next to accomplished amateurs in a wide range of concert settings.

The importance of community support for the local brass bands was a factor from the beginning. Bands and towns saw a need for each other, and contemporary newspaper articles emphasize diversion for the young men during the long winter evenings.[21] Articles mention assistance being needed from townspeople for purchasing instruments. Tiede suggests two major elements in the situation of Minnesota community bands at the time: "one being community involvement and support needed for such enterprise, and the other being the fact that the men who made up the band were not professionals and didn't own their own instruments, but immigrant farmers, laborers and business men of an amateur standing."[22] To get the community involved was essential and a rather clever move on behalf of band leadership. It assured them an audience whenever and wherever they performed. If the townspeople were to get their money returned or get a return for their money, they would have to make sure that the band had opportunities to play and audiences to play for. This community effort and support was significant in establishing the band's social role. It was a key element for a band to be given the label of a "community band." Although military bands existed in Minnesota at the time, they apparently didn't extend their support toward the development of community groups. "Our first community bands, at least in Minnesota, were truly the product of civic groups, civilian organizations, or personal enterprises."[23]

---

[1]Many steamship, passport, and birth certificate databases can be accessed via the Internet through the Institute of Migration in Turku. *www.migrationinstitute.fi/*

[2]Oskari Tokoi, *Sisu: The Autobiography of the First Premier of Finland* (New York: Robert Speller and Sons, 1957), 32.

[3]Clayton Tiede, "The Development of Minnesota Community Bands during the Nineteenth Century" (PhD diss., University of Minnesota, 1970), 214.

[4]"Amerikan Albuumi, Pictures of Finnish-American Life" Brooklyn, Kustantaja Suomalainen Kansaillis-kirjakauppa" (*Kuvia Amerikan suomalaisten asuinpaikoilta*, 1904), 46.

[5]Emil Saastamoinen, "A Word About Finnish American Music," *Airut* (published by the Sibelius Club, Monessen, Pa. 1921), 3.

[6]Alaine Pakkala, "The Finnish-American Bandsman," *Suomen Silta,* 4 (1985), 1.

[7]Conversation with Simo Westerholm, Finnish Folk Arts Centre, Kaustinen, Finland, January 19, 1999.

[8]Kauko Karjalainen, *Suomalainen Torviseitsikko–Historia ja perinteen jatkuminen* (*The Finnish Brass Septet—History and Living Tradition*). (Tampere, Finland: Tampere University Press, 1995).

[9]*Nivala News* (*Nivala lehti*), Nivala, Finland, Wednesday, December 17, 1975, 1.

[10]Pakkala, "Finnish-American Bandsman," 4:36.

[11]Leona Lampi, *At the Foot of the Beartooth Mountains: A History of the Finnish Communities of Red Lodge Montana* (Coeur d'Alene, ID: Bookage Press, 1998), 47.

[12] Pakkala, "Finnish-American Bandsman," 4:37.

[13]Ibid., 4:38.

[14]*Raittiuskansan kalenteri* (Temperance Society Calendar) was published annually for in Hancock, Michigan by the Finnish Lutheran Book Concern.

[15]Pakkala, "Finnish-American Bandsman," 4:37.

[16]Hans R Wasastjerna, ed., Toivo Rosvall, trans., "History of the Finns in Minnesota," *Minnesotan suomalaisten historia* (Duluth, MN: Finnish-American Historical Society, 1959), 298.

[17]See Hibbing Socialist Workers' Band Collection.

[18]The Berkeley Socialist Workers' Band collection, housed at IHRC, is probably the largest intact Finnish-American band collection in existence (15 linear feet), and includes mostly American band publications available at the beginning of the 1900s.

[19]Instructions to Young Music Teachers (Airut), Sibelius Club Journal, 1921, translated by Paul Niemisto.

[20]Margaret and Robert Hazen, *The Music Men–An Illustrated History of Brass Bands in America* (Washington: Smithsonian Press, 1987), 31.

[21]Tiede, "Development of Minnesota Community Bands," 11.22Ibid., 14.

[23]Ibid., 15.

Chapter Three
BANDS IN MINNESOTA

Many cultural changes in Northern Minnesota took place over just one generation at the turn of the 19th century. Northern Minnesota's early written history starts in the middle 1800s, with readings from notebooks of churchmen who were in contact with native Ojibwa, and from the diaries of voyageurs.[1] Written history has included only brief descriptions of life in the first remote villages of Superior and Duluth. By 1880, some mining and lumbering activity was begun, thereby spurring those developments with which this current study takes an interest: the founding of towns, the opening of new mines, the arrival of European immigrants in throngs, the establishment of public education, and the fostering of musical and cultural life on the Iron Range.

The oldest recorded Minnesota bands were in the southern part of the state, and include the Fort Snelling Military Band, (1850), the German Brass Band of St. Paul (1852), the Owatonna Brass Band (1859), the Mankato Saxhorn Band (1862), Burt's Band of Minneapolis (1877), the Cokato Cornet Band (1880), Tuzzi's Band of Minneapolis (dates unknown), the Aitkin School Band (1900, formed by a retired circus cornetist), and the Beaver Creek Band (1910).[2]

The dates included above note when there was a record of playing activity, and do not necessarily indicate founding dates. Among earlier immigrant groups in Minnesota, most band activity was concentrated in the Czech-Bohemian and German communities. In 1870, a band was organized in New Prague, Minnesota, by Joseph Smisek and Albert Wencel. A catalogue of the part books from this band is at the Immigration History Research Center, University of Minnesota. It includes opera overtures, social dance music, and marches. Additional Czech-Bohemian bands were formed in New Prague by the turn of the century, such as the Bohemian Brass Band formed in 1905 by Jan Komarcek. The German settlement of New Ulm still celebrates German music festivals with band music today. A brass band in New Ulm was formed in the 1870s, and was followed by several others in Minnesota's German communities. These continued to play in the old tradition, especially dance music and marches, until about World War I. Revival groups of the old German brass band tradition can be heard now, usually at festivals and county fairs in Southern Minnesota.

The photograph of Frank Danz and his band of Minneapolis, Figure 14, shows two particularly interesting instruments: an American-style double-bell euphonium and Viennese-style ventilhorn (rotary-valved french horn). You can find a copy of this photograph on the wall in the offices of the Minnesota Orchestra. Frank Danz, Jr. was the first concertmaster of the Minneapolis Symphony Orchestra and director of the Danz Band and the Danz Orchestra upon the retirement of his father, Frank Danz, Sr., in 1884. Frank, Jr. had been a noted violinist with the Theodore Thomas Orchestra and the New York Philharmonic before his return to the Twin Cities.

In 1891 Danz established a series of band concerts at the Lake Harriet (Minnesota) pavilion that became very popular. His orchestra ended their performances during 1902-03. The following season found Danz and most of his men playing in the newly formed Minneapolis Symphony Orchestra under the baton of Emil Oberhoffer.

Figure 15. Frank Danz and his band. Undated. Photo courtesy Harrowgate collection.

The very earliest Finnish immigrants to greater Minnesota included some adventurers arriving in the Red Wing area via the Mississippi River before 1860. Small Finnish Laestadian religious congregations settled in the Cokato area in the 1860s, and some farmers and woods-workers came to the New York Mills area prior to the Iron Range mining boom. None of these earlier arrivals had a brass-band tradition, since they arrived in Minnesota years before such bands had been established in Finland.

The first-known Finnish band musician to arrive in Minnesota wasPeter Esko. Emigrating from Finland in 1876, he and his family ultimately founded the village of Esko, near Cloquet. Not much is known about his musical career, other than that he played cornet in the Helsinki Guards Band. Although he apparently did not continue with any brass-band playing in Minnesota, his descendants were involved in music making.

Details about the founding of the very earliest Finnish bands in Minnesota are not well documented and have often been found to be contradictory. The earliest Finnish bands established in Minnesota, starting with Soudan and Duluth in 1888 and Ely in 1889, were sponsored by the local Finnish temperance societies. A few Finnish bands were independent of socio-political sponsorship, and provided music for all Finnish organizations.

The pioneer Finnish immigrant bands formed before 1900 can be seen as the first period of this history; these bands were the "seitsikko," the Finnish brass septet comprised of an E-flat soprano cornet, two B-flat soprano cornets, an E-flat alto horn, a B-flat tenor horn, a B-Flat euphonium, and a tuba (either E-flat or BB-flat.). Bands that had more than seven players would have the extra players doubling one or more of the seven parts. If a clarinet was added, it was to play the E-flat soprano cornet line. The second period of Finnish bands in America started after 1900, supplied by many newly arrived musicians discharged from discontinued Finnish military bands. These bands often adopted more standard mixed instrumentation in the style of the American bands of the time and primarily played American repertoire. The local Finnish socialist halls usually formed and supported those bands formed after 1900. The bands discussed in this chapter reveal a geographical and chronological flow from northeast to southwest with first period bands being formed in Ely, Soudan, Virginia, and Hibbing by 1895. Second period bands were in the more western towns such as Chisholm, Nashwauk, Bovey, and some non-mining communities, excepting the Crosby band.

Regarding other early Finnish bands, Finnish immigrants were in Duluth somewhat earlier than in Iron Range towns, but no sustainable Finnish bands were formed there until after 1900. Duluth is rather conspicuously absent from this research in part because early historical records are very scanty, and those bands that were known to exist weren't very successful. Duluth may actually hold the record for the oldest Finnish band formed in Minnesota with the Duluth Toivon Tähti (Star of Hope) Temperance Band being established in 1886 under Nicolai Miettunen. However, historical records indicate that this early attempt at a band did not go well and followed the fate of its sponsor, the "Star of Hope No.1" Finnish Temperance Society, which faded within a year. Duluth Finnish socialist bands appeared to have been formed after 1905, under the direction of newly arrived veteran military musician Frank Lindroos, who was then active as a musical leader among Duluth Finns for another fifteen years.

Minnesota's "Iron Range"

The "Iron Range" is a region of Northeast Minnesota, which is mostly contained in St. Louis County, but ends in the Grand Rapids area of Itasca County on the west, and at the Lake Superior shore on the east. As early as 1880 Finns were the fifth largest immigrant group in the entire state, preceded only by Germans, Norwegians, Irish, and Swedes, and most of them were in the north.

Minnesota reached a population of one million at that time, and 36.5% were foreign-born immigrants. Finns came to be considerably larger in number than any other immigrant group that came to the Iron Range.[3] This emigration was surprisingly large, if calculated as a percentage of total Finnish population. Almost every Finnish family today has some distant relatives living in the U.S. or Canada. A synthesis of several tallies shows that 23,000 came to the U.S. in the late 1880s, 36,000 in 1892 alone, 23,000 in 1902, and 19,000 in both 1909 and 1910. As late as 1980, almost a century after the immigration, St. Louis County, Minnesota, had the largest population with Finnish ancestry in the United States (17,394)

The Northern Minnesota communities identified for inclusion in this study showed significant evidence of band activity during the period of immigration. For many of these communities 1885 was an important year because of the completion of the Duluth, Messabe, and Northern Railway main network between the Vermilion Range mining towns in the east and the Mesabi towns in the west. About then, a large group of Finnish miners and their families began arriving on the Iron Range from other mining centers in Northern Michigan. Soudan Location was the destination of the first group that arrived in 1882. Many of these "skilled miners" were Finns who had initially landed in Northern Michigan a few years earlier. In those few seasons they had already been rapidly "converting parts of the Upper Peninsula in to a new Finland."[4] Apparently these newly arrived miners and their families were seeking the better opportunities that Northern Minnesota offered.[5] The founding dates of some Iron Range villages may have preceded the arrival of the first Finnish immigrants, but often only by a few months or a year. After 1895, further immigration exploded and the development of communities in Northern Minnesota occurred rapidly.

The Finnish-American brass bands' connection with their immigrant communities helped define their function and value at the beginning. However, the American-born citizens of Iron Range towns also had certain expectations about the role the brass band played in the wider community, even if those communities were just barely established by the 1890s. Many Minnesotans, both American born and immigrant, who settled in newly formed Iron Range towns, had already developed a taste for brass band music from previous locations. Many mining company executives were originally from states on the eastern seaboard and from communities where brass bands had been important for decades. They began promoting brass bands in the Range communities. At the beginning of the 1900s, the important Finnish contribution to band history in Iron Range Minnesota-and in other industrial or mining regions of North America-was that of music pioneer. The Finnish immigrants' passion for brass band music moved across the Atlantic and contributed to band culture in early twentieth-century America.

The Finnish men who mined actually had almost no experience as miners in Finland, but they demonstrated a skill using woodsmen's axes and mauls that could easily be transferred to a miner's pick. With new possibilities for mining work rapidly developing in Minnesota's Vermilion range, many Finnish miners and their families moved from the Copper Country[6] or Upper Peninsula iron mines near Marquette: Ishpeming, Republic, and Negaunee. But by 1900, the demand for miners and other laborers on the Range became so great that the word spread to Europe, and increasing numbers of direct immigrants arrived. The 1910 census reported that 14.1% of the children in St. Louis County outside Duluth were foreign-born, and foreign-born adult males over 21 outnumbered native-born males four or five to one![7] Note the variety of ethnic origins of the copper miners posing at the end of a work shift in a photograph taken around 1900 (Figure 16).

Figure 16. North Tamarack Mine near Calumet, Michigan, ca. 1900. Niemisto family collection.

It would be tempting to hope that bands from other ethnic groups paralleled the history of Finnish bands on the Iron Range. However, the populations of European immigrants to Northern Minnesota were not evenly represented in the band communities. Even ethnic groups with known band cultures were apparently unable to sustain their music traditions upon arrival in Northern Minnesota. By 1900, 4,600 Finns were settled in Northern Minnesota along with 2,600 South Slavs, 2,050 Swedes, 850 Italians, 650 Norwegians, 600 Cornwall English, 325 Germans, 255 Irish, 125 Russians, about 100 Canadians, 100 Polish, and 75 Danes.[8] Photographs of Slovenian brass bands have been found in Ely, and Ely's Scandia Band is a known example of a Swedish-speaking band: these groups represent the two next-largest immigrant populations after the Finns. Bands of other ethnic groups appear not to have been formed, because the supporting populations were too small although Italian bandsmen were found in almost every community band. The formation of local Italian bands would seem likely, but there is no evidence of such.

The Range-wide miners' strike of 1907 caused great numbers of Finnish-born miners to be blacklisted and forced to find work elsewhere. A newly arrived population who came directly to Minnesota from Finland, not by way of Michigan as previously, quickly replaced the pre 1900 Finnish immigrants in the mines. The mining industry, however, was very surprised to find that these newly arrived Finns were even more politically astute, more experienced in labor activism, and in general, more of a problem to management than the ones they had just blacklisted. It was from this second group of immigrants that most of the socialist halls and their bands emanated. The blacklisted Finns had thus become more politically invigorated and also became associated with the socialist movement, many in rural non-mining communities such as Sturgeon Township, Cromwell, and Embarrass.

In 1910, the immigrant population on the Iron Range had grown to 41,000. More than 10,000 of those were Finns, who were the largest foreign group in many towns, such as Soudan, Biwabik, Eveleth, Gilbert, Kinney, Mountain Iron, Virginia, Bovey, Chisholm, Hibbing, Keewatin, Nashwauk, and Taconite (Alanen in Clark, 1989). However, the four largest cities of the region-Virginia, Eveleth, Hibbing, and Chisholm-had significant representations of all ethnic groups and were surely the most multinational communities in Minnesota at that time.

A roster from the Hibbing City Band that went to the Minnesota State Fair in 1915 shows that many Italian immigrants were sitting beside Finns on the journey to St. Paul. The band's roster included Emil Wuorio, J.W. Moore, Joseph Pouter, Ben Setterland, Hemming Hautala, D.J. Rogers, H. Hamori, John Smith, Peter Aho, Tony Santini, William Nurmio, Charles Sandquist, Louis Sabbatini, Ed Sabbatini, Guy Tourassoni, George Martin, Joseph Olivadoti, Alex Eckstrom, Charles Gambauch, G.H Kohrt, Irwin Klizzman, G.S. Blake, J.E. Sawler, F. DiMarco, and conductor William Ahola.[9] It is not possible to know the ethnic background of all Hibbing band members, but there are clearly six Finnish surnames and six Italian surnames, with thirteen members whose origins are not as obvious. Ameriikan Poijat cornetist Don Hakala, who grew up in Chisholm in the 1950s and 1960s, remembers playing in the Chisholm City Band "as the only Finn sitting next to all the Italians."[10] Italian musicians were a part of

America's band history in many regions, and were very evident in the rosters of the Iron Range bands, including on the podium.[11]

The events of the second decade of the 1900s, including World War I, prompted the United States Government enforced more stringent immigration procedures, signaling a more isolationist stance intended to protect the American labor force and limit the arrival of potential subversives. Finnish independence was declared in 1917, creating a new hope for the poor landless Finn, who had previously been the most common class of Finnish émigré. Both of these major occurrences, happening in rapid succession, caused Finnish immigration to almost cease entirely. The Finnish immigrant communities in the U.S. began to diffuse and loosen their contact with the former homeland, although those ties would be quickly remade in the late 1930's, when the Soviet Union threatened Finland's existence during the early years of World War II. The Depression's impact on the Finnish American bands was both good and bad. Many of the older bands melted away in the 1930's as players moved around the country in search of work. Yet the rise of the socialist movement among Iron Range Finns, and the Federal Depression era programs that promoted rural cultural activity, both gave many of the Finnish band new hope and opportunity.

The decades prior to 1920 appear to be the most robust time for most of the Finnish bands, their "Golden Era." They enjoyed wide community participation, with active, national organizations sponsoring festivals and contests. In Minnesota, as elsewhere, this high point was fairly short-lived. Already by 1915, labor strife in the mines, changes in players' job situations, changes in the mining industry, and aggressive Americanization campaigns by schools and communities, encouraged the breakdown of many such ethnic cultural organizations. By 1920, the number of foreign-born Finns in Minnesota numbered about 30,000. That peak year, 1920, was also the end of Finnish immigrant population growth in Minnesota.

After 1920, most Finnish bandsmen had begun to abandon ethnic bands and blend into the larger musical community, and some had done so much earlier. In addition, some of the bands suffered from the many immigrant bandsmen giving up on their American adventure, returning to Finland with their pockets full of new dollars earned in the mines and lumber camps. The Finnish bands in America sustained further blows to their stability in the aftermath of World War I and Finnish independence. The war sapped the bands of many skilled personnel who left for the American military. The formation of the new Finnish state suddenly made emigration to America unfashionable and thus essentially shut down the source of new brass players from the old country. In tracing the histories of bands in Minnesota, it has usually been easier to pinpoint the year in which a band was formed, but much harder to determine exactly when a band ceased to exist. Probably many of them just slowly faded away.

As the older of Finnish ethnic bands faded, municipal bands were called upon to play when music was needed for the large, annual Finnish summer festivals, although significant numbers of Finnish musicians performed as members of those community groups. Finnish regional celebrations and music-making continued to go on nevertheless, and "about every town on the Range with a population of more than 500 had a band, and every town had a summer celebration in which all bands participated."[12]

The Iron Range Communities with Finnish Bands

Figure 17 is an historical map that shows the relative locations of communities where Finnish bands were most common on Minnesota's Iron Range and other nearby communities. The map does not include every town mentioned in this study. In general, the oldest Finnish bands started in Ely and Soudan in the northeast, and subsequent bands were formed along a southwestern path.

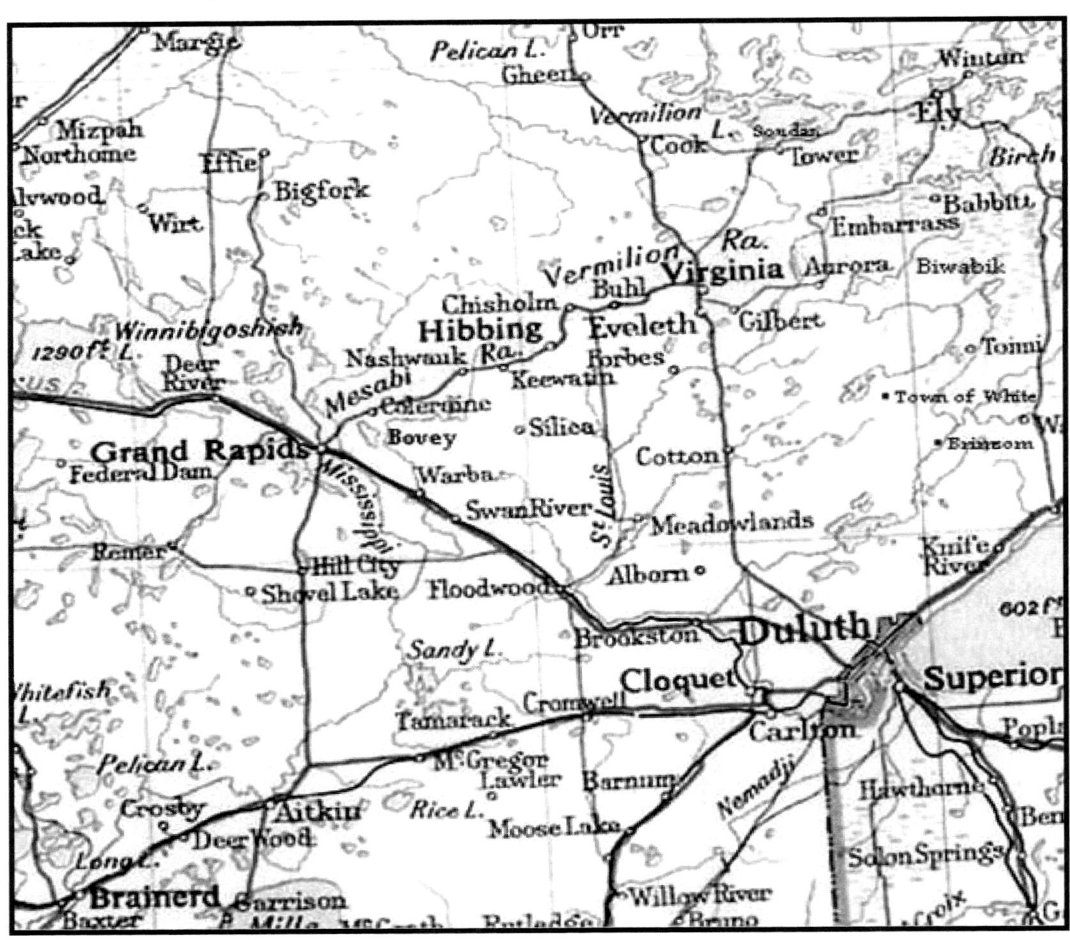

Figure 17. Map showing the location of communities where Finnish bands were most common on Minnesota's Iron Range and other nearby communities.

Ely

Ely developed as a village quickly after the discovery of iron ore deposits at the Pioneer Mine site (1886). Its status as an organized village was established in 1887, and it was incorporated as a city in 1891. Winton, a nearby smaller village, shares its history with Ely. Some suggest that Winton, with a Finnish population of mostly forest workers who had arrived before the miners, had a well-established community years before Ely was developed. Soudan and Tower also had close associations with Ely

In nearby Tower, the first town settled north of Duluth and the site of the oldest iron mine in Minnesota, the first miners arrived in 1882 (the same year as neighboring Soudan). Earlier exploration of this region by American prospectors and settlers occurred as early as 1875, but no mining operation had been established. In 1884, the first leg of the mining railroad from Two Harbors to Tower was completed. Then the Soudan mining settlement received a large Finnish population with a mass arrival from Northern Michigan. Tower's population contained more of a concentration of Swedes, Cornwall English, and others. A Tower native, Leo Wiljamaa, related, "Some of those in Soudan came from Quinnesec mine in Michigan in 1885 by the trainload...there were Finnish, Cornish, and Slovenians."[13]

Ely (Winton) and Soudan were the earliest Iron Range towns to have brass bands, Finnish or otherwise. As with the brass bands in Finland, they were formed under the sponsorship of social organizations that provided funds for instruments, practice halls, and performance opportunities. In Soudan, the Finnish Temperance Society was established in 1887. Pekka Westerinen organized their band in 1888. Wasastjerna writes about this pioneering effort: "It was conspicuously successful. It was the first of many Finnish bands to be founded in Minnesota."[14] This was the only time that this pioneering Finnish choral music leader in America, Pekka Westerinen, is mentioned in conjunction with bands: mostly known in Northern Michigan, most of his activity in Minnesota was with western Finnish communities as a choir conductor. Wasastjerna's reference to Westerinen and the Soudan band has not been corroborated by any other sources thus far. However, since the Finnish Temperance Society in Soudan was Minnesota's oldest, with its unusually shaped oval hall already having been constructed in 1887, it is certainly possible that a band was formed there from among newly arrived Finnish miners who had previously played in bands in Northern Michigan. A newspaper article, however, announced a contrary report that Ely citizen Oscar Castrén had formed a Soudan Finnish temperance band in 1895. It is not known if there were two Finnish bands in Soudan, or if the first one collapsed and was then revived by Castrén. What is possibly the oldest Finnish band in Minnesota has left almost no historical records to examine.

Not helping to clarify this sketchy history, the 1904 Amerikan albuumi states that the first Minnesota Finnish band was organized by Nicolai Miettunen in Ely in 1889, and that band was associated with the Ely Finnish Temperance Society. This publication, and possibly other sources, was apparenly unaware of the Soudan band under Westerinen as being first, and it is not known why this earlier example was overlooked. It is known that the Soudan Band continued as a community group for many years, although few details are available.

Besides the information that Miettunen started a band in 1889, there are no other records found to support when and if other Finnish bands were formed in Ely. It is known that "Professor" Castrén, another of the early Finnish band leaders in Minnesota, moved to Ely from Northern Michigan in 1890. The first mention in the press of the "Ely Cornet Band" was December 26, 1891. An early photograph of the "Ely City Band" is dated 1893. The connections between these bands, if they were in fact different, and any connection between Miettunen and Castrén, are all lost to us. However, we can speculate that they were mutually involved in some way, merely because they appear to have been active at the same time in the same city. By 1895, press announcements mention the Ely City Band and the Finnish Temperance Band in the same program, with Castrén playing and leading. No press article, or any other document, has been found that includes both Miettunen and Castrén in any mutual activity.

Nicolai Miettunen also came to Ely from Northern Michigan in 1889. Finnish language accounts state that he founded the Elyn soittokunta (Ely City Band), although the accounts confuse whether the band in question was the Finnish temperance band or a town band that he formed, or if they were the same. Being one of the first bands in the region, any new band surely served many social and musical purposes and certainly must have also been well known outside Finnish circles. Two of the earliest newspaper articles about Ely bands are shown below. Both date from the season when the Finnish Temperance Hall ("Finn Hall") was just completed. In the July program there is reference to the "Temperance Band" and in the October program to the "Finn Band." It is likely that they were the same band and were directed by Castrén, but that is not certain.

Figures 18 and 19 show musical selections that are consistent with American tastes in concert band programming at the time, with solos, novelty numbers, and excerpts from popular operas, marches, and overtures. Only a few items of a particularly Finnish nature are included in either program, except some national songs rendered by the "Finnish Quartette." It can be speculated that Castrén, already in the United States since youth, was much at ease with the American band tradition whereas Miettunen, trained as a military musician in Finland and recently emigrated, was of the old school and probably spoke very limited English. The audiences for both entertainments were drawn from the Finnish community as well as the wider community. At the time, the Finn hall or "Pink Hall," so called because of the color of its exterior, had no known political connotation and was the only facility in Ely large enough for such public events.

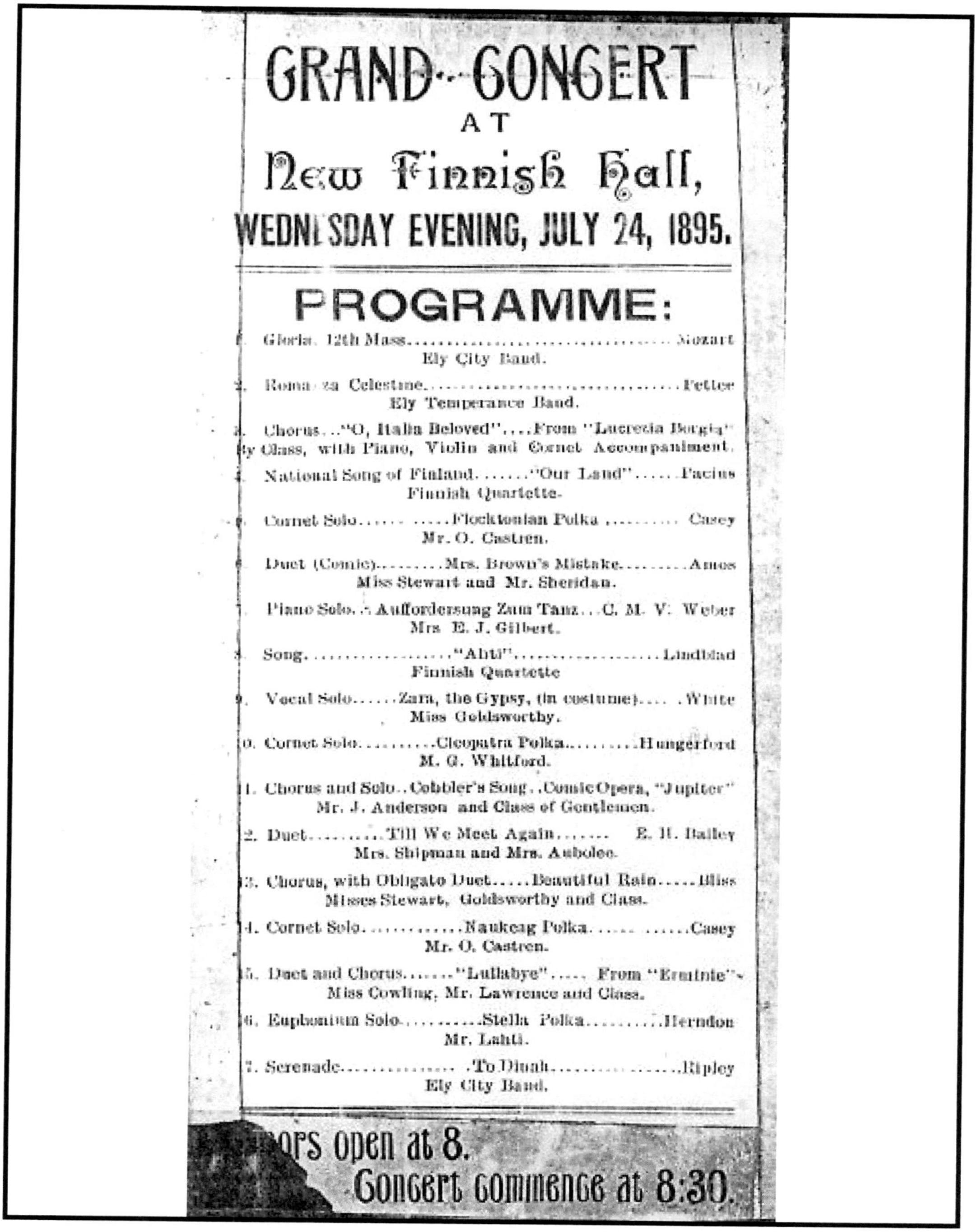

GRAND CONCERT

AT

New Finnish Hall,

WEDNESDAY EVENING, JULY 24, 1895.

PROGRAMME:

1. Gloria. 12th Mass.................................Mozart
Ely City Band.

2. Romanza Celestine.................................Fetter
Ely Temperance Band.

3. Chorus..."O, Italia Beloved"....From "Lucrezia Borgia"
by Class, with Piano, Violin and Cornet Accompaniment.

4. National Song of Finland......."Our Land"......Pacius
Finnish Quartette.

5. Cornet Solo...........Flocktonian Polka..........Casey
Mr. O. Castren.

6. Duct (Comic).........Mrs. Brown's Mistake.........Amos
Miss Stewart and Mr. Sheridan.

7. Piano Solo.-Auffordersung Zum Tanz...C. M. V. Weber
Mrs E. J. Gilbert.

8. Song...................."Ahti"...................Lindblad
Finnish Quartette

9. Vocal Solo......Zara, the Gypsy, (in costume).....White
Miss Goldsworthy.

10. Cornet Solo..........Cleopatra Polka.........Hungerford
M. G. Whitford.

11. Chorus and Solo..Cobbler's Song..Comic Opera, "Jupiter"
Mr. J. Anderson and Class of Gentlemen.

12. Duet..........Till We Meet Again.......E. H. Bailey
Mrs. Shipman and Mrs. Auboles.

13. Chorus, with Obligato Duet.....Beautiful Rain.....Bliss
Misses Stewart, Goldsworthy and Class.

14. Cornet Solo.............Naukeag Polka............Casey
Mr. O. Castren.

15. Duet and Chorus......."Lullabye"..... From "Erminie"
Miss Cowling, Mr. Lawrence and Class.

16. Euphonium Solo...........Stella Polka..........Herndon
Mr. Lahti.

17. Serenade................To Dinah..................Ripley
Ely City Band.

...ors open at 8.

Concert commence at 8:30.

Figure 18. Ely Miner announcement of a concert featuring bands, July 1895.

Next Saturday Night.

The grand musical entertainment for the Bell benefit, will take place Saturday evening October 19, at the Finn hall. The best of local talent will take part and everyone knows what this means. The concerts heretofore put on by home talent have met with approval by all who attended and the entertainment Saturday evening will be one of the best ever produced. The Arions, the City band, the Finn band and the others taking part are recognized as entertainers and a large audience will greet them on the rising of the curtain next Saturday evening. The program is as follows and the admission has been placed at 50 cents:

PROGRAMME.

Overture.........Crown of Victory..........Ripley
Ely City Band.

Overture...............Midland...........Finn Band.

Song...............The Serenade...........Schmidt
The Arion Club.

Vocal Duet..Gently Sighs the Breeze...Glover
Miss Eva Stewart, Mr. L. McCullers.

Tripple tongued polka...Geraldine....Gaylord
Ely City Band.

Fantasia.....With Forepaughs.......Finn Band

Cornet Duet...Lathord Watch..........................
Masters Joe. and John Seraphine.

Song.....Sleep Gentle Mother...from Trovatore
The Arion Club.

Solo and Chorus......Poor Jilted Jonathon
R. Lawrence accompanied by Messrs.
McCullers, White, Sheridan and Collins.

Challenge Concert Polka. (Bass Solo) with
band accompaniment..................Giovenini
Ely City Band.

Cornet Solo.. Flirtation Polka..........................
Prof. O. Castren with band accompaniment.

March....................................Ely City Band.

Figure 19. Concert at Finnish Temperance Hall ("Finn Hall"), Ely Miner, October 2, 1895.

Figure 20. Ely Finnish Temperance Band, March 20, 1905. Photograph courtesy IRHC, Gilbert, MN.

A favorite legend concerns the Ely Finnish Temperance Band, and while mentioned by many, is not verifiable. The midsummer temperance parade was held on a hot June day. After completing the long march while playing brass instruments and dressed in hot woolen uniforms, the Ely Finnish Temperance Band made a right-face at the parade terminus and marched directly into a saloon. Figure 20 shows the band playing at a ceremony in the snow, March 20, 1905.

In 1904, Charles Kleemola began to lead a Finnish band in Ely. Kleemola called it the Sampo Band, and it was probably under the same sponsorship as the 1890s Temperance Band, but with a new name chosen by the new conductor. Photographs show it to be a large and well-appointed band, and it was quite famous on the Range. The band's history during this decade is closely tied to the activity of its director Kleemola, whose biographical details are discussed later in this chapter.

Figure 21. The Ely Sampo Band, 1904, led by a young Charles Kleemola. The roster includes: Bottom row, L to R: Jack Houssa, Ben Kanniainen, Jake Pietila, Nels Paavola, Ed Lampinen, unknown, Onni Koivunen, Toivo Martilla; Second row, L to R: Amalius Stenlund, John Mäki, Henry Sirpiniemi Charles Kleemola, Matt Herranen, Anton Slogar, Theodore Partti; Third Row, L to R: William Jylhä, unknown, Toivo Partti, Erik Marttila, Henry Pietilä, John Mäenpää; Top Row, L to R: unknown, John Johnson, John Lepisto, Mike Laitala, Andrew Watilo, Charles Hendrickson. Anton Slogar was Slovenian. All the rest are thought to be Finnish-born. Photograph courtesy Kleemola family.

Figure 22. Ely Sampo Band, Charles Kleemola conducting, ca. 1908. Photograph courtesy Kleemola family.

This unusual photograph, figure 22, shows the Sampo Band of Ely performing in a rainstorm. It is most likely taking place at a Midsummer celebration. Only such an important community event would bring a band into very inclement weather. It should be noted, however, that all the instruments pictured are brass, so no risk was felt by the players. However, seeing this photograph reminds one of many old rain-stained band books in the Helsinki Guards' band archives. Conductor Charles Kleemola would have weighed the possible danger to his valuable sheet music before venturing into the rain. It was most certainly an important event. The citizens offering help with umbrellas, the proud demeanor of bandmaster Kleemola standing in front, and a general sense of vital action captured in the image, all give this photograph a special quality and make it a standout among all those discovered during this research.

The Scandia Band, founded in the early 1900s in Ely, included Swedish-speaking immigrants, either from Sweden or Finland, who constituted a substantial population in Ely and other Range towns. The band rosters indicate that some musicians played in both the Scandia Band and the Sampo Band. There was significant community activity among the Iron Range's Swedish-language churches and other cultural organizations. Among the organizations sponsored by Swedish immigrants, the Runeberg Society was a widespread social and benevolent association that specifically represented the Swedish-speaking Finns in North America. Their national yearbook summarizing Swedo-Finnish activity in 1908 mentioned several local clubs, including some in the Minnesota communities of Chisholm, Hibbing, Eveleth, and Ely as well as many locations in Northern Wisconsin and Northern Michigan. Many of these clubs had bands and choirs similar to the Scandia Band of Ely. Very little has been recorded about the activity of the Ely Scandia Band, but the few preserved photographs always show the band in summer outdoor activities such as parades and picnics, and connected with Midsummer celebration.

Figure 23. Ely Scandia Band, 1907. From left to right: John Ekening, Otto Tjaden, Frank Anderson, Dick Hodge, Amelius Stenlund, John Dist, Dave Nyman Hanson, Gust Peterson, Oliver Sundholm, Carl Anderson, William Berglund, Fred Hanson. Photograph courtesy of Iron Range Historical Center, Gilbert.

Biwabik, a village not far from Soudan and Tower, was a mining location as early as 1891. By 1892, the new village had 267 citizens. Biwabik's Finnish Lutheran Church and Temperance Society were established by 1895. Biwabik had a significant Finnish population, but not as high in proportion as in many other nearby mining communities. Finnish band activity there is not well documented, but there is the one instance discussed later in this chapter within the section about Victor Taipale

Eveleth

Eveleth was incorporated as a village in 1893, with 200 citizens. Nearby Fayal Township has a parallel history and figured in the Finnish brass-band story. Finns began arriving in both communities at about the same year. Eveleth has been an active band town for a century, and not only among the Finns. It also is known for having regionally famous town and school bands. From early in the century, the Eveleth City Band had a strong reputation under Italian bandmaster Joseph Moroni, and was a rival group to the legendary Virginia municipal bands under Vernon Malone. Finnish bandmaster Victor Taipale was one of the Eveleth Band's original leaders, and second-generation Finnish-American Emil Ikola was its director after the 1930s. Ikola grew up playing with the Kaiku (Echo) Band of Eveleth. The Finns living in Eveleth and the Fayal Township area apparently had at least two active bands operating simultaneously, the Kaiku Finnish Temperance Band and the Fayal Band.

While the Fayal Band was ostensibly a municipal band for the nearby mining location, its early membership was almost exclusively Finnish. The first Eveleth Finnish Band was sponsored by the Eveleth Finnish Temperance Society, which "allowed the free use of the Temperance hall, provided the musicians became members of the temperance society." The year the band was founded is thought to be 1895 or 1896, which coincides with the founding of similar temperance bands in Virginia and Hibbing. The founding bandmaster was Alex Koivunen.

> As small as the Finnish population was in the mid-1890s, plans for starting a brass band were already being discussed at a meeting at Charles Nieminen's shoemaker's shop in October 1895. A committee was appointed to procure musical instrurnents and managed to buy them, second hand, in Chicago. Others joined the search for a director and had to go outside Eveleth to contact one Alex Koivunen, who had recently come from Finland and was living in Negaunee, Michigan; he agreed to move to Eveleth. The final problem of rehearsal quarters was easily solved by all the potential musicians joining the temperance society, which then gave them free and unlimited use of the hall. When Koivunen left the band, he was followed

briefly by Herman Lindberg, and then permanently by Filemon Jacobson. [15]

The Eveleth Finnish Temperance Society was later reorganized under a new constitution and a new meeting hall was dedicated in 1905. It was with this later temperance group that Victor Taipale developed the *Kaiku* Band.

Figure 24. Eveleth Kaiku Band, date unknown but after 1910. Photograph courtesy Lager Family collection.

No roster has thus far been found for figure 24, but there are several of the same players who are clearly in another photograph of the Kaiku Band taken earlier (see figure 43, chapter 5). The three women, unusual particpants for any Iron Range band at the time, pictured here are discussed in Chapter 6. According to correspondence from Iron Range historian Finny Lager, Emil Ikola, who became the Eveleth City Band director in the 1930s, is pictured here as the young cornet player on the far right. Many members of this Eveleth Kaiku Band appear to be young contemporaries of Ikola, who was born in the United States in 1896. His membership in this band, as a schoolboy, indicates that the involvement of Finnish youth was very important in keeping the tradition alive. Interestingly, very few of the veteran Finnish military musicians mentioned in connection with the early Kaiku Band are any longer pictured in this later photograph. Many of their names, however, can be found on the rosters of various other Iron Range Finnish and municipal bands. Some may have left the region entirely or simply stopped playing after they moved away from the larger mining communities. Their departure from the Eveleth band took place within a five-year period, coinciding with two developments that may have hastened such personnel changes: Victor Taipale's departure as the bandmaster, and the start of a public school band program in Eveleth. Trained young school musicians apparently provided a new source of talent.

Virginia

Virginia was incorporated as a city in 1893, but it had already been a location for miners and lumbermen since at least 1890. In early 1893, the wooden buildings of Virginia burned to the ground as a part of a regional forest fire and it was as a newly rebuilt city that it received its municipal charter. The Virginia Finnish community was just being established at the time of the fire. Trying to comprehend Virginia's elaborate Finnish band history illustrates the complications of tracing ethnic organizations when their situation was constantly in a state of change. The Virginia Finnish Temperance society (Valon Tuote -- Ray of Light) founded its brass band in August 1895, with a substantial 35 musicians under the direction of John Haapasaari. Membership in the band was then open only to members of the temperance society. The first public appearance was made in a November 1895 concert, with band members dressed in new gray-blue uniforms piped with dark-blue braid. Note that several of the players in figure 25 are quite young, including one woman. The photograph is undated, but the dress fashions suggest 1900 or earlier. The Virginia Finnish Temperance Band apparently remained active for several years, but when the Virginia City Band was formed many of the members transferred into that new organization. Soon however, a few of those who had joined the City Band changed plans and organized an independent Finnish band named Jyrinä, (Thunder) which performed at both the Temperance Society and the Socialist Hall events. The Jyrinä band was also in great demand for community funerals, including those of Italians and Slovenians. Many such events provided this band with some extra compensation, and made membership in it more attractive. In 1907, Jyrinä chose to affiliate with the new Virginia Socialist chapter as the official band for their grand new opera hall. These Finnish band musicians probably had differing personal opinions about temperance philosophy, leftist politics, and wanting to connect with the larger Virginia musical community, but followed the path that led to the best music-making opportunities.

Some anecdotal information about the early Finnish bands of Virginia comes from Emily Hobhouse (1860-1926), a social reformer and anti-war activist who was on a lecture tour in Northern Minnesota in 1896. Born in Cornwall, she was an avid spokesperson against the Boer War in South Africa, and later, against World War I. She was a popular public speaker who traveled widely. The following letter mentions her hearing a Finnish band in Virginia while on a lecture circuit.

Figure 25. Virginia Finnish Temperance Band, ca. 1900 or earlier. Photograph courtesy Kaleva Hall, Virginia, MN.

> January 2, 1896: 'I knew I had to address a crowd of men. For nearly a week I had not been able to speak much above a whisper. The Hall was full, it holds nearly 300, and almost all men, only a sprinkling of women, and just before my speech all the business men came down and filled it till there was not standing room, and as soon as I had finished they went away again. I had prepared my address very carefully, but I had neither mind nor voice, so it was a great effort. They listen wonderfully. If it is known I am going to open my mouth the men all come. It is a dreadful position to be in. I gave it to them so hot last night that I almost fear to walk down the street this morning. The dear Finns were there, so proud to play their band for us. Fancy 25 Finns playing brass instruments all out of tune. They wanted to play 6 tunes for me, but I assured them we would not think of troubling them for more than 3 selections.[16]

The "hall" mentioned in this memoir was not named, but was likely Crockett's Opera House. The later Virginia Finnish Temperance Hall, still in use today, was finished in 1906, and no other hall could accommodate the crowd she described. This Hobhouse commentary, about the newly formed band in Virginia (started one year earlier), should be interpreted with some caution, and not be taken as evidence that all the Finnish bands played badly. Keeping in mind that she may have been familiar with the more polished industrial and

Salvation Army bands in England, and that this newly formed amateur group in Virginia may have rendered to her their second or third public performance ever, one should temper how her negative reaction is interpreted. No doubt, that indoor performance in the small hall probably was a bit rough, and probably rather loud.

Leroy Hodges, an immigration official on a fact-finding tour of the Iron Range in 1906, was clearly impressed by the squalor of the living conditions found among many mining families in Virginia and elsewhere. He was equally impressed by the vigorous socialist activity among the Finns. His rather reactionary report, with the unusually candid photographs that he took, is a unique document about life in turn-of-the-century Iron Range towns.

Hibbing

Hibbing (or, earlier, Stuntz Township) was already an established lumber and sawmill center before the War Between the States as a "tent city" for seasonal forest workers. Mining of iron deposits began there in 1891-92, and it was incorporated as a village in 1893. The first Finnish Lutheran Church and the Finnish Temperance Society were formed in 1896

Hibbing's Finnish bands show a continuing saga of changing affiliations and name changes similar to that of Virginia's. The formation of an "Independent Finnish Band" in Hibbing was discussed in the spring of 1895 by interested Finnish miners and lumbermen. They elected a slate of officers with John Haapasaari as chairman and bandmaster, Gust Järvi as secretary, and John K. Mäki as treasurer. Haapasaari was also active in Virginia, where he founded a Temperance band that same year. Given financial support for buying instruments and uniforms by the Lake Superior Mining Company, the independent group then called itself the "Lake Superior Cornet Band." They performed within the Hibbing Finnish community and for the mining company. After Haapasaari's departure, there was no official musical director for a few seasons, which necessitated the band members to take turns with the musical leadership.

The band continued to play and raised enough money through performances to buy "splendid uniforms" to wear in their parades and concerts. These are shown in Figure 26. Without a leader, however, the interest among the membership threatened to wane. The band then found Victor Taipale, newly arrived bandmaster from Finland, and appointed him the new director in 1901. This was Taipale's first position in Minnesota and may have been what drew him from Pennsylvania.

Figure 26. Hibbing Finnish Tapio Band with its new uniforms, 1900.

Figure 27 was found in the Hibbing Historical Society collection and includes a typewritten comment above the photo: Finnish Temperance Society Band 1903. "And how those boys could play!" The players' names were added below, probably by a proud family member of one of the musicians. The text was typed some years later than 1904. Any text written at the time of the photograph would have been in Finnish, the language spoken by everyone in the group. Sitting to the left of bandmaster Taipale, who is second from the left in the center row, is the very young William Ahola who would later become the conductor of the Hibbing City Band and have a musical career in various Iron Range Communities.

Figure 27. Hibbing Finnish Tapio Temperance Band, 1903. Photograph courtesy Hibbing Historical Society.

Receiving encouragement but diminishing financial support from the Lake Superior Mining Company, the band under Taipale sought to change its affiliation. Having been given encouragement and the free use of the Tapio Temperance Society hall for rehearsals, the band renamed itself Tapio, a Kalevala spirit of the forest and a typical Finnish name with clear nationalistic connotations for a band.

The members included several musicians who had already held membership cards from temperance societies in other communities, particularly from Mountain Iron. An earlier Hibbing temperance band, organized in 1896 by Alex Mattson, had temporarily ceased to exist, creating the need that was met by Taipale's group.

In 1903, when the city of Hibbing donated $100 for playing during the Fourth of July celebrations, the band showed its gratitude by once again changing its name, this time to the Hibbing City Band. Under the leadership of Taipale, still somewhat maintaining a Finnish identity, the Hibbing City Band took part in several regional events, winning the second prize in the Ishpeming Michigan Finnish Festival in August of 1903, in which eight bands participated. This band also won additional prizes during the next three years of Finnish regional festivals: second prize in Hibbing in 1904, first prize in Ely in 1905, and again first prize in Ironwood, Michigan in 1906.

By 1905, the Hibbing Concert Band became the official city band and was included in the town budget. Taipale was succeeded by William Ahola in that year and he led the band for the next ten years. He was later succeeded by another Finnish musician, Helmer Frankson, who in 1931 was also mayor of Hibbing.

Hemming Hautala became a long-time resident of Hibbing and in 1930 he started another independent band there, primarily to give local Finns an opportunity to play together for recreation and to foster musical activity among the younger generation. It is not known what this band was called or how it was sponsored, but it probably had a connection with the prevalent Depression-Era initiatives and the St. Louis County Rural Band Association. Wasastjerna writes that Hautala began to invite musicians from the wider community to fill the new band's ranks, and eventually the band included players from eight different national backgrounds. If Wasastjerna's information is correct, this would essentially have been a second community band in Hibbing. When the Virginia Finnish Chorus was planning to take part in the Chicago World's Fair, Hautala's "young generation" band gave several concerts to help them raise money for travel expenses. The band also played at Finnish festivals in Duluth, New York Mills, and Ely. Up to their end, in 1937, they had also given 50 outdoor band concerts and had appeared in numerous parades. It is not clear exactly how Hautala's band was related to the Hibbing City Band or to the bands in the Hibbing schools. No other records are thus far available to clarify.

Hibbing, as with the other larger regional cities, had a Finnish Socialist Workers' Society that sponsored its own band almost as soon as the society was formed. As with most of the Socialist groups on the Range, the Hibbing leftists later precipitated into a "schism" around the interpretation of socialist philosophy, and the original band became associated with the larger of the two divisions, "The Worker's Club," an organization referred to as "the Cradle of the Finnish-American Socialist movement." According to Wasastjerna, "the cultural activities rather than the political faiths are what these societies are best remembered by, and the Workers' Club, which had 140 members even after the schism, engaged actively in the usual patterns of auxiliary cultural endeavors."[17]

The Hibbing Socialist brass band was formed in 1905, with the first leader being Waldemar Eklund. Later directors include some names we regularly see in Iron Range Finnish band histories: Alfred Hongel, Nurmio, Edward Gröndahl, William Ahola and Hemming Hautala, all of whom had other band leadership responsibilities in Hibbing. Edward Gröndahl, who directed just prior to World War I, also organized an apparently independent band named Kaiku (Echo), which also rehearsed at the Workers' Club hall and which included many members of the Socialist club among its players. How this independent band functioned in the Finnish community is not known. During most of the time it existed, the smaller and more radical Socialist Chapter, "No. 2," also sponsored a band, which was under the direction of the same Mr. Gröndahl. Hugo Rosendahl was also in Hibbing and led "some other bands" as well as Aapeli Laitinen, both of whom were involved in the Socialist bands. Nothing more is known about these other groups. The record then suggests that Hibbing had at least three separate Finnish Socialist bands functioning at one time!

Figure 28. Hibbing Concert Band, William Ahola, director, ca. 1910. Photograph courtesy Hibbing Historical Society.

Figure 28 is of the Hibbing City band in its early years. The membership list includes several Finns, as well as several Italian immigrants, who were involved with this band at its formation: Steve Chounaird, Horace Jaynes, Jack Scherding, Louis Sabbatini, Helmer Frankson, Bill Moyle, Al Crowley, Dante Bechetti, Sanford Hill, Cecil Shea, Angelo di Bernardi, Harry Johnson, D. Roschon, Joe Curtis, Joe Panter, Emil Wuorio, Ben Sutherland, George Martin, S. Kontio, Ed Eckstrom, Al Newman, Jerry Cein, John Smith, Hemming Hautala, Frank di Marco, Irving Kleffman, Oscar Widstrand, David Bloom, Guy Tommasoni, and Ahola the conductor.

A profile of early twentieth-century Finnish band activity in Hibbing is a challenge to understand clearly because the written histories are incomplete and conflicting. In addition to the Hibbing temperance and socialist bands that came and went and changed their names, there were apparently also some independent Finnish bands that served some needed musical functions in the community. All of the other large Iron Range cities (Ely, Eveleth, Virginia, and Chisholm) sustained a sufficient population of musicians that allowed for such changing band configurations and reconfigurations. Each city has a somewhat confusing Finnish band history, but none seems cloudier, or busier, than that of Hibbing.

Chisholm

Chisholm's early history was that of a lumber town with no connection to Jesse Chisholm's famous cattle trail from Mexico to Abilene of the mid-1800s, but by 1900 it had begun to develop as a mining community, although on a smaller scale and a bit later than the other communities discussed here. Chisholm had a substantial Finnish population prior to 1910, during which time they maintained a lively cultural activity. Churches, socialist halls, and temperance societies were formed. The Chisholm Finnish temperance society was started in 1901. Nicolai Miettunen formed their band in that same year, after having just arrived from Ely. Other well-known Finnish leaders succeeded Miettunen during the band's short history: Charles Kleemola, Alex Koivunen, and Victor Taipale. Unfortunately, the entire city burned to the ground in 1908, but it had mostly recovered by 1910. The miners' strike of 1907, followed by the fire, scattered many of the Finnish immigrant families to locations outside of Chisholm.

The Chisholm Finnish Workers' Society dates from 1904. The society started a band, with J. G. Hulme as the first bandmaster. Hulme also was a central figure in Finnish workers' choirs in Chisholm for several decades. The familiar traveling conductors Kleemola, Taipale, Koivunen, and Hautala all took their turns leading the Chisholm Finnish Workers' Society (Socialist) Band, sometimes directing the Chisholm Temperance Band and the Socialist Band at the same time. The Socialist band, while directed by the very busy Victor Taipale, was awarded a prize at that first Finnish midsummer festival held in Chisholm in

1904. Note that, for that same festival, Taipale also led the Eveleth Temperance Band. It appears that Finnish Socialist and Temperance musical groups often played in each other's events in the early years of Finnish-American band activity. This Finnish Socialist Band (figure 29) provided the core of players that later developed into the Chisholm City Band. Hemming Hautala's biography has him appearing as a leader and player in many Iron Range Finnish communities with bands for several decades, Chisholm being only one. The subsequent history of the Workers' Society in Chisholm followed an already established pattern, with dissention leading to a split in 1915 and to a subsequent weakening in all its activities, including bands. By then, many Finnish residents of Chisholm had moved onto other locations, fleeing the strike and the fire.

Figure 29. Chisholm Finnish Workers' Band, between 1904 and 1907. John Wilenius is the tuba player second from left in back row; no one else is identified. Photograph courtesy Wilenius family.

Figure 30. Chisholm City Band, ca. 1910. Photo courtesy IRRC, Chisholm.

Comparing Figures 29 and 30, taken in Chisholm within five years of each other, one can see the dramatic change that occurred in that community during that very short period from about 1905 to 1910. Figure 29 shows the well-appointed Finnish Socialist brass band that soon disappeared after the 1907 miners' strike and the subsequent exodus of many Finns from the city. The

1910 photo shows a city band with new uniforms, a mixed instrumentation with several woodwinds, and not much to relate it to Figure 28. If there are any players who appear in both photographs, they are not immediatelty obvious.

Nashwauk

Nashwauk, on the western edge of the Iron Range, saw the first Finnish immigrants arrive around 1902, the same year that the village was organized and registered a post office. In a common pattern for villages formed after 1900, Nashwauk's foremost Finnish organizations were first socialist labor groups, representing the miners, although many Finns in Nashwauk also worked in the lumber industry. Nashwauk's first band was probably both the town band and the Finnish Socialist band, with the playing membership interchangeable between the two bands for a time. John Colander was the first bandmaster, to be followed by August Miettinen, then by Victor Taipale. The names are not identified in the 1903 photograph (figure 31), but it can be assumed that the leader, John Colander, is third from left in the front row. This band later became the core of a municipal band. The socialist organizations in Nashwauk kept excellent records and minutes, including expense sheets for their ceremonies and entertainments, which document the expenses of the band. This includes stipends to the players and other costs, such as music and instruments.

Figure 31. Nashwauk's first band, 1903. Photo courtesy Nashwauk Eastern Itascan.

The members of the Nashwauk City Band were mostly new Finnish immigrants, but it also included many Italian immigrant musicians. An early roster includes Louis Saccoman, Raymond de Petro, Peter Larro, George Kokko, Arvo Lindevall, August Miettinen (the bandmaster at the time), Victor Taipale,

B. de Petro, Charles Sulonen, Frank Lindfors, Elmer Lindevall, David Korhonen, Hemming Varonen, Hugo Lilja, John Rokala, Charles Kaminen, John Toivola, and Eero Matara.

As with almost all of the Range's Finnish communities, the Nashwauk Finnish Socialist Club also sponsored other cultural activities, such as a chorus and a particularly popular and successful dramatics group. The dramatists' presentations became an important money-earner for the society, with 60 or so plays successfully produced over its lifetime. There were also men and women's gymnastics clubs, which completed the normal profile of Finnish community social organizations. The unusual success of the Nashwauk Finnish Socialists in organizing community activity had the unfortunate effect of delaying the development of a temperance society, or even a Finnish Lutheran church in the early years of the community. More information about the Nashwauk band history can be found with Victor Taipale's biographical notes in the next chapter.

Cloquet

Cloquet, a lumber and paper-mill city south of Duluth, has been included in this study even though it is geographically not among the Iron Range mining communities. Cloquet has had a significant Finnish population with a geographic proximity to the Range towns that allowed for regular cultural interaction with the mining Finns. In 1879, it began as a lumber town and that industry attracted the Finnish immigrants starting around 1880. The most traumatic event for the town and surroundings was the catastrophic forest fire of 1918, which swept through the whole region just south of Duluth, with the loss of 559 lives, 11,000 families left homeless, and 2000 square miles in ashes. This included 25 communities, including some Duluth suburbs. The Finnish immigrant yearbook of that year estimated that the majority of those who suffered were from the Finnish immigrant population.

A Cloquet Finnish temperance society was formed in 1890, with its hall erected by 1895. That society sponsored a band, a chorus, and a drama group in the pattern of many other temperance societies. A socialist workers' society was developed in the early 1900s, with their hall constructed in 1905. No specific mention is made of any band sponsored by the socialist group, but it is likely there was one since available Finnish players were certainly present in the community.

Comparing figure 32 with figure 33 taken a decade later, it is possible to identify many of the same players. Some of the names recorded in the later photograph include Luukkonen, Laaksonen, Wikstrom and Hoffren. The instrumentation, except for one clarinet, is identical in both. Compared to other Iron Range bands, such continuity of membership over a decade is unusual. It suggests a very tightly knit and loyal organization, rather rare among such bands. Unfortunately, no archive documents, sheet music, or other artifacts from this band have as yet been found.

Figure 32. Cloquet Raikas Finnish Temperance Band, before 1900. Courtesy Carlton County Historical Society.

Figure 33. The Cloquet Raikas Temperance Band, 1910. Courtesy Carleton County Historical Society.

The *Pine Knot*, a Cloquet community newspaper, makes the first mention of a municipal band in 1898, but it is likely to have been started earlier. An extended 1906 Pine Knot article stated

> The Cloquet Band is re-organized largely through the efforts of L. A. Hanson. Prof. Chauncey Mills, who led a similar organization in the city about two years ago has returned to Cloquet and taken up instruction of eighteen players. With the city band revived and an already efficient body of Finnish players, Cloquet is particularly well supplied with music.[18]

This newspaper item does not make clear whether the "body of Finnish players" was a group (or groups) unto themselves, but presumably these Finnish musicians played in both their ethnic bands and in the early Cloquet City Band. Mills was a very active bandmaster, having done community and school band work in Buhl and Ely as well as Cloquet.

Figure 34 shows a Cloquet City Band of the next decade, with many new and youthful faces. In fact, there is no obvious personnel match when comparing this 1917 image with the earlier Raikas photographs. Clearly the 1917 band is a new generation of players, essentially a youth band. The conductor is Louis Gerin, seated in the center. William Syrjälä, a young trumpet player in the Cloquet bands, is in middle row, second from left; he is discussed in more detail in the next chapter.

Figure 34. Cloquet City Band, ca. 1917. Courtesy Carlton County Historical Society.

The following smaller settlements have also been a part of Finnish band history in Minnesota. Their development took place a decade or more later than the "Big Five" Finnish communities of Ely, Virginia, Eveleth, Hibbing, and Chisholm. Some were not directly associated with the mining industry. The Finnish families that left the larger mining communities usually formed new communities based on agriculture or forestry. The miners' strike of 1907 involved the entire Iron Range region and caused many miners to be blacklisted from the industry. Many of the blacklisted Finns left the mining communities and settled or homesteaded in nearby farming or lumbering areas.

Bovey

Figure 2 is an illustration of the socialist Finnish brass band that was organized in Bovey in 1906. Like almost all Finnish bands that started after 1900, it was connected with the local Finnish Socialist Workers' Society, which was organized in Bovey in the same year. The town of Bovey was formed in proximity to a newly opened iron mine in 1904. It has always been closely associated with the larger neighboring town of Coleraine, both having been formed at the initiative of the local mining company. Finns began to arrive and settle in the region soon after these communities were formed. Bovey had a bit of a rough and rowdy reputation in the very early years, with 26 saloons on a rather short main street. A Finnish Temperance Society was formed in 1908 in reaction to Bovey's dominant tavern culture. There is no record of the Bovey Temperance Society having sponsored a band, and, with the relatively late date of formation, it is unlikely. This is one of those rare instances on the Iron Range where the Finnish Temperance Society was formed after the Finnish Workers' Society. Bovey native Marvin Loff refers to the same group of players pictured as the "Trout Lake Finn Band," which was a new name for the group after the Socialist Hall disappeared, since they then rehearsed at the Trout Lake Finnish Hall. Trout Lake is a major landmark near Bovey and Coleraine. The original Trout Lake Finn Band, which apparently was the old Bovey Socialist Band with some added players, lasted until about 1930. The group disbanded "due primarily to the retirement from playing of older immigrant members. Some, like euphonium player Matti Koski and cornetist Severus Ruuhela joined the Coleraine City Band. From six to eight members became the nucleus of the Bovey City Band which I believe was formed in 1932."[19]

As seen in many small Iron Range towns, the 1930s brought a renaissance in cultural activity, including bands. Spurred by Depression-era cultural programs, the "Iowa Band Law" and regional band organizations, every village now had a band that played year-round. Summers were especially active. Loff remembers that "the county fairs provided venues for concerts by town bands. For instance, Coleraine always celebrated July 4 and Bovey always celebrated Labor Day (known as Bovey Farmer's Day). Farmer's Day brought bands in for the parade and concerts throughout the day from Deer River,

Grand Rapids, Coleraine, Marble, Calumet, Nashwauk and Keewatin as well as the National Champion Chisholm Drum & Bugle Corps."[20]

The Bovey School Band in figure 35 shows one of the many successful public school band programs on the Iron Range, with typical American uniforms and instruments. Director Hemming Hautala, discussed in more detail in the next chapter, came from a very traditional band background. The photograph is not dated, but uniform fashions and Hautala's apparent age suggest it was taken just before World War II. This band's membership included many ethnic groups from the community and appears to be composed of mostly high school musicians.

Figure 35. Bovey School Band, Hemming Hautala, Director. Courtesy of the Lager family.

Iron Range community bands from smaller communities generally practiced once a week during the cold weather months and played one winter concert. From Memorial Day through Labor Day, the bands generally did not rehearse but performed either a hometown outdoor concert or participated in some town celebration every weekend, playing from a repertoire of repeated and mostly memorized music. On one July 4th, Loff remembers playing four concerts and then marching in a parade. These concerts of the Bovey Town Band were in nearby communities of Coleraine, Marble, and Calumet, plus a concert and parade back home in Bovey. He then adds, "After that I played in a combo for an evening dance and still got a shift in at the Danube Mine. All because of an understanding mine foreman and rehearsal schedules that let me play with 4 bands. This was not unique."

Sturgeon Township

The Finnish settlers who formed the Sturgeon Township Band were homesteaders who arrived in the wilderness lowlands north of Chisholm right after the 1907 miners' strike. These Finnish mining families from Chisholm chose to settle the region as a rural farming area, and at the beginning made up the total population of the communities of Sturgeon Township, Alango, Idington, and surrounding areas. John Wilenius was a tuba player in the Chisholm Finnish Socialist Band and then became the first leader of a band in this newly settled area. John's brother Swen played tenor horn in both the Chisholm Band before 1907 and the Sturgeon Band afterward. The Sturgeon Band always seemed to have had an affiliation with workers' or socialist political groups, probably emanating from both the musicians' mining backgrounds and the political sympathies of that community. The band in its first form almost ceased to exist after a catastrophic event:

> Eva remembers that the Sturgeon Social Hall located across from the Eino Eskola house and tavern, and was the first community building in the Alango-Sturgeon area. She remembers that it was built prior to WW I, but after her birth in 1907. Both confirmed that it had indeed burned down during the time the brass band was still in existence. Eva recalls that Eino's daughter had related to her a few years ago that her father had burned down the Socialist Hall because it was interfering with his tavern business.[21]

This event may sound like an indicator that arson and anarchy among the Sturgeon Township Finnish-Americans was common, but it is noteworthy to see how common such violent acts were in many Finnish communities around the U.S. during the period of political conflict. The social halls of many a political stripe were set on fire during the height of the tension between socialist factions and the rest of the Finnish-American community in the post-World War I period. This kind of vengeance was part of many community histories.

Gladys Koski Holmes continued to write about how a brass band in the Minnesota Finnish countryside functioned:

> Bill said they (the band members) owned their own instruments, and both Eva and Bill concurred that they played "by ear." However, my third cousin, with whom I just had a phone conversation, still has the E flat Saxophone that her great uncle, Toivo, played in the Sturgeon Brass Band. There was some sheet music with it, too, attesting to the fact that Toivo at least read music, but it might be from a later time when he played in a dance band with his brother and nephew. Bill thought it was mostly

Finnish music that they played, and Eva could not remember anything about the type of music except that it was very loud.

> Eva remembers that her uncle, Nick Ketola, was the drummer. (He took his family to Russian Karelia in 1932 and died of a heart attack there a few years later, according to a letter sent to the Ketola family.) Toivo, her father's cousin, and Andrew Roine played sax, and Bill couldn't remember what John Kontio played. Besides Jon Wilenius and these four, Bill thought there were several others but couldn't remember who they were.
>
> Bill still remembers the time in 1924 when the band was practicing at the Alango Hall, around a half-mile down the road from School 46 where he was in the fifth grade. The teacher, Nora Lynch, let the whole school, grades one through eight, go and listen. He remembers how impressed he was with their ability.
>
> Eva remembers that the band played at the funeral of John Ketola, her father, at the Sturgeon Town Hall in October 1928. She said her uncle, Nick Ketola, who was the band drummer, had arranged for the music. She said it was the one and only time the band ever played at a funeral.[22]

After the Sturgeon Socialist Hall burned in the mid-twenties, bandmaster Jon Wilenius lost interest in continuing the band. It may also have been that some music and equipment was lost in the fire, making continuation difficult. Apparently some players re-organized into a dance band that continued to play for a few years.

In 1929, with energy from the growing Socialist movement, the Sturgeon Township band was re-organized with Toivo Nordquist as director. Andrew Roine, who was very active in political circles of the Finnish farmers of the region and a member of the older Sturgeon Band, was one of the key persons in the re-organization.

Ernest Koski, in his youth, was the drummer in the newly re-formed Sturgeon socialist band. Koski went on to become a very well-known Socialist organizer as well as musician. He was for several years the editor of one of the most successful leftist Finnish newspapers, the "Työmies" (Working Man), published in Superior, Wisconsin. He later wrote about some reminiscences of the Sturgeon Band's earliest history:

> Most rehearsals were held at the Sturgeon Hall and, at times, at the Roine's farm house. There were about 20 in the band and most of the instruments had come from the Chisholm Finnish Workers' Club, which had ceased functioning about 20 years earlier when most of the Finnish farmers staked out homesteads and purchased farm lands in the Alango-Sturgeon area, 25 miles north of Chisholm. They were mostly blacklisted iron ore miners, consequently class-conscious Finns eager to

pursue the cultural activities that they had participated in the mining towns of the Mesaba Range.[23]

His youthful enthusiasm for music and politics, which among the Sturgeon Socialist bandmembers became united, is obvious: "The Heino road wasn't much of a road. Half of the way was through swampy country where the road was the typical corduroy base with a meager amount of gravel on top. But it was a thrill to be in a band group where most of the band music was workers' marches including, naturally, the Internationale. 'Arise ye prisoners of starvation, arise ye wretched of the earth,' we'd sing at times."[24]

The revival of the Sturgeon-Alango Band conveniently coincided with the establishment of the Mesaba Co-operative Park Association on the west side of Chisholm. The park, discussed in more detail in Chapter 5, was an important gathering place for Finnish socialists during the inter-war period. Koski remembers the band going to the first midsummer celebration at the new Socialist park:

> "...We rode on Roine's hay truck which had an extra long platform, so more than 20 band members could conveniently fit with our instruments. When we arrived in Chisholm, on our way to the park, while riding down Main Street, we played at full blast the Internationale and De Marseillaise and many of Sousa's marches. Then we drove through Buhl and from there to the Mesaba Co-operative Park, where already over a thousand Mesaba Range workers and farmers had congregated for the first summer festival. Our band played several times during the daylong celebration, giving it a real working-class musical impetus and enthusiasm."[25]

No one seems to remember exactly when the Sturgeon Band stopped playing, but it is known that World War II brought an end to many such groups, with many of the younger generation joining the military. The communities that the young Finnish-American men returned to after the war had changed, and many of the old band traditions did not survive the interval.

Cromwell

Cromwell, as with Nashwauk and Bovey, had a later start than other nearby towns, and so its cultural history begins with the founding of a Finnish Workers' Society in 1906, when the "Kyntäjä" (Plowman's) society was born in a meeting held at A. A. Parviainen's farm. This was shortly after the first Finnish immigrants arrived. Cromwell, in Carlton County, is not in the Iron Range district, but has always been a farming community with a predominance of

Finnish settlers. Its proximity to the Iron Range towns allows for inclusion in this study.

While political leftists seemed to be in large numbers among the Cromwell settlers, the community also started some small Lutheran congregations quite soon after settlement, with the first services held in farmhouses. Interestingly, the Cromwell Finnish Temperance Society didn't begin until after prohibition was repealed, apparently responding to regional Finnish community traditions or to local conditions of alcohol abuse. That temperance group was formed after an inspiring speech by Heikki Moilanen, a visiting member of the Minnesota Temperance League. It functioned until after World War II, one of only six such Finnish groups on the Iron Range that survived after the repeal of prohibition.

By 1912, the "Plowman's Society" had developed the plan to build a social hall and had purchased land for that purpose. They dedicated their new building, "Plowman's Hall," on Midsummer 1913. In that same year, Cromwell settler William Paananen organized a chorus and a brass band for the Society, for which they purchased new instruments. Arvid Kastel was the first bandmaster, and was succeeded by Johan Aho and later still by William Paananen's son, John W. Paananen. All of these members were from the Cromwell Eagle Lake Finnish community, and many have living children still in the area.

As with the other communities discussed, the Finnish socialist schism also developed in Cromwell, a division between the communists and the more traditional cooperative ("Co-op") oriented socialists. Nationally, this rift was made final after World War I, when international communism became more robust. The communist group eventually took control of the Cromwell Plowman's Finnish Hall. This led, as in many communities, to the development of a second socialist hall association, the "Cromwell Farmers Co-operative Hall Association." With the later demise of the Cromwell Communist organization, they turned the Plowman's Hall over to a local "Raju Athletic Club," which used the Plowman's Hall until 1953 when the building was torn down.

Crosby

Crosby is a town on the Cuyuna Iron Range in Crow Wing County and was one of the few communities in that region with a substantial Finnish population. Mining communities to the immediate west of the Mesaba and Vermilion Ranges attracted Finnish settlers somewhat later. The Cuyuna Range was mined later than the others and Crosby wasn't home to any substantial Finnish population until after 1910. By 1911, a Finnish Socialist Workers' group was formed and by 1912 constructed its hall. A band was initially formed sponsored by the Socialist group, but when the Socialists developed into two clubs, the band declared itself the Crosby Independent Finnish Band "Ahti," and played for all Finnish groups in the community. It is not known how long the band was kept going, but the Workers' Club that sponsored some of its activity, and owned the instruments, lasted until 1952.

Figure 36. Crosby's "Independent" Finnish Band, Eero Matara, director, ca. 1918. Courtesy IRRC, Chisholm.

Eero Matara, the leader of the Crosby band and presumably the founder, was a very active cornet player and bandmaster in several Iron Range communities. Nothing more is known about him and no death or immigration records have been found thus far in Minnesota archives. He is in the center of an undated, but about 1918 photo of Crosby's "Independent" Finnish Band (figure 36). Other names identified in the picture are August Ulvinen, William Laine, Matti Suvanto, Arne Pelto, Isaac Talvitie, Frank Lehto, and Lehto's young son with the clarinet.

St. Louis County Rural Band Association

Some Finnish village bands on the Iron Range began or were revived during the Depression era. The St. Louis County Schools sponsored a "Leisure Education" program in the rural areas, promoting vocational-academic education, crafts, dramatics, dancing, music, and community festivals. The formation of the St. Louis County Rural Band Association was a project associated with that effort. The Leisure Education program was particularly targeted to unemployed young adults who were 18-year old high school graduates or no longer attending a public school. The rural county schools supported two corps of teachers during this time: the standard "day staff" and the evening "Leisure Education" staff, which offered any course or program requested by at least 15 local people. "Out of this movement came projects such as Laskiainen (winter festival) and Snow Queen Contests, and I suspect many of the local agricultural fairs."[26] This county-wide program was very successful and enjoyed some fame as a model for youth development in other communities during the 1930s.

Three of these community bands are of particular interest to this study. The Leisure Education program had a positive effect on almost all town bands in Northern Minnesota, including the many previously existing rural bands. These programs offered the bands the benefit of financial and institutional support. This unusual program is of particular importance because it offered a breath of new life for the band culture of the more remote areas of the region; these three villages are of particular interest to the history of Finnish bands because the participants were almost all of Finnish heritage. One of the community bands, the Bassett Township band, is discussed in more detail within William Ahola's biographical notes later in the chapter. The other two, Embarrass and Town of White are discussed here.

Embarrass

In correspondence from Helmer Hanka, a 94-year old native of Embarrass, are reminiscences of the Embarrass Community Band. Hanka recalls memories of the band's founder Nielo Hakala, and how the band came to be. Neilo was an extremely rare case of a buttonbox accordion player taking an interest in forming a wind band. Hanka suggests that the WPA Leisure Education program gave Hakala the idea and opportunity:

> That was in the early years of the Great Depression, when President Roosevelt's recovery programs began to take effect. Many St. Louis County schoolteachers were unemployed and were hired for directing evening recreation programs. One teacher, who was a children's daytime instructor at School #72, a half-mile from my home, gave Neilo his first instruction in music reading. He soon decided that he needed some knowledge from more advanced people and went to a university in Chicago. After completing his studies there, he joined two other performers, where Neilo used his accordion, and they sang, at bars in Chicago. They had high-class stages: I was in Chicago at the time and heard them a lot. Then I got myself inducted into the army.
>
> Our Embarrass Community Band was entirely organized, instructed, and conducted by Neilo. It was a pretty classy brass

band with a dozen or maybe few more members. All instruction was done in English. We did community concerts and were associated with about six other local groups, and we gathered every summer for a band festival (St Louis County Rural Band Association). It was really great entertainment and fellowship.

Neilo Hakala, who was advocating for a community band, started the Embarrass Band. Some of the new members already had horns; I think I bought my trombone for $5 or $10-equipment was reasonable priced during the Depression. I sold my valve trombone to one who said he'd become a band member. He never amounted to anything but I lost my valve trombone, which I enjoyed playing for my own pastime. That deal I really rued.

Neilo never taught in a classroom but he did all teaching during practice session evenings. Some of the instruction was unconventional. For instance, Neil talked my brother into playing the tuba. He protested that he didn't know anything about music but Neil assured him that he'd learn. So he began practicing and learned to play. But he played his "toots" a sort of elongated, so finally Neilo began to try to correct the problem. He told Hugo, 'That's not the way you play the tuba.' Hugo said, 'Well that's what I told you: I don't know anything about it.' Neil began instructing by saying, 'Hugo, you've taken care of a dairy cow a big part of our life and you know that in the springtime when they are first let to pasture their innards get sort of runny from fresh grass. So when they were walking they would drop the refuse with a splat-splat-splat-now that's the way you play the tuba. Well, Hugo made use of the illustrative teaching and became really good. So good, in fact, that when we were at one of our band festivals, the other tuba men gathered behind Hugo to give a listen.[27]

Helmer continues:

Who were the members of the Embarrass Band? Helmer Hanka (trombone), Hugo Hanka (tuba), Leonard Stone (trumpet), and a pair of brothers Johnson (one played trumpet one played baritone). We had two clarinets but I can't remember who the players were.There was a drummer-can't remember the name. All were beginning taught by Neilo, except I don't know about the clarinets. The Johnson brothers were in some sort of school in Faribault for part of the year, where they received their music training. I think there was a couple more but I don't remember what they played. It's sixty or more years ago. But when Neilo left, that was the end. He designated that I should

> then lead but I very shortly left for Chicago too. It's sort of sad, when I think of it.
>
> I played dance music with Neilo and drummer Johnny Korpela of Aurora, plus occasionally we had Bill Walker who was a radio announcer at WMFG-Virginia, and WHLB-Hibbing, where we went on air Sunday afternoons. Those were the earliest radio stations in Virginia and Hibbing: we aired from both.
>
> The brass band was "The Embarrass Community Band." There was nothing of Finnish connection with that band except that the majority of the participants was of Finnish extraction and, at that time, was fluent in both languages. It was an excellent sounding band, attributed to Neilo's talents, which were put in motion by his father William.[28]

It appears that the Embarrass Community Band was not long-lived, lasting until the beginning of World War II. No photographs or other memorabilia of the band have been found thus far.

Numerous Finnish-Americans with strong socialist sympathies demonstrated their enthusiasm rather dramatically during the 1920s by opting to immigrate to the Finnish-speaking regions of the western Soviet Union known as Karelia. The dramatic saga of their experiences as Americans in the Soviet Union is a story beyond the scope of this study, but yet is an element of the history of how those bands connected with the Socialist halls evolved and ceased. There are records of brass bands formed in the Karelian SSR including players who came from the United States. Socialism, as a political philosophy, had a rather wide following in the United States in the 1930s. Many Finnish-Americans were also enthusiastic adherents and major participants. However, the popularity of Socialist political activity among all Americans, including the Finns, took an immediate downward turn with the receipt of new information regarding Josef Stalin's atrocities among millions of his own citizens. Also, very dramatic news for the Finnish-American community was about how badly the sojourners to Soviet Karelia were mistreated. This news further elevated the growing mistrust of the Soviet idealistic world order and raised fundamental questions among Finnish Socialists about their continued support. It was a blow to the Finnish Socialist movement and for any bands associated with it.

The traditional band that Nicolai Miettunen put together in Ely in 1889 was quite a different ensemble from Hautala's Bovey school band, with its clarinets and saxophones (Figure 35). Yet they form the temporal bookends of the Finn Band Era in Minnesota. Each year fewer and fewer Finnish bands were heard at the large Finnish celebrations, though there were numerous American Finns actively playing in community bands all over the Iron Range. But by World War II, the "Finnish Band in America" had disappeared, and memories and records of it were also rapidly being lost in time.

[1]Timothy Lawrence Smith, "Factors Affecting the Social Development of Iron Range Communities," Immigration History Research Center, University of Minnesota, 1963, 12.

[2]Margaret and Robert Hazen, *The Music Men–An Illustrated History of Brass Bands in America* (Washington: Smithsonian Press, 1987), 13.

[3]Timo Riippa, "The Finns and Swedo Finns," *They Chose Minnesota: A Survey of the State's Ethnic Groups*, June Drenning Holmquist, ed. (St. Paul: Minnesota Historical Society Press, 1981), 303.

[4] Article in the *Ely Miner*, September 10, 1899, 1.

[5]Työmies Finnish Newspaper, Ishpeming, Mi, August 26, 1892, 5. Translated: "Large numbers of workers are coming from Michigan and Wisconsin to work in Tower."

[6]"Copper Country" is the region of the Keweenaw Peninsula of Upper Michigan, with significant copper mining in sites near Houghton, Hancock, Calumet, and South Range.

[7]Thirteenth United States Census (1910) (Washington, DC,, 1913), 624-28.

[8]United States Census, St. Louis County, Minnesota, 1900. Note that while the number of Italians in 1900 was only 850, that number exploded to about 5,000 by 1910.

[9]Hibbing City Band archives, Hibbing Historical Society.

[10]Conversation with Don Hakala, a brass player who grew up on the Minnesota Iron Range, 2002.

[11]Hazen, *Music-Men*, 53.

[12]Conversation with Marvin Loff, Iron Range musician, March 2002.

[13]Interview with Leo Wiljamaa, 90 years old, March 2002; the 1885 date he mentions is probably incorrect.

[14]Hans R. Wasastjerna, ed., "History of the Finns in Minnesota," Toivo Rosvall, trans., *Minnesotan suomalaisten historia* (Duluth MN: Finnish-American Historical Society, 1959), 352.

[15]Ibid., 495.

[16]A. Ruth Frye, *The Life of Emily Hobhouse*, (London: J. Cape, 1929), 221.

[17]Wasastjerna, "History," 335.

[18]Cloquet, MN, *Pine Knot*, July 16, 1906, 2.

[19]Interview with Marvin Loff, musician raised in Iron Range Minnesota. March, 2002

[20]Ibid.

[21]From correspondence with Gladys Koski Holmes, a Sturgeon Township resident and member of the Wilenius family. 2003.

[22]Ibid.

[23]Ernest Koski, "Tune of the First Festival," *Fifty Years of Progressive Cooperation, 1929–1979* (Mesaba Range Co-operative Park Association, Superior, WI: Työmies Society, 1979), 3.

[24]ibid., 4.

[25]ibid., 7.

[26]Interview with Harry Lamppa, Iron Range historian, Virginia, Minnesota, January 2002

[27]Interview with Helmer Hanka in 2002, with subsequent written correspondence in the author's possession.

[28]Ibid.

Chapter Four
Finnish Bandsmen

The Finnish bandsmen in this study can be classified into three general categories. The very earliest examples include John Haapasaari, Nicolai Miettunen, Peter Westerinen, and Oscar Castrén, whose biographies are mostly lost to us, and who were active before 1895. Occasional mention of them and their work can be found in some of the newly established newspapers, but there is not much detail. An earlier Finnish settler, Peter Esko, known to have been a cornetist in the Helsinki Guards Band, had settled in Minnesota as early as the 1870s, but there is no evidence that he continued to play in this country, nor to associate with other band musicians, and thus his story ends. He and his family were founders of the village of Esko, Minnesota. The backgrounds of the earliest Finnish-American bandmasters appear to have two general patterns. Nicolai Miettunen and John Haapasaari seem to have had formal training in military band music in Finland prior to arriving in the United States. Peter Westerinen and Oscar Castrén appear to have more extensive experience in American culture, as revealed by the available documents of their musical programming. Castrén arrived in America as a boy. Westerinen's available biography is very sketchy, but it is known that he was a very active musical leader among the Finns in Michigan's Copper Country region prior to his arrival in Minnesota.

The second group, the main body of immigrant Finnish brass players and leaders, arrived in America between 1895 and 1905. Wasastjerna cites a roster of the members of the Fayal (Eveleth) Band in 1904. The following list of players is a rare example in the literature. No other such detailed roster has been found.

> Taipale ... in 1901 managed to recruit fifteen musicians who all had experience behind them in Finnish military bands: Waldemar Eklund, A. Kyllönen and Knut F. Öhman, from the Helsinki Guard Regiment; Lauri Husgafvel from the Uusimaa Battalion; Kalle Kajander from the Turku Battalion; John Paavola and Jacob Pehkonen from the Vaasa Battalion; Matti Huru, Emil Kauppinen, August Miettinen, Ville Penttilä and Kaarlo A. Sarviranta from the Oulu Battalion; John Collander and John Toivola from the Häme Battalion, and Arthur Rehnström from the Viipuri Battalion. Other outstanding musicians in Taipale's band were Kalle Kleemola, Victor Parkkonen, August Potti, Hilding and Peter Sholund and Oscar Yrjölä.1

This Eveleth band roster suggests that many of the Iron Range Finnish bands of the early 1900s were being populated by the cadre of trained military musicians coming directly from the recently dissolved Finnish military bands. A similar roster to the one above, but with less-detailed information about the players, can be found for the Finnish band in Duluth, which was formed in 1905 under Frans Lindroos.[2] Although the Fayal band lists players for one specific midsummer event, several of the names are subsequently found with many other bands on the Iron Range, as both conductors and players.

The third and later category of Finnish bandsmen includes the musicians who came to the United States as small children or were born here. It was after the great migration that these younger musicians were included in the bands. Many were trained in Minnesota in the normal apprenticeship manner or came out of public school band programs that were increasingly common on the Iron Range after 1910. As usual in the Finnish village bands, a young and enthusiastic recruit would sit beside a veteran player and learn the necessary skills through imitation. Charles Kleemola, Hemming Hautala, William Ahola, and Emil Ikola represent this category. These "third wave" musicians were usually fluent in English and were able to mix well with the community beyond the Finnish enclave.

While three distinct groups of Finnish-American bandsmen have been identified here, it must be remembered that the period of time between the earliest and the latest is less than thirty years. This knowledge confirms the fact that cultural life on the Minnesota Iron Range was rapidly changing during the time the immigrant communities were establishing themselves.

Pekka Westerinen

Pekka Westerinen is the earliest known, active Finnish immigrant musical leader thought to have formed a viable brass band in Northern Minnesota. Although his activity in Minnesota appears to have been primarily with Finnish choirs, Wasastjerna indicates that Westerinen founded a Finnish Temperance Brass Band in Soudan in 1888. A former cantor-organist from Kiuruvesi in Finland, Westerinen organized the first Finnish chorus in America in Calumet, Michigan in 1884. He then moved to New York Mills, Minnesota, in 1886 to organize choral activity there. A newspaper announcement poster from May 1887 has his choir presenting a "Grand Concert in Finnish by the K. K. Chorus assisted by Prof. Ormsby's Orchestra." By July 1888, Westerinen was ready to leave the community because Astoria, Oregon, had offered him more money. If Wasastjerna's claim that Westerinen formed a brass band in Soudan in 1888 is correct, then his time in Oregon must have been similarly brief to his time in New York Mills, or he delayed his departure, or never actually went west at all. Westerinen's name does not appear in any immigrant records, ship registers, or other similar listings involving Minnesota. He may have died in Ely, Minnesota, but that identification is not certain.[3] The Westerinen family name was known in the Ely area, although no other details about his musical leadership in that region have emerged from any other sources.

Nikolai Miettunen

Nikolai Miettunen, also one of the earliest Finnish bandmasters to arrive in Minnesota, was born in 1862 in Finnish Lapland. He joined the Oulu Battalion Brass Band as a cadet in 1881. In 1885, he completed training at an organ academy in Oulu, and soon thereafter immigrated to Duluth, Minnesota, where in 1886 he started a Finnish Temperance Society Band, a part of the newly formed "*Toivon tähti*" (Star of Hope) Society. If the date is correct, the Duluth Temperance Band would be the oldest Finnish Band in Minnesota. No photographs or other records of this band have been found thus far, but it is known that the *Toivon tähti* temperance group did not fare well in its development, and so the band's life would also have been short. In 1888, Miettunen moved to Ishpeming, Michigan, an iron-mining area, where he organized another Finnish brass band. No records of this band have been found either. For that one year, he apparently traveled between Duluth and Ishpeming, managing to direct both. This was not unusual: many of the active directors regularly took trains from one band town to another.

In 1889, he moved to Ely.[4] Some Ely natives, however, say he is thought to have arrived at the nearby town of Winton, which was also an active Finnish community in 1889.[5] That was the same year that Ely formed its own Finnish Temperance Society. These conflicting references may be due to the rapid growth of Ely during the decade that followed, as Ely soon overshadowed Winton, the older settlement. Miettunen "brought along with him several other Finnish bandsmen and started the Ely Finnish Band,"[6] in all likelihood the temperance band for the newly formed organization. It is not certain if Miettunen "brought along with him" some of the players from the defunct Duluth Finnish Temperance Band or from Ishpeming, or perhaps both. Figure 37 is an 1889 photograph that appears to have been famous among Finnish-Americans nationwide as it is found in several publications of that period. It became an advertisement for the Ely Finnish Band in other regions, thereby attracting more brass players to the town, and traveled with musicians during the Spanish American War. Finnish publications of that period also identify this photograph as the "Ely Band," as though it were the city band. That designation is not certain, but it appears to be the earliest band in Ely. This would make it the second oldest Finnish-American band and the first one photographed. Miettunen, with his cornet, is seated in the center; no other names have been identified.

Miettunen, as with most Finnish bandmasters, needed a steady income outside of music. He opened a soft-drink bottling works in Ely in 1892. He probably stayed in the community for several years as a bottler and musician, but there is little documentation about his life during that time. He is not mentioned as being a part of any band activity with Castrén, or later with Kleemola. He does not appear to be in any other photographs or rosters except the one shown in Figure 37. The next instance was his starting a new band in

Chisholm and then in Buhl, a mining town near Chisholm. By 1901, he had apparently moved to Chisholm, leading the band for the new Finnish Temperance Society. "In Buhl he started a community band, which consisted of twenty members; and we got together and hired a Finnish pop salesman by the name of Miettunen. He had played in the Old Country, even in the Russian band. He was a crackerjack cornetist; he could play with one hand and direct with the other. We paid him twenty dollars a month... so that was the Band everybody was so enthusiastic about".[8]

Figure 37: Ely (Winton) Finnish Band, 1889.
Photograph courtesy Kleemola family.

Miettunen was succeeded as the Buhl bandmaster by two other Finns, Alex Koivunen and John Niemi; the latter remained until 1911. Besides Chisholm and Buhl, there is no other record of Miettunen being active with any other bands after he left Ely. The Polk city directory notes that he continued operating a bottling works in Chisholm, but appears to have also operated a "saloon," was a woodworker and miner during those years after Ely. In his later years he apparently was a farmer, and his obituary presents him as "a pioneer citizen of Chisholm."[9] His time with the Ely band seems to have been relatively short, and his time with the Buhl band even shorter. He died in Chisholm in 1930. A "crackerjack cornetist" with good musical training could be expected to have had more musical success, more visibility in the history books, and more photographs of his activity. The untold parts of Miettunen's story are some of many mysteries connected with this research.

Oscar Castrén

Limited biographical information has been found about Oscar Castrén, who is thought to have started a Finnish band in Ely by 1890, making him one of the earliest. He was born in Finland on September 16, 1866, and came to this country as a five-year-old, settling in Northern Michigan. His father, David Castrén, a Finnish schoolteacher, arrived in Calumet in 1873 to develop Finnish language education among immigrant children.[10] Oscar is thought to have moved to Ely by 1890, a twenty-four-year-old with many years experience with both music making and the English language in America. In these regards, he was unique among the early Finnish bandmasters. It should be of little surprise that his Ely band programs contained almost exclusively American material. His training as a cornetist and bandmaster in the Michigan mining settlements would probably have taken place during his membership in the Finnish and community bands there. His name is also mentioned as a leader of the Hibbing Tapio Temperance Band at about 1900, but it is not known if he settled in Hibbing, or how long he directed that band. He settled in the Eveleth area (Leonidas location) in 1907 and remained there for the rest of his life. There is no record of his having been involved in the bands in the Eveleth-Virginia area during his years there. He died in 1937 at the age of 71.

John Haapasaari

John Haapasaari, as the founding leader of Finnish bands in Virginia, Hibbing, and perhaps other towns around 1895, is a primary pioneer in the Finnish band movement in Minnesota. However, his name does not appear again in the history books after these initial instances, and it seems he may have moved out of Minnesota shortly after. The normal reference resources, Polk City Guides, death certificates, and census lists, do not make any reference to him. In fact, Haapasaari, a fairly rare Finnish name, does not appear in any Minnesota death records statewide. No success has come from efforts to trace him to other American locations, or even back to Finland. Haapasaari's pioneering work took place at about the same time the first local newspapers in Virginia and Hibbing were being founded, explaining why news of his arrival in these cities is not recorded, but the later formation of his bands was noted.[11]

Charles (Kalle) Kleemola

Charles Kleemola was born in coastal Ostrobothnia on May 15,1880, and came to the United States with his family as a youth. His granddaughter places the family's initial arrival in the mining town of Monessen, Pennsylvania, sometime after 1895, when he was in his teens. It is not clear if Kleemola might have received some musical training with a village brass band in Finland before emigrating, or if he started playing with the Finnish bands in Pennsylvania; either is possible. His father was a farmer who ultimately settled his family in Bessemer, Michigan, by about 1897 where the father "also worked in the mines and with the railroad."[12] By that time, Kalle had apparently achieved a high level of proficiency as a cornet player. He and his trombone-playing brother were taken into the Michigan National Guard Band in Ironwood around the time of the Spanish American War (1897-98), where they met other Finnish musicians who had settled in the Upper Midwest. Some of them were from Ely and had played with Miettunen's temperance band. Levander says the photograph shown in Figure 37 of the Ely (Winton) Finnish band was seen by other Finns in that National Guard band, and this contact persuaded Kleemola to move to the Ely-Winton area. The photograph was found in the Kleemola family collection, taken home by Kalle after he was in the Guard Band in Ironwood. The R.L. Polk *Range Cities Directory* places Charles Kleemola in Ely for the first time in 1903, listed as a sales clerk in the Vail Clothing Store.[13] He was married in Ely in 1904, and was already actively involved as a player and conductor with various Finnish or other bands in Ely. Figure 38 is a boyhood photograph of Kleemola with the unlikely instrument, a helicon, on his shoulder. Kleemola was only known among his contemporaries as a brilliant cornetist, so this photograph was probably a stunt. However, if he had access to such a band instrument in Northern Michigan, he was in the company of band musicians during that important time in his development as a musician.

Figure 38. Charles Kleemola, with a helicon, probably Bessemer Michigan, before 1900. Photograph courtesy Kleemola family.

Figure 39. National Guard Band stationed in Ironwood, Michigan, during the Spanish American War. Photo courtesy Kleemola Family.

Figure 39, a rare photograph of the National Guard Band stationed in Ironwood, Michigan, during the Spanish-American War, probably includes a significant proportion of immigrants, considering the population of Northern Michigan and Wisconsin at that time. Charles Kleemola is at the lower left.

Kleemola's granddaughter Mary Ellen Levander recounts that he "started the first Ely School Band in 1906," and suggests, based on city folklore, that it was the first school band in the state of Minnesota. "Mr. Pierce came after my grandfather. He had it for maybe 6 months after starting, since grandfather didn't have teacher training."[14] The details of Kleemola's career from about 1904 until his early death in 1918 are not clearly documented. It is known that he and other Ely Finnish brass players traveled occasionally to Red Lodge, Montana, to play with the famous Red Lodge Military Band. The Red Lodge Band made a tour in 1909 that included Minnesota, during which time they participated in the regional Finnish Temperance Midsummer Festival in Eveleth and the regional Finnish Socialist Workers' Festival in nearby Virginia. Levander also claims that "Kleemola went and played with the Ringling Brothers' Band, and played with the Sousa Band, too" but neither membership can be verified. He is listed as a player in various other Iron Range Finnish bands from time to time, and is included in several photographs and band rosters used in this study. Travel between Iron Range towns was quite easy and fast by rail, allowing an ambitious cornet player to hold membership in several bands at the same time. Kleemola may not be unique in this matter of mobility, but it is clear that as a cornet player and bandmaster, he traveled very frequently and would seem to not have stayed at home in Ely for very long before again going out of town for another rehearsal or performance. The trips to Red Lodge would have taken weeks. His name is also seen as a conductor on band programs in Monessen, Pennsylvania, probably as a guest conductor.

Kleemola composed and arranged some music for his bands, although the only work found is a march he wrote in honor of the local spring log harvest reproduced as Figure 40. The title refers to the action of the boom that pulls logs out of the water, or "heaves" them upward: *Hopsikko!* ("Up she goes"). He must have received some training in theory and composition, perhaps while with the National Guard band. He is said to have received some formal music training in Chicago; if true, the most likely possibility would have been at the Vander Cook Cornet School, where many aspiring bandmasters of the time studied.

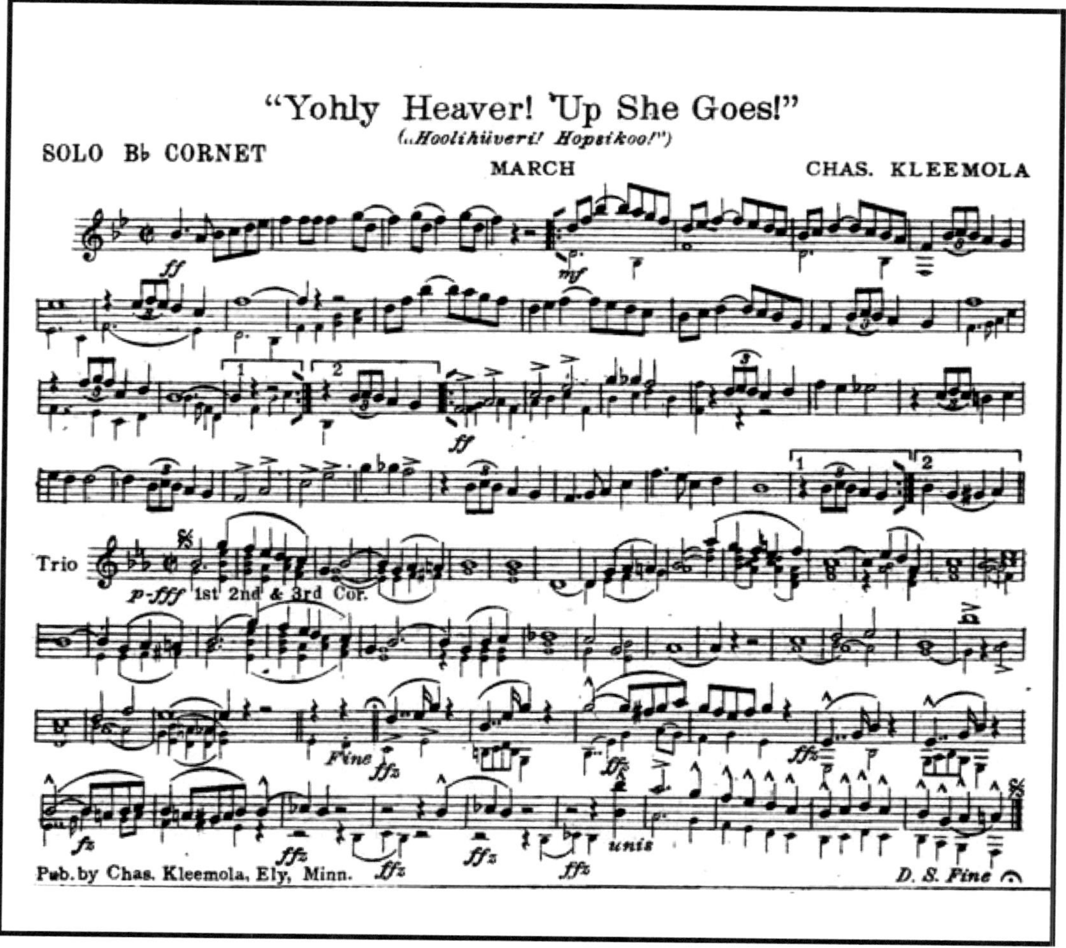

Figure 40. Cornet part, Yohly Heaver! 'Up She Goes!.
Photograph Courtesy of the Kleemola family.

Ely's Finnish Temperance Society band in the 1900s was named *Sampo* (meaning "magic mill" from Finnish mythology), a name apparently chosen by Kleemola. Its membership was almost entirely young adult male Finnish immigrants who had apparently learned to play prior to arriving in Ely.[15]It is probable that this band was a continuation of the original temperance band formed under Miettunen. This *Sampo* Band is first mentioned more than a decade after Miettunen's original band was formed. Some *Sampo* members were newly arrived from the disbanded military or town bands in Finland. Interviews with former members also suggest that Kleemola instructed some of the younger band members himself.[16]

Kleemola's *Sampo* Band continued until 1913. The Ely newspapers contain fewer and fewer instances of the band's activity after 1911, indicating that the band was probably deteriorating, with players joining other bands. It would appear that Kleemola's activities in other bands outside of Ely might have been part of the reason the band was less active. In 1913, Kleemola resigned from leadership of the *Sampo* band, to accept an opportunity to "direct several bands" in Stockett, Montana. The *Ely Miner* notes that "Mr. Kleemola is a director of no mean importance and musical circles in this town will miss him. He expects to remove his family to the new home providing he is satisfied with the new place."[17] Apparently Kleemola left his family back in Ely when he went to Stockett, as he made regular trips to return home. His last trip was to attend the funeral of his daughter, who died of illness. Kleemola himself died on April 16, 1918, in Duluth, while on his way back to Montana after his daughter's funeral.

With a view to the fragile conditions under which ethnic and community bands existed at the time, with the knowledge that community bands endured a constant flow in and out of players and leaders, with the understanding that musicians were trying to develop careers and make music under very difficult circumstances, and that there was competition between municipal and ethnic bands, Kleemola's story is a telling example of conditions at that time. It provides insight into why many of the Finnish bands on the Range had ceased to exist by 1918.

William Ahola

William Ahola, born in Finland in 1881, immigrated with his family to the U.S. in 1892, living first in Northern Michigan. According to his 1931 obituary, the family had moved to Hibbing by 1904,[18] but there are some questions about the accuracy of that information since there are photographs of Ahola as a very young player in the Hibbing Finnish Temperance Band, assuming the 1903 date and the names attributed to the photograph are correct (see Chapter 4, Figure 27). The photograph shows him under the directorship of Victor Taipale in that Temperance band. Taipale may also have been involved in Ahola's development as a bandmaster, since he was a known music educator. The family has no records or memories of his having taken any formal instruction in music, but it is likely he was involved with brass bands as a cornet player in Michigan before arriving in Minnesota or he would not have been able to assume the position of director of the Hibbing City Band by 1905 at the age of 24.

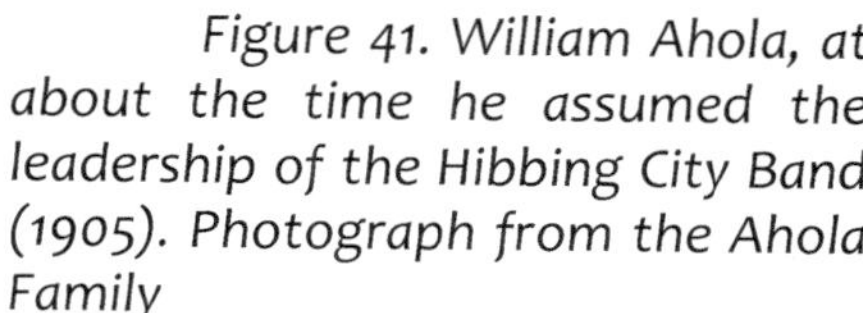

Figure 41. William Ahola, at about the time he assumed the leadership of the Hibbing City Band (1905). Photograph from the Ahola Family

Ahola resigned from the band in 1915 due to some disputes about financial support. An editorial in the *Hibbing Journal* at the time summarized his work and reputation in the town:

"Ahola has made the Hibbing band the best amateur band in the state of Minnesota and was acknowledged by the music loving public, band directors, and the members of the Hibbing Concert Band as one of the most capable directors Hibbing has ever had. Ahola worked tirelessly to perfect the organization into the stage it has now reached, and his many friends will regret to hear of his resignation."[19]

After leaving Hibbing, he moved to Fairbanks, Minnesota, in the forested region east of the Iron Range. He became a store manager for the "Finnish Supply Company," a general merchandise firm, and also started a town band in Bassett, a nearby village, in 1917. The band performed at the dedication of the Bassett Town Hall in 1917. A note by Signe Sandstedt Beckman summarizes Ahola's work:

> A debt-of gratitude is owed to Mr. William Ahola for his work in promoting music in those early days. Being a professional musician, he directed his efforts toward developing the talents of the young people interested in music. He was instrumental in organizing the Bassett Band in the 1920s. There was a sense of pride in this band and the town hall was always filled to capacity when they played.[20]

He and his family remained in the Fairbanks–Toimi–Bassett area until 1927, when he moved to Orr to become manager of another merchandise firm. As far as is known, he did not continue any band activity in Orr, and died four years later at the age of 50. His descendents still live in that community.

Victor Taipale

Victor Taipale emerges as the most active and successful of the Finnish bandmasters in Minnesota. He was unlike many others in that he resided for most of his career in only a few locales on the Iron Range. A brief biographical entry of him appeared in 1949, after he had left the Iron Range for a short period in Detroit. He then subsequently returned.[21]

Taipale was born January 21, 1875, in Nurmo, a village in Ostrobothnia. He received the basic grammar-school education available at the time, and then enlisted in the Vaasa Battalion Military Music School from 1889 to 1894. He then spent two years at the Rauma Teachers Seminary before moving to Helsinki. In 1896 he joined the Helsinki Guards Band under Adolph Leander (1833-1899), and played in the Helsinki Symphony Orchestra. He also enrolled in the Helsinki Music College where he studied military music and band directing under Leander. When the military bands were dissolved, he enrolled in church composer Emil Sivori's "School for Choir Leaders, Choristers and Organists" in the eastern city of Viipuri from 1898 until 1900, after which he left Finland for Minnesota as certainly the best-trained and most experienced musical leader and teacher to arrive among the Finnish immigrants.

Coming to the United States in 1900, Taipale first arrived in Worcester, Massachusetts, where he directed the choral and band activities for the Finnish Temperance Society for a year. In 1901 he arrived in Hibbing, Minnesota, and found an active group of Finnish brass band players that needed a leader. He is listed in the Polk Directory as a miner for that first year.

In 1902 he is listed as the leader of the Lake Superior Cornet Band. The Finnish journals refer to the same band as the "Hibbing Finnish Band" (see chapter 4, figure 26). He was also involved in band leadership in Eveleth by 1903, but still active with the Hibbing Band, apparently commuting.

Descendents of Biwabik Finns have suggested that Taipale started the school band there in 1902, and they have pronounced it the oldest school band in Minnesota rather than Ely.[22] It has been difficult to verify this, since the first Biwabik newspaper was published five years later, in 1907. The fire that destroyed most of the high school and the school's archives in 1985 has made further verification of any history difficult. The earliest school yearbook preserved was for 1968, in which the then sitting superintendent, Victor Reishus, wrote a school history. The village, organized in 1892, built its first school in 1893. Reishus does mention Taipale:

> Four bands were formed and functioned to some extent in Biwabik's early history. The first was organized in 1893 under

> the direction of Prof. Snyder, an itinerant piano-playing musician. About 1898 or 1899 another band was formed under the directorship of a Swede named Charles Swanson. It functioned for a while. The third group, formed about two years later [verifies the 1902 date] was organized by a Finn cornetist, Victor Taipale. It didn't last long.[23]

Biwabik was not a strong center for Finnish immigrant miners at the time, so it might have been difficult for Taipale to generate a Finnish band there in the style of his ensemble in Eveleth. Reishus does not confirm that Taipale's work in Biwabik was specifically with a school band, but it was certainly not with a "Finn band," and probably was not another community band to compete with Swanson's existing City Band. A Biwabik school band under Taipale starting in 1902 is a possibility, but why it didn't continue is not known. It could be assumed that the post "didn't last long" because Taipale began to see other opportunities with his Fayal Band and in Virginia and other places, and he probably left for those opportunities. Taipale's English language skills are unknown, so it might have been challenging for him, barely two years in the U.S. to instruct a group of young musicians in Biwabik whose common language had to be English. Taipale's next school band position, in Nashwauk–Keewatin, was some years later. In the meantime he may have obtained some teaching certificate, although the circumstance for his obtaining such training is not known. This is about the same time that Kleemola was starting the Ely band under similar circumstances, and he too was quickly replaced with a certified music teacher.

Taipale certainly had a significant role in fostering the development of the popular Finnish midsummer festivals in Minnesota, which began with his involvement in Eveleth in 1904. These regional festivals (held around St. John's Day, the midsummer observance in Nordic countries) were hosted each year by a different community. Eveleth was the host for Minnesota's first festival. As related by Wasastjerna,

> The proposal had first been made in a meeting of the Otava Chapter Knights of Kaleva and immediately after that had been mentioned again at a program evening of the Järvenkukka Temperance Society in September 1903. Matt Porthan proposed for discussion the sponsorship by the society of a huge midsummer festival in which all Finnish organizations would participate. The proposal was unanimously accepted. A committee was appointed, to make contact with all temperance societies in the shore area... The minutes of a meeting three weeks later showed that the societies of Soudan, Eveleth, Biwabik and Hibbing, together with their bands and choral groups, had accepted the proposal, and that that the Ely

temperance society was to decide where the festival was to be held, and it decided on Eveleth.[24]

The 1904 Finnish Midsummer festival began early in the morning at the Eveleth railroad station, where out-of-town visitors were greeted by a reception committee, a guard of honor of 50 Finnish temperance ladies in white blouses and blue skirts, standard bearers with decorative flags unfurled, and a crowd of festival attendees and Eveleth citizens. When the train rolled in, Taipale's *Kaiku* band played the Star Spangled Banner, the Finnish National Anthem, and the city mayor gave a welcome speech in English.

The combined Finnish bands from Chisholm, Ely, Eveleth, Hibbing and Virginia then played a Lutheran hymn; a Finnish pastor offered a prayer, followed by the combined bands rendering yet another hymn. Then, from the train station, everyone lined up to parade through the city to the festival grounds, where the program was continued.

In 1904, there were about 5,000 in attendance. The program continued all day, with bands playing, choruses singing, speeches and readings being given into the evening. After an intermission for lunch, the competitive phase of the festival began:

> The mixed choruses, then the male choruses, sang and were judged and ranked, and then the bands followed suit, while athletic teams on another part of the field competed in track events. That evening brought the final phase, a festival concert held at Fayal Hall, with the participation of the Chisholm band, the mixed choruses joined into one massive group, the Virginia band, the Eveleth mixed chorus, the Ely band, the Hibbing band, interspersed with trumpet solos by Jacob S. Saari.[25]

Figure 42. Eveleth Kaiku Temperance Band, ca. 1906.
Courtesy Iron Range History Center, Gilbert.

Figure 42 shows the Eveleth *Kaiku* Temperance Band in an undated photograph, but probably about 1906. Director Taipale is standing on the right, and Charles Kleemola is kneeling in the center. See also figure 24 in chapter 4 for a picture of the same band several years later.

Taipale's involvement in the 1904 and 1907 Midsummer festivals is further documented in the printed festival programs that have been preserved.[26]

There is limited evidence that Taipale collaborated with other Finnish bandmasters on the Range. He does appear as a playing member of the Virginia City Band and the Nashwauk Band, confirming that he also played in other bands outside Eveleth during the years that he conducted. We have no evidence that Taipale ever met Miettunen, but Taipale's choice of profession in Eveleth soon after arriving in Minnesota,of soft-drink bottler, does seem an unusual coincidence.

There is no exact information about how long Taipale stayed in the Eveleth area, but it seems it was until after 1910. Polk lists him again in Hibbing by 1909, this time as a "driver," and then in 1910 as a "miner." By then, there are newspaper references to a Mr. Scott conducting the Fayal Band. Taipale's connection with the Eveleth *Kaiku* Temperance Band and the Fayal Band appears to have lasted only a few years.

By 1915, he is listed as a resident of Chisholm, from where he must have commuted to Nashwauk, where he was then engaged as a school and community bandmaster. His record in Nashwauk includes starting the school band in September 1914.[27] By 1917, the Nashwauk-Keewatin High School Band was invited to play at the Minnesota State Fair. A contemporary newspaper article mentioned some of the names in the 1918 photo of the band: George Kokko, Claude Extrom, Hugo Sutonen, Walmer Kuru, Nick Gentile, Russell Tweed, Neil McEachin, Ernest Galley, Mennie Wirtanen, John Tarro, Sulo Rantala, Toivo Nurkka, Ralph Verre, Sam Shapero, John Morris, Hans Latvala, Helmi Taipale, Carl Gentile, Seppo Taipale, Carl Backlund, Kenneth Bright, Rufus Johnston, Theodore Schuirman, Peter Beloti, Henry Rokala, Ernest Johnson, Väinô Mäki, Rudolph Raattamaa, Eino Karkkainen, Charles Lundquist, Carl Ranta, Lawrence McEachin, Gabe Schuirman, and Eli Tuomala.

It is not known when Taipale started directing the Nashwauk City Band, but it was at least as early as 1914. An article in the *Nashwauk Herald*, May 22, 1914, announced the band's "fourth spring concert" under Taipale, including the repertoire. The article included an announcement of the meeting electing the band's officers for 1914: George Kokko, President; Oscar Yrjölä, Treasurer; Hugo Lilja, Treasurer; John Raattama, Business Manager; John Rokala, Assistant Manager; Victor Taipale, Leader; and George Sulonen, Assistant Leader. The article announced that there was $1.60 in the treasury, prompting the question why this group of Finns would need two treasurers and a business manager.

Figure 43. Nashwauk-Keewatin School Band, Victor Taipale, director, 1918. Photograph courtesy Latvala family, Nashwauk.

The Taipale family resided in Nashwauk after 1917 and Victor's wife was the postmaster during this time. His children's names appear in school band concert programs as late as 1921. Figure 44, taken from the 1924 Temperance Society Yearbook shows the Taipale Family Orchestra in 1923. Victor is behind the tuba, daughter Helmi at the piano, Pacius with the cello, Voitto with the French horn. His wife stands in the back, not performing. The saxophone on top of the piano is Helmi's, and the euphonium on the floor belongs to Pacius. Taipale's name re-appears in the Hibbing directory by 1922, and yet it is certain that he directed the Nashwauk school band until 1925. At that point, he and the family moved to Monessen, Pennsylvania, where he directed the famous Louhi Band for one year.

It is difficult to trace Taipale's career accurately through the Finnish communities in other states, but if we infer from the better-documented biographical example of Finnish bandmaster George Wahlström of Ohio, it can be assumed that Taipale's journeys outside of Minnesota were mostly occasional and not long in duration. One exception was a five-year directorship of the 182nd Field Artillery Band in Detroit Michigan, from 1926 to 1931.

He and his family moved back to Minnesota soon after the Detroit military band period, where he is next found directing a small village school band in Bassett Township while residing in Chisholm. By1938, Taipale's name is back in the Hibbing "Polk" community directory, listed as both a musician and a watchman at the St. Louis County Garage. By 1949, he is listed as a resident of Duluth, and he may have moved out-of-state after that, since no death record or social security records have been found in any Minnesota archives.

His obituary has not as yet been found, but a 1949 *Who's Who Among Finnish Americans* has the following tribute: Taipale "trained the younger generation in music, band and orchestra for almost 40 years; organized numerous school bands in Minnesota; director, various bands and choirs, in

Michigan, Ohio, Minnesota and Pennsylvania, and editor of the Finnish newspaper *American Sanomat*, 1909-13.[28]

Figure 44. Taipale Family Orchestra, 1923.

Taipale, a very active and successful bandmaster and teacher with connections to the community, still seemed to follow the itinerant pattern that has been observed among many of the immigrant leaders: his longest time in any one place was in Nashwauk, which lasted about ten years. It is unknown whether this tendency to travel was merely to accept new opportunities or the expected pattern for a Finnish-American bandmaster.

Hemming Hautala

Hemming Hautala was born in 1890 in Evijärvi; apparently his original family name may have been Dahlbacka, which was Finnicized in the fashion of the time to *Hautala*. He attended school in Finland, and played in a *Nuorisoseura soittokunta* (Youth Society Band); he must have received additional musical training and experience during his twenty-nine years there. He arrived in the U.S. in 1919 and played in several Iron Range bands, including the 13th Regimental Band in Duluth, which operated on the home front in Minnesota during World War I. He conducted the Hibbing City Band for a while and then moved to South Dakota, conducting the Frederick Town Band and *Savo* Band there. The Frederick band won the South Dakota State Fair prize in Aberdeen in 1925 under his leadership. Several players in the Frederick band were from the *Savo* Band and later the two combined.

A brief biography of him in the Sibelius Club *Airut* magazine states that he attended the VanderCook Musical College in Chicago, but his name does not appear in the VanderCook archives. He probably attended the VanderCook Cornet School, an earlier institution that preceded the Musical College, whose records were less detailed.[29] He must have received a music education certificate from VanderCook, since he then served as school music teacher in Ord, Nebraska, and later in the Hibbing schools, where he also ran a music store. He must have begun to work in Bovey in the 1930s, where a photograph of him is seen with the school band. He is also seen in the same decade as a player in the Hibbing City Band.

Wasastjerna lists Hautala as "Chairman of the St. Louis County Rural Band Association," a position he held while he worked as an instrumental music teacher in smaller village schools during the Depression. Leo Wiljamaa, a retired schoolteacher, remembered Hautala as a traveling music teacher to rural schools in the 1930s:

> I taught for four years in St. Louis County—and Hemming Hautala was band director—he came to each school; lot of stories about him. He had skis; we'd have an hour off for lunch, and he'd ski around Brookston–Toivola and all those places. I saw him once a week–I knew Hemming Hautala well. When he retired from the county he ran a piano store in Duluth. I visited the store there and had a long talk with him. He traveled around St. Louis County rural schools. He stayed all day in one school: they were all in a row: Brookston, Elborne, Meadowlands, Toivola, Cotton. He had a band on the Range.[30]

Figure 45. An undated Hemming Hautala photograph. Courtesy Immigration History Research Center, University of Minnesota.

Figure 46. Hibbing City Band, 1931. Photograph courtesy of the Hibbing Historical Society.

Hemming Hautala is seated behind the tympani in a photo of the Hibbing City Band in 1931 (Figure 46). At the end of his career, Hautala settled in Duluth, where he had a music store. Several contacts in the Iron Range recall visiting that store in the 1950s, where many bought their parlor pianos. He died in 1959.

William Syrjälä

William Syrjälä from Cloquet is included on this list of Finnish bandsmen because he is an example of the musician who made the transition from the old band tradition to the modern popular dance music of the time. Born in Finland in 1898, he came as a child to Minnesota, where his family settled in Cloquet, and where his father worked in the paper mill. He learned about music making within the community, and played in Finnish and community bands throughout his youth. In high school he showed great promise as a musician, both on violin and trumpet; in 1918, his graduation year, he started the school band, which "has helped make basketball games lively and tuneful." He also performed in the Cloquet High School Orchestra; he is shown seated at the left playing violin in a photo from the 1918 yearbook (figure 47).[31]

CLOQUET HIGH SCHOOL ORCHESTRA

Figure 47. The Cloquet High School orchestra, 1918. Courtesy Carlton County Historical Society.

Syrjälä joined the Alger-Barnes Circus band in 1920, and then studied music at Valparaiso University for some time from 1922 on. After 1927, he began an active career as a dance musician, with tours to Finland and around Finnish communities in North America.

Syrjälä's name is still known in Finnish-American music circles as the husband and musical partner of the very popular dance accordionist Viola Turpeinen. Finnish-American musicians coming from Iron Range bands in the early 1920s often embraced the music of the swing era and the dance combo, leaving their traditional brass band roots behind. Syrjälä and Turpeinen produced a substantial number of 78-RPM records of Finnish dance music, and kept a touring schedule going from one Finnish dance hall to the next that lasted into the early 1950s. That often annual itinerary took them through almost every Finnish community in the East and Midwest, and into Canada with repeated appearances at the same Finnish dance halls. Viola Turpeinen died in 1957 and Syrjälä died in Florida in 1996.

Other Minnesota Finnish-American Bandmasters

While information about their work is limited, some other bandmasters should be included in this study:

Little is known about **Emil Ikola**, who was born in Minnesota in 1896 and had an active career as a musician and bandmaster in Eveleth, Cotton, and other nearby communities. He is a cornet player in photographs of the Kaiku Band and is listed as director of the Eveleth Cuty band in the 1930s. No other biographical information about his musical career has been found, but Ikola may be the earliest of the "second generation" Finnish bandmasters: Ikola seems to be the earliest of the American-born school and community band directors with Finnish-American heritage who were common in mid-twentieth-century northern Minnesota. He died in 1968.

Neilo Hakala, an accordion player who formed a community band in Embarrass in the 1930s, but left for Chicago some years after forming the band. He submitted a letter to the *Finnish-American Reporter* in July 1994, reminiscing about his career as an accordionist.[32]

Jon Wilenius was an immigrant miner who formed the Sturgeon Township Band after leaving Chisholm.

Frans Lindroos was significant as a leader of Finnish musical groups in Duluth after 1913, and remained there until 1918. He came from Viipuri in eastern Finland and received some of his training in the Finnish military bands. It does not appear that he stayed in Minnesota after 1918.

Alex Koivunen, brought to Minnesota from Negaunee Michigan as a bandmaster in the Vermilion towns and Buhl, has a very short record in Minnesota, so he must have remained only a short time.

Several of the Finnish bandmasters had some training as musicians through the military. Had they remained in Finland rather than immigrate to America, some of them might have had careers as players or musical leaders in the communities of newly independent Finland. The social status of the

Finnish-American bandmaster within his own ethnic community is hard to determine exactly from written sources. The music men were valued and awarded a certain social position based on their important contribution to ceremonial and cultural activity in the community. At the same time, there seemed to be an inordinate restlessness among the bandmasters, as they all too often moved from one leadership position to another. Was it that the bandmasters were not satisfied, or that the bands were seeking new leaders? It is not clear. The only available music-directing positions with any financial permanence that emerged on the Iron Range were those connected with municipal and school bands. Yet, rarely did even those positions have a full-time career status. There were some examples, such as Taipale, who would function as musical leaders in both school and municipal roles and were able to create careers in music. Yet even the most successful of these musical leaders were unable to sustain the activity as a breadwinning career throughout all their active professional years. Hemming Hautala, even when very active in school music, teaching, and municipal bands, still maintained a music store in Hibbing. All of the other music men discussed in this chapter had other wage-earning jobs, often menial, outside of music. They never reached the social and economic status in their communities that was enjoyed by, for instance, schoolteachers, businessmen, or clergy. The fantasy that they may have dreamed about in coming to America and becoming great bandmasters in the new land was only partially realized. They never were able to feed their families from it without some outside employment.

Bandsmen are rarely included in the two available "who's who" publications of Finnish-Americans in the early twentieth century.[33] Knowing that there were many active bandsmen in leadership positions at the time, their absence is conspicuous and makes a statement about the status of amateur music in the minds of these book editors. In the social circles of Iron Range cities, the status of the immigrant bandmaster was noted with cruel honesty, if verified by the Polk Directories. Almost all Finnish immigrant bandmasters were listed as common laborers or shopkeepers. The grand uniforms, parades, and ceremonies seemed to have been part of a fantasy lived out for the local Finnish communities. To the surprise and regret of the Finnish bandmasters and players who arrived in America with high hopes, the appreciation usually did not extend very far beyond the front door of the Finn hall.

---

[1]Hans R., Wasastjerna, ed. , "History of the Finns in Minnesota," Toivo Rosvall, trans., *Minnesotan suomalaisten histori.* (Duluth MN: Finnish-American Historical Society, 1959), 465.

[2]Ibid., 246.

[3]"Westerinen, Peter, 10/09/1892, Ely," Minnesota Death Index; identity not confirmed.

[4]*Airut*, Sibelius Society publication, Duluth, 1917, 46.

[5]Conversations with Mary Ellen Kleemola Levander and David Kess, Ely natives, December 2, 2001.

[6]Translated from the Miettunen biography in *Airut* p. 46.

[7]"Nick Miettunen opens pop factory," *Ely Times* 6/24/1892, 5.

[8]John Pustovar, "History of Bands in Buhl, Minnesota," (thesis, Bemidji State University, 1972), 23.

[9]*Chisholm Tribune Herald*, Nov 27, 1930, 1.

[10]Armas Holmio, *History of Finns in Michigan,* trans. Ellen M. Ryynänen (Detroit: Wayne State University Press, 2001), 385.

[11]"John Haapasaari–leader of first Hibbing band," *Hibbing Sentinel,* February 2, 1897, 6.

[12]Kleemola Levander interview, 2002.

[13]R. L. Polk, *Range Towns' Directory* (Duluth, MN: R. L. Polk, 1903), 197.

[14]Interview with Mary Ellen Kleemola Levander, granddaughter of Kleemola; Jan. 7, 2002.

[15]Ibid.

[16]Lyle Klein, "A History of Instrumental Music in Ely Minnesota" (thesis, Bemidji State University, 1977), 20.

[17]*Ely Miner*, September 26, 1913.

[18]*Duluth Herald*, Duluth, MN October 16, 1931, 8.

[19]"Band Leader is Through," *Hibbing Journal*, Hibbing, MN, December 22, 1915, 1.

[20]Signe Sandstedt,, *Brimson-Toimi Legacy* (Iron, MN: Glensco, 1995).

[21]*Who's Who Among Finnish-Americans*: "A Biographical Directory of persons of Finnish descent who have made noteworthy contributions to the pattern of American life" (Fitchburg, MA: Raivaaja Publishing Co., 1949).

[22]Wasastjerna, "History," 482.

[23]School Yearbook, Biwabik, Minnesota, 1967, 9.

[24]Wasastjerna, "History," 470.

[25]Ibid., 472.

[26]Minnesota Finnish-American Historical Society collection at Iron Range Research Center, Chisholm, MN.

[27]Nashwauk School Yearbook, 1921, 40.

[28]Ayer's *American Newspaper Annual and Directory* (Philadelphia: N. W. Ayer & Son, 1913.

[29]Correspondence from VanderCook College of Music, Chicago.

[30]Leo Wiljamaa, 90 years old when interviewed in March 2002.

[31]Cloquet High School yearbook, 1918.

[32]The *Finnish American Reporter* is a monthly English language journal established in Hancock, Michigan, in 1986 that is still publishing in 2010.

[33]Werner Nikander, ed., *Amerikan Suomalaisia* (Finnish-American Biographical Dictionary) (Hancock MI: Finnish Lutheran Book Concern, 1927), and *Who's Who among Finnish-Americans* (Fitchburg, MA: Raivaaja Publishing, 1949).

Chapter Five
BANDS IN POLITICS, RELIGION, EDUCATION, AND SOCIAL ORGANIZATIONS

Political and Social Activism among the Finnish Immigrants

The Finnish immigrants who came to America usually polarized into two very contrasting social groups that were clearly split between religious adherents and those who left religion behind for political causes. It might seem to be oversimplifying to declare that this division over religion/temperance and politics was the main factor in how Finnish-American society was organized, but it appeared to be true. Regarding the development of bands, these two main sponsors of Finnish-American cultural activity, the temperance groups and the leftist political groups, generated almost all of the band activity. The tension between these two major Finnish-American cultural movements was at first negligible but eventually developed a rather bitter opposition to one another.

Some elements of this social division were already emerging in Finland in the 1880s, prior to emigration. It first developed within a conflict between two opposing agendas for the emergence of a new Finnish social order: a traditional nationalism vs. a working-class socialism.[1] In its original Finnish manifestation, this division was defined by an important language element. The Swedo-Finns, 1.5% of the population who had always dominated the main franchises of commerce, government, religion, and education, were the strongest early proponents of a new nationalism and of the role of a state sponsored Lutheran church. This "Fennoman" movement's mission was the promotion of Finnish language and culture, yet the most active early organizers of that group were Swedo-Finns who promoted the concept of a Finnish-language nation as a potential foil to continued Russian domination. Commonly at that time, the names of ardent Fennomen were changed from Swedish to Finnish, such as *Liljeström* to *Lumme* or *Järnefeldt* to *Rautavaara.*

The remaining 98.5 % of the Finnish population, the poor, common laborer, almost always spoke Finnish. As literacy increased through adoption of universal education in the late 1880s, Finnish-speaking landless workers began to seek political solutions to their poverty in the midst of an economic recession. The rise of socialism during these decades was partly in step with the rise of a Finnish national identity, but must also be understood separately as "an ethnolinguistic conflict, and an element of its class character"[2] "As the country became more urban, the first leftist organizations in Finland were simply trade unions trying to improve working conditions, especially in larger towns . While Swedo-Finns saw a Finnish national identity as a possible strategy against further Russian interference, many Finnish-speaking Finns were more interested in a future Finnish independent nation as part of a new social order that would hold promise for the economic betterment of the common laborer. The intensity of these political differences would become more acute during and after Finland's independence in 1917, when they developed into a bloody civil war in the spring of 1918.

Socialism was still an early emerging phenomenon in Finland when most emigrants left for America in the 1890s. It was still an unformed movement, but slowly evolved on both sides of the Atlantic. Many of the later arrivals among the immigrants to America already had significant experience with labor conflict and the socialist party in Finland, thus adding more leadership and skill to the growing movement. They had a more activist demeanor, were often better-educated and had significant experience with labor strikes and protest organizations in Finland.

Historians point to the "February Manifesto" of Governor General Babrikov in 1898 as a major catalyst for the rapid growth of social activisim among the Finns in both Finland and America. That manifesto's terms were designed to quickly russify all of Finland, squelching any nationalist tendencies. It was a harsh decree: the Finnish army would be dissolved; Finns would be conscripted into the Russian army; laws giving native Finns certain rights in their own land were abolished; the Russian language would become the official language of government and university; native Russians could be employed in the Finnish civil service; and certain Finnish customs, including the printing of money, would be abolished.

The manifesto drew many immediate responses within Finland, but one of the strongest was the massive working-class adoption of the socialist cause, which at that time more clearly defined itself as linked to the working man's interests in the struggle for national identity. Another response, of course, was a surge in the exodus of thousands to North America. At a time when political turmoil was shaping a new Finnish nation, it is notable that many potential participants in that historic process were boarding steamers and heading abroad.

The Babrikov manifesto had an equally profound result on the socialist movement among American Finns. Immediately after the edict was announced, the American Finnish community organized efforts to support the independence movement back in Finland by encouraging state and national legislatures to apply pressure on the Czar. Food and other aid was collected and sent to Finland. "Opposition to political conditions in Finland and resistance to military service played a large part in their decision to leave. These more sophisticated and politically conscious immigrants plunged right into the life of Finnish-American communities."[3] Prior to 1898, the socialist movement in Finnish America was at best embryonic and localized. While other important socialist causes, such as dangerous and unfair working conditions in American mines, contributed to the rise of Finnish-American socialism, the Babrikov manifesto gave it the greatest single early impetus.

Finnish Churches and Temperance Societies

Knowing that the Finnish immigrants to America were primarily Finnish speaking working classes, one might assume that they all had socialist tendencies. However, most of the earliest waves of immigration were Finns whose background was more connected with agrarian culture and the church. The Finnish churches established in North America were also closely connected with the newly popular temperance hall movement in the new communities. Temperance was also a popular social movement across the United States during the time when Finns began arriving.

In Minnesota, the churches developed quickly after the first Finns arrived in the Vermilion Range towns, in part because many new arrivals to the region came as families that had been established previously in Northern Michigan. But with the families came the many unwed young miners as well as the single girls looking for work as domestics. Support from the Finnish-Lutheran clergy for temperance activity was direct and often specifically aimed at those unwed miners who often showed rather rowdy habits.

While Finnish immigrants were involved in other church congregations in Minnesota, the majority of them were Lutheran. Lutheranism among immigrant Finns took on several forms. A pietistic group, followers of religious leader Lars Leevi Laestedius, was already present in Minnesota and Michigan in the 1870s and continues to be an active congregation in many Finnish-American communities to the present day. A "Finnish National Lutheran Church" was formed in 1890, as an alternative to traditional "Church of Finland" Lutheranism, or the Suomi Synod. That "Finnish National Church" developed traditions and practices that eventually were incorporated into the American Missouri Synod Lutheranism. The Suomi Synod was an American exponent of the state-sponsored Lutheran Church in Finland, with the clergy and other institutions having close ties there. The Finnish state church initially provided trained clergy as missionaries for the many Finnish-American communities until Finnish-Americans could be trained for the ministry from local institutions. The Suomi Synod eventually evolved to become a part of the current Evangelical Lutheran Church in America. During the era of immigration, all branches of Finnish-American Lutheranism jointly supported the Finnish temperance hall movement. While the Suomi Synod (the largest group) held the major role in the temperance movement, the temperance hall may have been the one place where differing religious factions met on common ground to sing in choirs, act in plays, and play in bands. While Finnish brass bands were not known to have played in churches, either in Finland or in America, their association with the temperance halls somehow has connected the cornet with the pulpit. The summer music festivals always had bands playing traditional hymns for outdoor congregational singing. The level of scrutiny regarding participating bandsmen's personal religious convictions and alcohol habits varied somewhat from community to community. In general, it appears that musical ability usually took precedence over other moral factors. Finnish bandmasters and bandsmen seem to have participated without restriction among the various socialist halls and temperance societies.

While the temperance movement among Finnish-Americans had some roots in Finland, it should be seen mostly as an American phenomenon, and a cause that many immigrant church workers and social reformers embraced. It was established among Finnish-Americans years before the rise of organized socialism in the same communities. Many of the first immigrants to arrive in the 1870s were young single men, recruited to lumbering and mining camps or factories. The "wild west" social life was already well in place when they came, and boisterous Finnish boys joined in enthusiastically. Akseli Järnefelt Rauanheimo, an early historian of Finnish America, told of the saloon culture as a basic behavior of that time for the Finns. As seen in any favorite Western movie, the social life, business, and entertainment of the immigrant men in the 1880s all took place in the tavern. This rough social environment continued until the arrival of Finnish clergy and women to the communities. Carl Ross suggests this situation can been seen as a step in the evolution of the Finnish-American cultural life: "One need not condone hard drinking to suggest that before associational life developed, the Finnish immigrant contrived to find a mutual bond of cultural and social solidarity in this setting."[5] However, the level of Finnish drinking, knife-fighting, and lawless behavior became legendary within the American communities. A perusal of the newspapers in Iron Range towns of the time will show numerous and regular instances of drunken Finns brawling in public places.

When Finnish temperance societies first began to be established about 1885, their mission was immediate and clear: to provide an alternative activity to the saloon culture. These societies were formed rather quickly wherever Finns had settled. This was due partly to a sudden change in the gender profile of the immigrant population, as larger numbers of young single Finnish women began to arrive, primarily as domestic servants. The development of the temperance movement had the added effect of uniting the Finnish-American population into a nationwide, organized whole. The temperance movement was already well-established in American society, and Finns initially joined existing temperance societies of the time, such as the Good Templars. However, the sheer number of Finns in many of these communities precipitated the formation of independent Finnish temperance groups. Northern Michigan was the first region to develop Finnish temperance societies with the support of Finnish Lutheran congregations in the 1880s. However, within a few years, Iron Range Minnesota Finnish communities and other centers around the country established similar institutions.

Finnish immigrant bandsmen, having already played in fire brigade, *Nuorisoseura*, and *Kansanvalistusseura* (KVS) bands in Finland, were quickly formed within the structure of the Finnish-American temperance organizations.

This story is repeated for almost every early band, except for a few that organized either independently or under the sponsorship of a mining company. Even the independent bands participated in Finnish temperance events.

The division of Finnish-American society into the temperance societies and the newly formed Finnish-American socialist clubs was gradual. The initial reaction to the Babrikov manifesto was to unify the immigrant community nationwide, with all voices speaking as one. In its first stages, socialism shared many goals with the temperance movement, with both organizations sharing meeting space and membership. It should not be construed that Finnish-American socialists condoned the tavern culture. Carl Ross observes that the socialist movement grew as a germ within the body of the temperance movement in some communities:

> Probably nothing facilitated socialist growth as much as a continuing relationship to the temperance movement, with which the socialists shared secular leadership among the Finnish-Americans. The socialists endorsed the temperance principle, and in many areas led a struggle to clean up the drink and vice-ridden industrial communities. Clergymen and business leaders continued to dominate top-level leadership of the temperance clubs, but they could not check the drift toward socialism among the young and exuberant working class membership. Temperance societies, some as whole units, and their dramatic and musical groups, were caught up in the new crusading spirit. The socialists were advised by their leaders to remain with the temperance clubs and, as in the 1907 Wyoming state socialist convention, were advised to go slow in building new halls while intensifying efforts to gain control of temperance centers. In the Rocky Mountain States, where there had been some fifty temperance clubs, the whole movement was swept into the socialist camp.[6]

Co-operation with the temperance halls swiftly evaporated as the socialist movement expanded among the rising number of mobilized working-class Finns. Many Finnish communities have stories, part truth and part legend, of meeting halls and dance halls being mysteriously burnt, and of other demonstrations of antisocial activism between the two camps.

Figure 48 shows a program announcement for a Finnish temperance festival held in Hibbing in July 1904. Interestingly, this was the second large Finnish temperance gathering that took place in Minnesota's Iron Range, the other a month earlier in Eveleth. The participating Finnish choirs and bands were from Hibbing, Ely, and Chisholm, and Hancock, Michigan. The evening's entertainment included a band and choir competition, although this program does not list the contestants or repertoire. Programs for both festivals indicate that the bands active on the Iron Range attended both that summer.

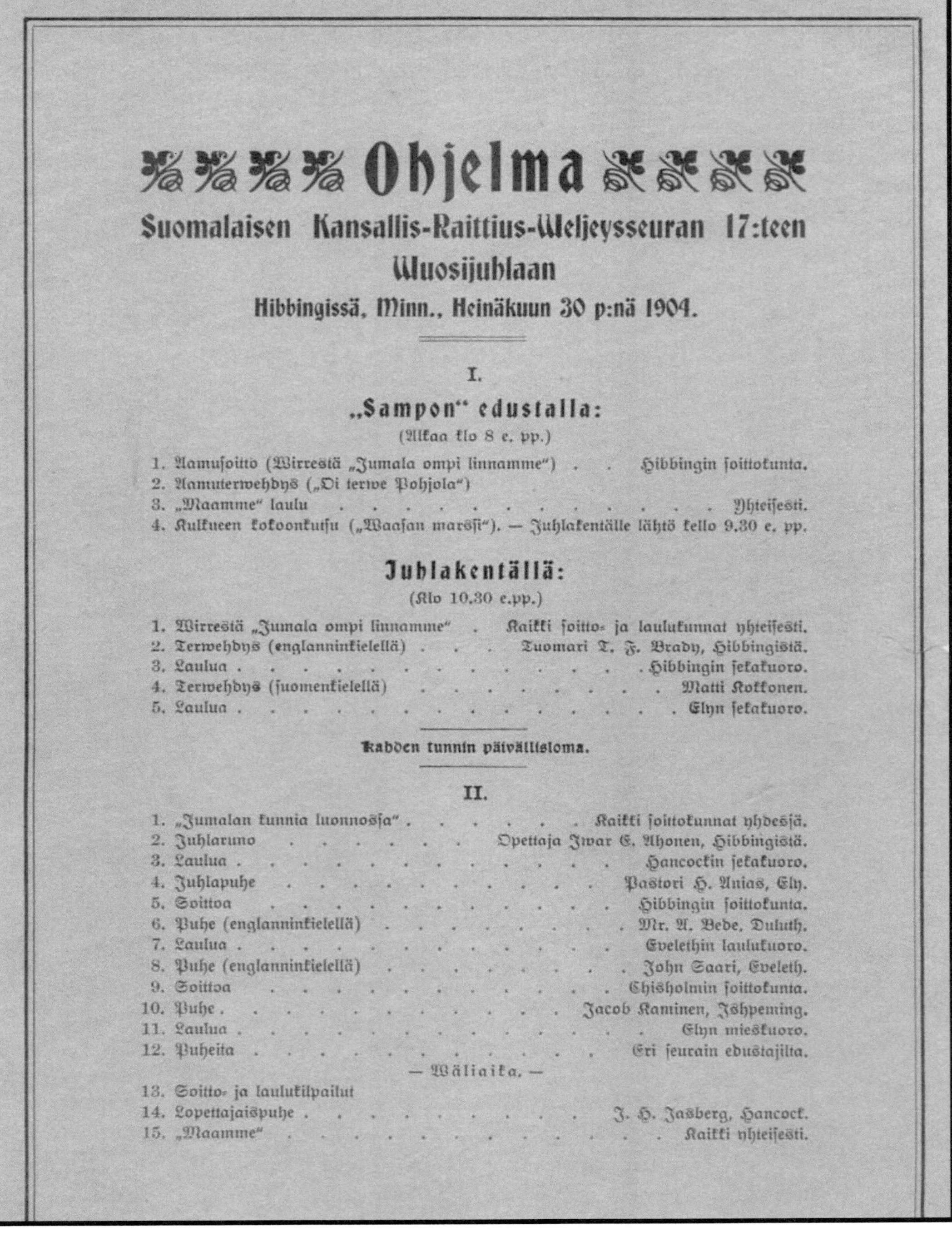

Ohjelma

Suomalaisen Kansallis-Raittius-Weljeysseuran 17:teen Wuosijuhlaan

Hibbingissä, Minn., Heinäkuun 30 p:nä 1904.

I.

„Sampon" edustalla:

(Alkaa klo 8 e. pp.)

1. Aamusoitto (Wirrestä „Jumala ompi linnamme") . . Hibbingin soittokunta.
2. Aamuterwehdys („Oi terwe Pohjola")
3. „Maamme" laulu . . . . Yhteisesti.
4. Kulkueen kokoonkutsu („Waasan marssi"). — Juhlakentälle lähtö kello 9.30 e. pp.

Juhlakentällä:

(Klo 10.30 e.pp.)

1. Wirrestä „Jumala ompi linnamme" . Kaikki soitto- ja laulukunnat yhteisesti.
2. Terwehdys (englanninkielellä) . . . Tuomari T. F. Brady, Hibbingistä.
3. Laulua . . . . Hibbingin sekakuoro.
4. Terwehdys (suomenkielellä) . . . . Matti Kokkonen.
5. Laulua . . . . Elyn sekakuoro.

Kahden tunnin päivällisloma.

II.

1. „Jumalan kunnia luonnossa" . . . . Kaikki soittokunnat yhdessä.
2. Juhlaruno . . . . . . Opettaja Iwar E. Ahonen, Hibbingistä.
3. Laulua . . . . Hancockin sekakuoro.
4. Juhlapuhe . . . . Pastori H. Anias, Ely.
5. Soittoa . . . . Hibbingin soittokunta.
6. Puhe (englanninkielellä) . . . . Mr. A. Bede, Duluth.
7. Laulua . . . . Evelethin laulukuoro.
8. Puhe (englanninkielellä) . . . . John Saari, Eveleth.
9. Soittoa . . . . Chisholmin soittokunta.
10. Puhe . . . . Jacob Kaminen, Ishpeming.
11. Laulua . . . . Elyn mieskuoro.
12. Puheita . . . . Eri seurain edustajilta.

— Wäliaika. —

13. Soitto- ja laulukilpailut
14. Lopettajaispuhe . . . . J. H. Jasberg, Hancock.
15. „Maamme" . . . . Kaikki yhteisesti.

Figure 48. Program, Hibbing Finnish Temperance Society's 17th annual festival, July 30, 1904. Courtesy of the Iron Range Research Center.

Almost every Finnish community on the Iron Range had both temperance and socialist organizations, with their separate meeting halls. Decades later, socialism among Finns took on two differing manifestations with the rise of the co-operative movement in the Finnish farming communities, and, in contrast, the more militant rise of organized labor and communism in the Finnish industrial communities. Both the temperance and the socialist organizations constructed social halls that were centers for cultural, educational, and athletic activity. These "Finn Halls" were the site of almost all public events in the Finnish community. The Finnish temperance movement mostly ended when prohibition ended, although the resultant "Finn Hall" culture and a socially active Finnish religious community previously associated with the temperance movement continued on.

Many of the halls that were constructed by Finnish temperance societies and socialist clubs have been torn down or burnt. Those that have survived have mostly been converted to other uses, such as Virginia's Socialist Opera House, and Ely Temperance Hall, often called the Pink Hall because if its brick color (now a bowling alley). Reino Hannula's *Album of Finnish Halls* lists and illustrates many of the important halls in the United States. In Minnesota, for example, Hannula lists Finnish halls in Aurora, Biwabik, Brainerd, Cloquet, Cokato, Cromwell, Crosby, Ely, Embarrass, Eveleth, Floodwood, Gilbert, Grand Marais, Hibbing, Lawler, Minneapolis, Nashwauk, New York Mills, Pike, Palo, Petrell, Virginia, and Zim.[7] The book has omitted many others for which Hannula may not have had information, such as Soudan, Sturgeon Township, Chisholm, Mountain Iron, Toimi, Cherry, and Rice River. Many communities had more than one hall, depending on how many political and social factions were active.

Among those halls preserved in their original form, one of the most notable is the Virginia *Valon Tuote* temperance hall, now called Kaleva Hall. The building has a large, upper story with a hardwood floor, a proscenium stage, and a vaulted ceiling. The room was used for multiple purposes, including concerts, meetings, dances, gymnastic events, and exhibits. Without fixed chairs, the floor can be used as a dance floor (see figure 49).

Figure 49. Finnish Temperance Hall, Virginia, Minnesota, 1906. Postcard courtesy Virginia Area Historical Society.

The Virginia Minnesota Socialist Opera House, built in 1913, was considered at the time to be "the most elegant building owned by the Finns in the United States."[8] It was used for club meetings, theater presentations, vocal and instrumental music concerts, and rehearsals for all the events. The calendar was so full that it necessitated hiring a full-time business manager. The building is still in use, converted into a labor union hall and co-operative society headquarters (see figure 50).

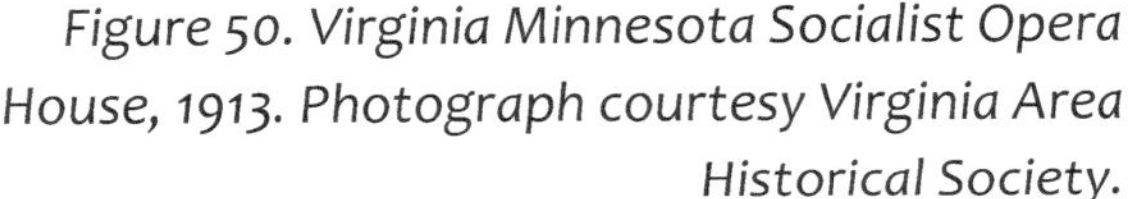

Figure 50. Virginia Minnesota Socialist Opera House, 1913. Photograph courtesy Virginia Area Historical Society.

Figure 51. Interior, Virginia Finnish Socialist Opera House. Courtesy Virginia Area Historical Society.

The view from the interior in figure 51 shows permanent seating. Dancing took place in the lower level, along with refreshment service. Bands and other musical groups frequently participated in the *iltamat* variety shows or provided incidental music to plays in this sumptuous space.

Notice the oval shape of the Finnish Temperance Hall in Soudan, Minnesota (figure 52): it was said at the time that a hall without corners had no place to hide the devil.

Pohjan Leimun haali perältä katsottuna.

Figure 52. Finnish Temperance Hall, Soudan, Minnesota, 1898.[9]

Both temperance and socialist groups fostered lively cultural activity, including dramatic presentations, choirs, gymnastic clubs, brass bands, and summer festivals. A careful study of photographs and rosters of the Minnesota bands, however, reveals that often the same brass player belonged to many bands, and might appear in gatherings of both camps. This sharing of good musicians had already been a pattern in Finland, where many bands were formed in small villages, and where it was said that a talented E-flat cornet player might have several band uniforms in his closet.[10]

Finns, Schools, and School Bands

Many of the local educational developments on the Iron Range coincided with the rise of Finnish brass band activity, both unfolding rapidly. The opening of a mine, development of a municipality, arrival of a Finnish immigrant population, and the establishment of public schools and civic organizations would all be completed in about two or three years. Evolving together, these important elements influenced each other. Newly established public schools afforded the opportunity for some Finnish bandmasters to start youth band programs in various communities, and provided instrumental music training to the immigrant's children. Qualifications and training required of a school bandmaster at the time apparently allowed for the hiring of immigrant musicians, even with limited English language skills and no American pedagogical training. This was perhaps because they were the only experienced bandmasters in town. All of the earliest school band positions, as filled by Finns such as Taipale, Kleemola, and Hautala, were part-time positions. The circumstances of Taipale's and Kleemola's initial and very short school band directors' tenures suggest that the qualifications for such positions were also quickly changing to require certified pedagogical training. Kleemola never repeated his first attempt to work with school bands, whereas Taipale clearly sought out necessary training and continued for many years.

When school systems offered more permanent positions for band directors, they were filled by bandmasters trained through American educational institutions. Not many immigrant Finnish bandmasters were able to make that transition and meet the requirements. They usually arrived in this country with somewhat inflated expectations of opportunity, and only a few were successful in developing longer careers of musical leadership in the general community. None of those Finnish bandmasters found positions that brought full-time careers in musical leadership. The chances, however, for part-time teaching band-directing positions continued to grow as more schools opened. The Eveleth school system "employed Frank Lepresto, an Italian, to direct, in 1913 the school band. Thereafter, in Range schools large and small, immigrant musicians generally fllled such positions, usually on a part time basis"[11]

The First School Bands on the Iron Range

All of the oldest school band programs in Minnesota were in the newly built Iron Range high schools. Charles Kleemola started the Ely School Band in 1906, though he turned it over to Chauncey Mills in the following year.[12] Mills, in turn, turned it over to Richard Pierce in 1908, following a short interval under the leadership of the Ely City Band director John Kinsman.[13] This, and other Iron Range school band programs, was several years ahead of any school bands in southern Minnesota.

Figure 53. Ely High School Band, Richard Pierce, director, 1909. Photograph courtesy Ely Winton Historical Society.

Wasastjerna suggested that Victor Taipale started the Biwabik school band in 1904, though his tenure in that position would have been very short. The instances where Finnish immigrants were involved in school band leadership were several. One unusual example was William Syrjälä, a Finnish-born trumpet player who graduated from high school in Cloquet, and during his senior year formed the first school band (Syrjälä is discussed in chapter 4).

Public Schools and the Immigrants

Iron Range public school development was heavily influenced by the enormous influx of immigrants from the very start. In the *Ely Times*, September 15, 1893, Joseph Schaefer editorialized about the disruption caused by the "overwhelming number of foreign children presenting themselves for admission at different times of the school year, not knowing a word of English." This was a dilemma for the public school in many Range communities. The editor of the *Eveleth News* on September 2, 1903 wrote: "We have several hundred children of foreign parentage who ought to be Americanized, and the surest way to do that is in the schoolroom. There is abundant taxable property to give Eveleth the best school system in the state."[14]

Mining company representatives and their wives were community leaders in most Iron Range towns. Aware of educational reform movements in Chicago, espoused by social activitists such as Jane Addams and Francis Parker, they began to see it as their mission to create educational systems to serve the entire population on the Range. Some officers from the Oliver Mining Company are listed on almost all Iron Range community school boards at the turn of the century. One of the first manifestations of this educational mission was the founding of numerous kindergartens, a popular new concept from the "Progressive Education" movements of the 1880s. The Minnesota Compulsory Education Act was passed in 1894, but it wasn't until 1900 that children under 8 years of age were actually required to attend primary school, ushering the kindergarten law into action. Smith sees Eveleth as a good example of the phenomenal growth in Iron Range school populations: in 1895, Eveleth was essentially a small, unkempt mining camp, but by September, 1903, 850 children "knocked on the school house doors."[15]

The reaction among American-born citizens to the large influx of immigrants was, at times, one of alarm. These attitudes were being formed just as public school education was being established in the area. Here is an editorial that appeared in the *Ely Times* in 1899:

> The Finns whom Russian persecution are driving from Finland are emigrating in large bodies to this country and dream of establishing themselves in colonies in our northwestern states where as they say, "Finnish customs and habits or thoughts can be preserved and a spiritual union among them kept up and strengthened." They would here establish a Finland with old-country customs and usage. While the desire of the Finns to preserve the traits of their nationality is creditable, that desire will be swept from the minds of the younger generation in the desire to become American, which is the inevitable result of contact with our people and our institutions. Germans, Irish and Swedish people have come to this country and while it has been tried, have never been able to withstand the American influence for any length of time and their old-world customs and manners have disappeared under the free tutorage accorded them here. No other race can resist the metamorphosing assimilating power of the America stock. No language can hold its own among the children of any immigrant against the English. No nation has as yet been able to plant on our soil a new Germany, Ireland, Sweden or other country and at this late day we are certain the Finns cannot turn certain localities into New Finland. This desire will be swept from the minds of millions before, born of Irish, German and Swede parentage who now resent any attempt to classify them other, than American citizens.[16]

The adult Finns who arrived in Minnesota had a 98% literacy rate, substantially better than most other immigrant groups coming to Northern Minnesota.[17] With their educational background and aspirations, the Finns were usually the largest ethnic group found in both the public-school classrooms and in the night schools for adults.[18]

The Lavishness of Facilities

Even today, travelers to Iron Range communities are often impressed by the imposing grandeur of the public school buildings built in the early 1900s. These schools were some of the most lavish and well equipped in the United States at the time. Economic conditions of the region and the values of the era precipitated the establishment of these superlative Iron Range school programs.

Before 1920, the school population on the Range was almost all primary and "grammar" school age. In the 1880s, the mining communities had quite small populations of school-aged youth, with only limited schooling programs in place. Compulsory education was until age 16. Most high school students would seek employment in the mines rather than continue to graduation. By 1900, the population of youth, immigrant and native, had risen significantly and new legislation establishing rural one-room schools was in force.[20] After 1905, the miners' communities, with the support of the mining companies, levied expanded school taxes, and the building of schools exploded, both in extravagance and in number. These schools, most dating from about 1910, offered elaborate services:

> They fumished instruction for the grades from kindergarten through high school, as well as for junior colleges in Hibbing, Virginia, Eveleth, and Coleraine, after the war period. Ample classroom and laboratory facilities were furnished, and additional provisions were made for auditoriums, gymnasiums, swimming pools, greenhouses, industrial and domestic science training, cafeteria, and similar facilities. Through the years, competent health and dental offices were added, and playgrounds with supervised recreation during the summer months were included as a part of a general health program. At the high school level extra-curricular activities included competitive athletics, clubs and organizations of various types, debate and public speaking, band and orchestra, drama, student publications, and the usual program of events found in such schools. Because of the sufficiency of funds, both the school structures and the educational program maintained in them were financed generously. Pupils and students were given a level of instruction and an extra-curricular program comparable to that to be found anywhere else in the state. Indeed, the Range schools secured a reputation for lavishness that made them the envy of school administrators elsewhere in Minnesota. [21]

The contrast between luxurious schools and relatively grim living conditions of many immigrant mining families was a daily reality for second-generation immigrant youth. Many first arrived at school with, at best, a limited knowledge of English. The acculturation of these children into American society became a common and zealous goal for all Range school programs. This process was supported by two established guidelines: "to practice complete non-discrimination between nationalities in their treatment of students," and to provide acculturating opportunities through the school that an immigrant family may otherwise lack. John Syrjämäki wrote that this was one motivation behind the Iron Range cities' exceptional effort towards developing such comprehensive educational facilities and programs.[22]

As community leaders strove to develop their municipalities and schools, they could not ignore their communities' immigrant populations. The schools and their curricula had to be planned with the immigrants in mind, both because of the immigrants' political clout at the ballot box, and because of the overwhelming number of immigrant children sitting in the classrooms. Virginia, for example, had the following breakdown for the nativity of its 1736 pupils' parents (25 Languages) in 1909: Finland (402), United States (343), Sweden (236), Norway (124), Canada (105), England (92), Poland (67), Russia (67), Germany (65), Austria ("including Slavic countries," 64), Italy (39), Iceland (32), Bohemia (26), Hebrews (25), France (18), Scotland (16), Hungary (10), 9 other nations (5).[23] Note that only about 20% of the parents were American born. Most other pupils spoke a mother tongue other than English at home. It must be kept in mind, however, that these public school enrollment statistics are separate from actual population profiles for Virginia in that year. Finns did not make up as large a proportion of the city population as they did of the school population. In addition, 196 out of 267 night-school students had Finnish parents.

The memories that Finnish immigrant children have shared about these school experiences confirm there was some degree of non-discrimination in their treatment, as prescribed in the guidelines. However, many of the Finnish children viewed this "non-discrimination" as an insensitivity to all non-American cultures and their manifestations. For example, speaking any language other than English on the school premises was forbidden in almost all elementary schools. It has become clear that this "highly evangelistic tone," as Syrjämäki noted, in the drive to Americanize immigrant children on the Iron Range, had an immediate and devastating impact on the perpetuation of ethnic cultural activity, such as musical culture being studied here. The abrupt jump between having a Finnish-speaking family and a school that wanted to erase ethnic identity often created tension within the child. Many others felt they were being considered "second class" because of their Finnish heritage, a common theme in Finnish immigrant memoirs. However, it appears that the schools' Americanizing zeal was broadcast evenly over all the immigrant groups. Students from cultures having more exotic languages may have felt it more. The impulse of immigrant families to advance their children educationally came not merely from the external pressure of Americanization, but also from their own internal hopes for their children's future success in the new land. This momentum was cause for the unusual success of the educational system on the

Iron Range, and for the significant role these immigrant children played in the schools.

The public school music programs were very successful cultural melting pots for immigrant youth of diverse backgrounds. Both school and municipal bands were mirrors of the ethnic diversity of the community. In situations where Finnish-born conductors became school bandmasters, they can be seen to have been eager to adopt teaching and programming tastes based on American models of the time.[24] Momentum coming from the immigrants toward developing fine music programs in the schools was considerable. Timothy Smith commented on Eveleth's exceptional instance: "Instruction in music, art, and dramatics likewise started out with aims familiar to educators of the day–to give youngsters from 'culturally deprived' homes an introduction to the refinements of civilization."[25] But they soon became powerful instruments for creating a feeling of solidarity among youngsters of widely divergent backgrounds. Songs and music, just as Colonel Parker[26] had urged, became indispensable vehicles of instruction in the elementary grades, and dramatics a method of learning rather than simply of performing. The teachers were quick to see and exploit for New World ends the resources of the Old World inheritance. At Eveleth, the school orchestra proved so popular among immigrant children, particularly the Italians, that it finally broke down the resistance of the school board there to substantial expenditures for educational 'extras.'[27]

Educational values of the time made a direct connection between developing a respect for authority and the performance of music. The Chisholm superintendent wrote about his view that the band or orchestra conductor could inculcate this respect for authority as few other situations could.

In their zeal to acculturate the immigrants, Iron Range educators expanded their scope to include heavily subscribed summer school programs and night schools. Night school programs were initiated at the very beginning of the growth of school districts, as they accommodated immigrant miner communities. Both the immigrant miners and their wives attended the night schools. While primarily intended to teach English, American history and civics, the curriculum expanded to include other offerings such as industrial arts and homemaking. Night school on the Iron Range took on a particularly keen importance during World War I, when immigrants were presented with a very strong mandate to obtain American citizenship. The alternative was often deportation, so night school became a vehicle for immigrants to obtain sufficient knowledge of English and American culture to be able to remain here.

The establishment of a school in each of the Iron Range communities took place in quick succession, with larger towns slightly earlier. Some communities with substantial Finnish populations had school band programs. Tower, with a population of only 1,200, established its first school in 1884 and a high school four years later. Ely (pop. 3,000) was next with a school in 1889, a high school in 1895. Virginia (pop. 2,500) and Hibbing (pop. 2,400) built their schools in 1893, with high schools following in 1904 and 1912. Eveleth (pop. 3,000) established its school in 1895, with the high school following in 1904. Soudan (pop. 2,000) built both a school and a high school in 1898. Similarly, Biwabik (pop. 1,000) and Aurora (pop. 1,000) built schools in 1900 and 1904, with the high schools following in each case seven years later.[28]

All immigrant groups showed a pride in the educational accomplishments of their children, fostering mild rivalry between the groups. "Finns wished their children to surpass the Swedes and Danes in public schools. German Catholics built their own secondary schools and supported Catholic Colleges like St. John's University, in direct competition with the Irish. Poles and Czechs withdrew from larger Catholic congregations and schools and formed their own."[29]

The Finns in Northern Minnesota established some of their own educational programs to promote and preserve their culture. For small children, the programs were often of religious orientation, where classes in Lutheran catechism and Sunday school included some basic Finnish grammar studies. The Finnish temperance societies and socialist halls both sponsored educational and recreational programs for all ages. Yet public schools were embraced by Finnish immigrants as the primary educational resource for their children, with their own ethnically oriented programs only providing a small supplement. No Finnish private schools are known to have been established. The two secondary institutions in Finnish America at the time, the Workers' College in Duluth and Suomi College in Hancock, Michigan, did not attract a large number of college-bound Minnesota Finnish youth. The newly formed community college system on the Iron Range and other universities in Minnesota were more common choices.[30] Three known examples of early Finnish-American bandsmen who sought further education include Hemming Hautala (VanderCook in Chicago), William Syrjälä (Valparaiso in Indiana), and Victor Taipale, the details of whose training in the United States is not known.

The Iron Range school band programs of the early 1900s had access to fine instruments and to the published band music that was being produced so prolifically at the time. Very little of these older music collections have been preserved today, but programs found in newspapers and yearbooks provide a sense of musical tastes. Taipale's school band programs, performed primarily by second-generation Finnish children, show a taste for the American popular band repertoire of the time, including many transcription from orchestral and opera sources, and there is no Finnish music. Perhaps he chose the music to present an American program and not represent any ethnic orientation of the performers.

Finnish-American Bands in a Gender Context

The discussion so far has dealt with "bandsmen and bandmasters," and little attention has been paid to any women who may have been involved. The early bands (those before 1900) were the first ensembles in many of the towns where they were formed. The popularity of band music among the general Iron Range public also enhanced the opportunities for Finnish bands to perform in the wider community, usually before other municipal musical groups had developed. Because the trained players tended to be men from the Finnish military, and because they were the predominant gender among the mining and lumbering Finns who first arrived, the bands were male organizations. Women who joined the Finnish mining and lumber settlements usually joined the mixed choruses, which were often more common than bands. The Finnish American choirs frequently had as short histories as many bands.[31]

The participation of women in the Finnish-American bands was fairly rare, although it was not nearly as rare as it was with the Iron Range municipal bands of that time. Women are almost never found in early band rosters or photographs of town bands in Virginia, Eveleth, Hibbing, Ely, or Chisholm. After the Iron Range school bands began training girls on instruments, the pool of new players for municipal bands included both young men and women. Among Finnish groups, women are found in the rosters of at least the Eveleth *Kaiku* Band, the Virginia Finnish Temperance Band, the Aurora Finnish Socialist Band, the Cromwell *Raju* Athletic Club Band, and the Brimson Community Band. The earliest of these, the Eveleth *Kaiku* Band in about 1910, included three women listed as "Mrs. Saari," a soprano saxophone player, "Mrs. Mäkivirta," an alto horn player, and an unnamed clarinet player.[32] Another photograph of the *Kaiku* band taken earlier shows the same unknown clarinet player and Mrs. Saari (figure 42). The inclusion of women in these early bands demonstrates that Finns have generally had a progressive attitude toward gender equality in society, as also demonstrated by their being the first European country with women's suffrage. However, other than in family bands, photographs of early bands in Finland almost never show women players, probably because the Finnish band movement at first had such a close tie to the military, fire brigades and factories, all predominantly male settings.

A progressive attitude toward women in society was carried to America with the Finnish immigrants. One unique musical example was with the Finns in Red Lodge, Montana, which supported an all-women's band conducted by the pioneer bandmaster Oscar Suojanen.[33] It is not known which organization sponsored the Red Lodge Finnish women's band since there were three separate bands in Red Lodge with Finnish connections at the time, but it is likely to have had some Temperance Society affiliation. All-girl bands began to be formed in the United States at that time, and so Suojanen may have modeled the Red Lodge Finnish Women's Band after other known examples. Nevertheless, this Red Lodge group is apparenly a single example among Finnish immigrants and an indicator of the same tolerant attitude that allowed for the membership of women in the Iron Range Finnish bands discussed above.

Figure 54. Red Lodge Montana Finnish Women's Band, Oscar Suojanen, conductor, taken before 1909. Photograph courtesy Carbon County Historical Society, Montana.

Minnesota Finnish-American Bands and Other Ethnic Communities

There is ample evidence that Finnish-American bands played for the ceremonial occasions of other ethnic groups in the Iron Range communities. Wasastjerna's mention of the Virginia Finnish band *Jyrinä* being "in great demand at funerals of the southern Europeans" is certainly not an isolated example. Funeral notices and obituaries in the papers unfortunately rarely comment on the music of the occasion. The known instances were all around 1900, and providing such services to Italian and Slovenian communities by Finnish bands probably discontinued after municipal bands developed and were able to do it. The Virginia Finnish band participated in such a funeral processions. Figure 55 shows a funeral procession led by a Finnish band and followed by a cadre of fraternal brothers in uniforms and plumed hats carrying banners with the coffin hearse at the rear. The deceased person is not identified in any documents accompanying the photograph, but it was someone of stature in the Ely Slovenian community. The brass band appears to have a couple each of cornets, trombones, and euphoniums, with a tuba and a drummer. This was probably a minimum number of players for such a funeral procession, and does not include all members of the band.

Figure 55. The Ely Finnish Temperance Band playing for a Slovenian funeral. Undated photograph. Courtesy IRHC Gilbert, from the Brownell Collection.

Another specific instance of such support by a Finnish band for another ethnic community is a commemorative program that took place in Ely. Figure 56 shows a page from a program written in Slovenian that honors the most important Roman Catholic churchman of the region for his thirty years of priesthood. Father Joseph Buh (1833-1922) arrived in Tower by 1888, but had been ministering to a Slovenian community in Stearns County since the early 1880s. The program notes that music was provided by "an orchestra" led by the Finn, Charles Kleemola. In all likelihood, the orchestra was the Finnish *Sampo* Band, Kleemola's group from Ely. The band played a march entitled, "Our Celebrant (Nas Slavljenec)." The ceremony also included a Slovenian men's choir.

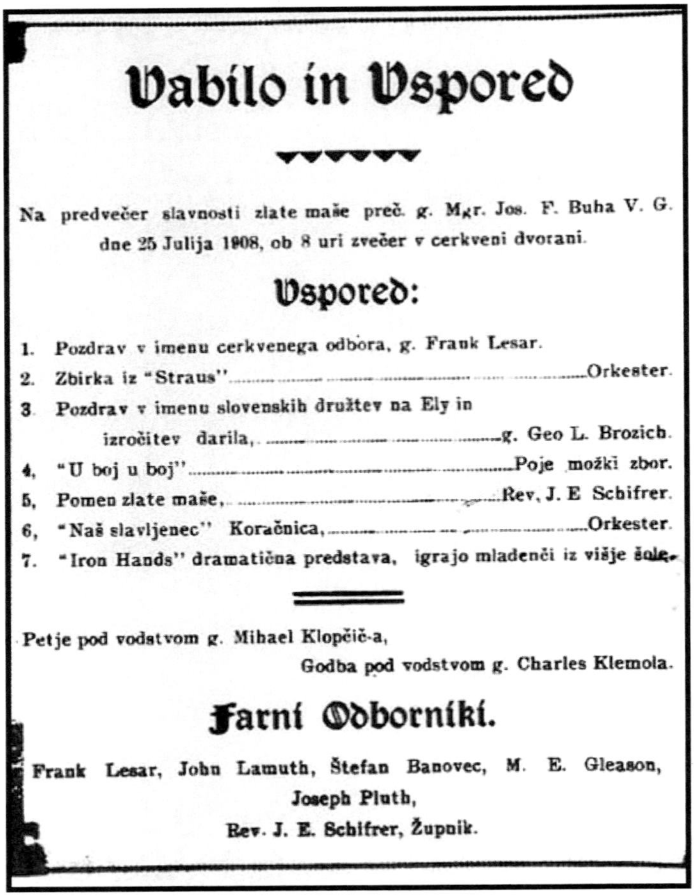

Vabilo in Vspored

Na predvečer slavnosti zlate maše preč. g. Mgr. Jos. F. Buha V. G. dne 25 Julija 1908, ob 8 uri zvečer v cerkveni dvorani.

Vspored:

1. Pozdrav v imenu cerkvenega odbora, g. Frank Lesar.
2. Zbirka iz "Straus" .... Orkester.
3. Pozdrav v imenu slovenskih družtev na Ely in izročitev darila, ... g. Geo L. Brozich.
4. "U boj u boj" .... Poje možki zbor.
5. Pomen zlate maše, ... Rev. J. E Schifrer.
6. "Naš slavljenec" Koračnica, ... Orkester.
7. "Iron Hands" dramatična predstava, igrajo mladenči iz višje šole.

Petje pod vodstvom g. Mihael Klopčič-a,

Godba pod vodstvom g. Charles Klemola.

Farni Odborniki.

Frank Lesar, John Lamuth, Štefan Banovec, M. E. Gleason, Joseph Pluth, Rev. J. E. Schifrer, Župnik.

Figure 56. A program honoring the 30th jubilee of Monsignor Josef Buh in the Iron Range Slovenian religious community, July 5, 1908.

These few instances are probably only samples of more interactions between ethnic communities. Unfortunately, no examples of band music have been found to provide information about just how international the folder of an Ely Finnish bandsman might have been.

The Finnish-American Brass Band and its Role in Communities

A central inquiry of this study has been the Finnish brass band's role in the communities they served. At first, many of the bandsmen who immigrated to America came from a community of musicians who had shared a common experience in Finland. Upon their arrival in America, they were embraced by the community of Finnish immigrants, a population that was already dividing itself into separate, polarized communities with differing positions on temperance and social order. Those communities, though in conflict, were of great importance to the bands, providing identity and purpose. In addition, Finnish immigrant communities were organized into geographical communities: on the village level, on the regional (Iron Range) level, and on the national level. Finnish bands played a part in Finnish-American communities at all of these levels. The Finnish bands or their individual members often became involved with a wider American community through local municipal bands. These associations with municipal bands lasted well beyond the demise of the Finnish bands themselves. The connection between the Finnish bands and the local schools' instrumental music programs varied from community to community but was usually significant. While only limited documentation exists, it shows that Finnish bandmasters often played the initial role in the development of school bands, which then fed the Finnish bands with young players. An attempt to understand the function of the Finnish bands within this broad "community of communities" results in seeing many contrasting forces at play, no doubt enhanced by the rapid evolution that all of these civic institutions experienced. Yet the bands kept playing. The Finnish musician's underlying desire was to make music. While there was some effort to maintain a Finnish identity within the bands, that ethnic fervor was always superceded by the desire to be musicians. That desire overshadowed any concerns about for whom and with whom to play.

The periods of American history that coincide with Finnish brass band activity have been called the Gilded Age (1870–1900) and the Progressive Era (1900–17). It was a time of some turmoil with industrial migration to cities, massive emigration from Europe, and a time when much of the country's social fabric was being stretched. Yet Robert Putnam views that era as a time of "extraordinary social inventiveness and political reform." In his book *Bowling Alone*, he measures the phenomenon of social capital as a vital positive element of American history, and suggests that it is a characteristic that has since been lost, as society has become more depersonalized.[34] Putnam defined "Social capital" as "the connections between individuals, their social networks and the norms of reciprocity and trustworthiness." Social capital was certainly in a healthy state among immigrant communities in America. Immigrants needed each other to survive in the new environment. In many cases, immigrant communities were more successful at resisting larger national trends toward the deterioration of social capital. By 1890, the "cacophony of strange tongues and strange customs of the newcomers" had triggered a national debate about Americanization and ethnic identity, similar in some respects to the debate about multiculturalism and 'English only' in recent decades.

The Finnish brass bands in northern Minnesota manifested how artistic activity was an integral part of social capital in a community. Most likely, bandmasters did not see themselves primarily as community builders, although all the bandsmen must have sensed the pleasure and pride they developed from their music-making. They might have looked back on their experiences in the multicultural Iron Range and agreed with Putnam's statements that "the arts are especially useful in transcending cultural barriers" and that "social capital is often a valuable by-product of cultural activities whose main purpose is purely artistic."[35] Thus, band music provided both for the bonding of a community within its heritage, and a bridging process that helped overcome the walls that may have developed between the ethnic group and the larger community.

---

[1]Peter Kivisto, *Pre-emigration Factors Contributing to the Development of Finnish-American Socialism* (New York Mills, MN: Finnish Americana Series, Parta Press, 1984) 5:23.

[2]Ibid., 5:25.

[3]Carl Ross, The Finn Factor in American Labor, Culture and Society (New York Mills, MN: Parta Press, 1977), 59.

[4]Akseli Järnefelt Rauanheimo, *Suomalaiset Amerikassa* (*The Finns in America*) (Helsinki: Otava, 1899), 273.

[5]Ross, *Finn Factor*, 19.

[6]Ibid., 71.

[7]Reino Hannula, *An Album of Finnish Halls* (San Luis Obispo, CA: Finn Heritage, 1991).

[8]Ibid., 88.

[9]From *Raittiuskansankalenteri.* Finnish Temperance Society Yearbook, Hancock MI, 1899

[10]From a conversation with Simo Westerholm, Finnish Folk Arts Centre, Kaustinen, Finland, 2000.

[11]Timothy Lawrence Smith, "Educational Beginnings, 1884-1910," (University of Minnesota: Immigration History Research Center, 1961), 4.

[12]Interview with Mary Ellen Kleemola Levander, Ely, Minnesota, January 5, 2002.

[13]Lyle Klein, "A History of Instrumental Music in Ely Minnesota" (thesis, Bemidji State University, 1977), 20.

[14]*Eveleth News,* September 2, 1903, 1.

[15]Smith, "Educational Beginnings," 161.

[16]"The Finns in America," *Ely Miner*, September 10, 1899, 1.

[17]US Commissioner of Immigration statistics report, Washington, 1900-1910.

[18]Leroy Hodges, "Report [on] the Vermilion and Mesabi iron ore ranges of Northern Minnesota concerning immigrant life and institutions" (typescript, United States Immigration Commission, 1909), 93.

[19]John Syrjämäki, "Mesabi Communities—A Study in Their Development" (PhD diss., Yale University, 1940), 384.

[20]Smith, "Educational Beginnings," 2.

[21]Syrjämäki, "Mesabi Communities," 386.

[22]Ibid., 391.

[23]Hodges, "Report," 93.

[24]Nashwauk-Keewatin High School Band concert program, 1923.

[25]Smith, "Educational Beginnings," 4.

[26]Col. Francis Wayland Parker (October 9, 1837 –March 2, 1902) was a pioneer of the progressive school movement in the United States.

[27]Ibid., 5.

[28]Duluth and St. Louis County: Their Story and People, American Historical Society, Chicago, 1921. In three volumes.

[29]Smith, "Educational Beginnings," 538.

[30]Paul Malm, "The role of the Range Junior Colleges in the Acculturation of the Immigrant 1916-1941" (PhD diss., University of Minnesota, 1991)

[31]Hans R. Wasastjerna, ed., "History of the Finns in Minnesota," trans. Toivo Rosvall. *Minnesotan suomalaisten historia* (Duluth MN: Finnish-American Historical Society, 1959), 297.

[32]"Range Pioneer recalls early Music Culture" *Mesaba Daily News,* Sunday, March 24, 1974, 12.

[33]Leona Lampi, *At the Foot of the Beartooth Mountains: A History of the Finnish Communities of Red Lodge Montana* (Coeur d'Alene, ID: Bookage Press, 1998), 67.

[34]Robert D. Putnam, *Bowling Alone: The Collapse and Revival of American Community* (New York: Simon and Schuster, 2000), 19.

[35]Ibid., 146.

Chapter Six
REPERTOIRE AND PERFORMANCES

The repertoire played by the first Finnish brass bands — social dance steps, opera overtures, military marches, even the Finnish patriotic songs — were all reflections of a strong European influence on the emerging Finnish music culture in the late 1800s. When many of the Finnish musicians came to America and quickly adopted the American style of band music, it was just a continuation of what had happened in Finland, becoming familiar with more foreign band music. That Finnish-American tastes in popular music later turned a cold shoulder on the old brass band in favor of the accordion band should be no surprise. An accordion was cheaper, more efficient, just as loud, and a lot less complicated for the many little Finnish dance halls across northern Minnesota. The chances of Toivola, Meadowlands, or Palo dance halls coming up with a couple of local accordionists was far better than of getting a dozen brass players together for every Saturday night dance. All was not lost for the bandsmen, however; if his Finnish band teetered or folded, the typical Finnish cornet player simply joined another group. It appears from all available sources that no Finnish brass players had any expressed regrets at the time, and just moved on.

Finnish repertoire had very little lasting impact on band music on the Iron Range. Taipale's music collection, now at the University of Helsinki (see Appendix A), was typical for an early Finnish brass band, and those schottisches, marches, waltzes, and polkas met the ethnic community's needs but were rarely heard by a wider audience. The Hibbing band library and the Hibbing Socialist band collection have only the few Finnish pieces published by the Sibelius Club. The influence of Sibelius Club publications on Minnesota Finnish bands is hard to measure, but apparently it was not very great outside ethnic festival settings. An Iron Range community band director of Finnish-American heritage, questioned about any evidence of "cultural residue" from the old Finnish bands in today's Iron Range bands, answered "None." Yet two generations ago "band music may have played a role in Americanization of the Finnish population, and the Finnish bands embraced American music, played for American celebrations."[i] Thus band music ingratiated the Finns to their American communities, as the Finnish bands, being the only band in town, were often called upon to contribute to ceremonies and concerts.

The contents of the old music folios known to be used by Finnish-American brass bands can be classified into five basic categories: dance music, ceremonial music, march music, concert pieces, and religious pieces. The religious works for band were the commonly sung Finnish hymns, for which players provided accompaniment at outdoor ceremonies. The Taipale collection in Appendix A includes several hymns arranged for brass bands. The temperance halls were usually large enough to accommodate a brass band for singing hymns. The Finnish churches were not known to use brass bands in religious services. It does not appear that brass bands played any other role in the church music of Finnish-Americans.

It is fortunate that, while available archive collections of Finnish-American band music are not numerous, they do represent these five musical genres and cover most activity periods, including the very earliest. That some dance tunes, marches, and other band material well known in Finland are absent from this material is also revealing about how and when these bands obtained their music in America. In Finland, the twentieth century brought new trends in popular and dance music, which influenced the brass bands there. However, the latest dance steps from Helsinki did not often get to America: no tangos, two steps, *humppas* (foxtrots), or other popular dances in early twentieth-century Finland have been found in any of the books, repertoire lists, or news articles of brass bands in Finnish America. Available recordings of other Finnish bands from the 78-rpm era, and recent recordings and live performances by groups such as the Red Lodge Band, make it possible to speculate about such performance elements as tempo, note length, rhythmic emphasis, and articulation heard one hundred years ago. The Red Lodge Montana Band, still in existence, is an important and unique resource for the study of Finnish-American band performance style.

The following is a review of some musical materials that Finnish bands are known to have played and a discussion about some of their normal playing situations. An examination of the repertoire and performance situations can further establish how these bands evolved and adapted musically in America, and may also provide some information about their ultimate demise.

The bands played for Finnish-American social dances during the few years before "dance orchestras" and accordions became more common. However, some bands continued to serve other functions such as ceremonies, parades, hymns for large outdoor worship settings and festival concerts into the mid-twentieth century. The music they played was a mixture of some older Finnish pieces as well as a full range of contemporary American concert-band publications. Even the very earliest bands used this combination of material, as confirmed through published repertoire lists of the Ely bands under Castrén and Kleemola in the 1890s. It is known that many of the early Finnish bands functioned in a variety of community settings, since they were often the first and only town bands for the general population. The demands of the community on the Finnish musicians prompted them to become quickly familiar with American band music.

Repertoire Sources for Finnish-American Bands

Material evidence of what the bands played in the earliest years in America is rather sparse, but what has been found is richly interesting. The

Finlandia University Finnish Heritage Center has perhaps the only American collection of musical material for bands written in manuscript before 1890.

Figure 56 shows the inside cover and a polka from an 1875 cornet book that was autographed by Emil Björnstadt and was apparently penned by a Swedish-speaking Finn. Nothing is thus far known of any names written in this set of three surviving books (the other names were C.M. Bergersen and P. Pederson). The age of this material easily rivals the oldest such brass books to be found in Finland, and coincides with the beginning of the brass septet movement outside of the military bands there. That these books are found in the United States and that they appear in the Finnish Heritage Center collection is a very unusual set of circumstances. As with many similar books found in Finland, they were probably used for a long period, with the first tunes written down in 1875, but then added to and used for many decades afterward. This set of books was possibly passed from father to son, and then it was the son who immigrated to America, when the books were already decades old. Observing the main years of emigration, it is almost impossible that these books were actually in the United States much before 1890, although they were probably still in use for many decades after that. This set of books is incomplete, so it is not definitely known whether the scoring was for septet or the common alternative, a Swedish sextet.

Figure 57.Emil Björnstadt cornet book, 1875. Finnish-American Heritage Center and Historical Archives, Finlandia University. Photograph by Paul Niemisto.

These books were found as a part of a larger collection of musical materials that was discovered at Finlandia University in the 1990s. The collection, which contains a large inventory of brass band material, had been stored unnoticed for many decades in a footlocker in the attic of an older college building. Other than some inconclusive clues from the various names and locations hand-written in the material, the footlocker's origin remains unknown. It is not known if the collection was from one source, or if various contributors had filled the footlocker. The oldest books contain the following musical selections, which is a typical nineteenth–century mixture of dance music, concert pieces, and military marches.

Contents of 1875 Brass Band Book, Finnish-American Archives, Finlandia University

1. April Polka af CM Borch
2. Valz, C.M. Borch
3. Marsch
4. Albertine Polka
5. Flora Vals, af Presto
6. Marsch, C.M. von Borch
7. Amusement Polka, Faust
8. Herslieben Polka Mazurka, Sekat
9. Geburs lago Gallop, C.M. von Borch
10. Mazurka
11. Frühligs Ewachen, af von E Bach
12. Reilander
13. Sancthans Valser, C.M. von Borch
14. Smålands Skarpskyttemarsch, Faust
15. Vaarblommer Mazurkka
16. Brudefarden Hardanger, Kjerluf
17. Den norske Garde in Bögeskoven, af Steen
18. Polonaise, af Helde
19. Française, af Larson
20. Polka, af B. Steenberg
21. Leonora Valz
22. Polka af Pariserlivet, af Offenbach
23. Marin Polka, Faust
24. Romance
25. Fredmans
26. Introduction And.-Epistel/ Anna Polka Mazurka
27. Gallopp af Oper. Orpheus, af Offenbach
28. Fahre Marsch
29. Valz
30. March

31. Faaren
32. Jegerne I Skogen
33. Andante con Moto, Schlummerker ur den Plumme, Auber
34. March
35. Polka, Schubert
36. Napoleons Död
37. Arie ur Opr Ernani, Verdu
38. March over Belmannske Sånge
39. Myrtenkronan Valz, af Berner
40. Gallopp
41. Kayser March, af Svaboda
42. Chouer af Oper. Trollflöten
43. Reilander
44. Gvinnans Lof
45. Andika Valz
46. Mazurka, af Schubert
47. Mazurka, af Lumbye
48. Polonaise
49. Sidonia Polka, Faust
50. Finska Fålksången
51. Hamburger Polka
52. Polka Mazurka
53. Polka, Fanders Overmand
54. Mit eget Kompani March, af Tru. Goffeng
55. Minde Ovad, af L. Lindner
56. Der Stander A Slot
57. Valders Mel
58. Kom Broder Mild Mel fr Valders
59. Den försk Guldterning, Norsk Fjeldmelodi
60. March der Flotte Geist, af Rosenkrands
61. Sturm Gallopp
62. Pelles, Frieri
63. Marsch (afver Fjelarna graa)
64. Halling
65. Polonais
66. Fiskaren
67. Marsch, af Lindberg
68. Barcarole Den Stumme i Portici
69. Gubben er gammel
70. Andante Religiöse
71. Elisa Gallopp, af Lindner
72. Naturen och Hjertat, af O. Lindeblad
73. Kinderlibe Française
74. Ekseser March

75. Locomotiv Gallopp C.M. von Borch
76. Normanna Marsch, af Lindborn
77. Serenade, af Vrangel
78. Sancthans Valz, C.M. von Borch
79. Sofi Ro, af Möring
80. Polka, arr af C.M. von Borch

The primary language in these music folios is Swedish, although the material is from many countries, including Norway. The waltz, galop, Française, polka, "Reilander" (i.e., Reinlander or schottische), and mazurka suggest the books were used for traditional, social dances, possibly in the potpourri (*purpurri* in dialect Finnish) setting.

Two other sets of books, from 1900 and 1910, are also in the Finlandia University collection. They are less extensive than this example, but are quite similar in content. They are "Band 1" New York 1910, Fritz Olofson, and "Arvid Windahl Album," Abo Finland, May 1, 1905.

Fashions in nineteenth-century social dance music were international, affirmed by comparing the list above with the one below collected from Ely, Minnesota. The Ely newspapers' social reports ran accounts of "calico hops," leap-year dances, holiday dances, masquerade dances, although none of the dances seemed to enjoy the success of the Fireman's Ball. The music for this event was played by a brass band. The dance program for the Ely Fireman's Ball in July 1892 is probably typical of dances held at that time. The order of dances reads as follows:[ii]

Grand March
Quadrille, Ladies Choice
Polka
Waltz
Schottische
Virginia Reel
Lanciers
Portland Fancy
Waltz
Polka
Schottische
Hungry Waltz Supper
Cicillian *(sic)* Circle
Quadrille
Waltz, (Ladies Choice)
Polka
Lady of the Lake
Tempest
Waltz Quadrille
Fireman's Dance

Boston Fancy
Polka
Dan Tucker

If a Finnish immigrant couple attended this Fireman's Ball, which was entirely possible, they would have had no trouble following the majority of the dance steps, the same as they would have known at a Finnish hall. The Finnish immigrant bands obtained some of their musical materials from their leaders, who brought some original arrangements with them from Finland. Some examples of this material were originally scored for brass, such as the example illustrated in Figure 56. Other sets of parts found were for a salon dance orchestra, an instrumental ensemble paralleling the rise of the accordion band as a dance-hall ensemble of choice. Appendix A contains a catalogue of Victor Taipale's music collection at the University of Helsinki. Several of the part books have notations indicating they were first used in the military bands of Finland. Other sets from the Taipale collection, assembled from various sources in Finland, were probably used or copied by the many brass bands in Minnesota that he formed and led after arriving in 1901.

This Taipale collection is a rare example of a performance library for Finnish-American bands from the early twentieth century. No other similar collection has been found. It includes three titles that were published in the United States by Carl Fischer and J.W Pepper; all others are manuscript materials or Finnish publications. Not found in this collection is any material published by the Sibelius Club. This may be because Taipale was using this collection's contents before the Sibelius Club began to publish or, that this discovered collection is only part of the material Taipale used. Most likely, the oldest materials in this collection were souvenirs of his early years, and he may have set them aside as his musical repertoire became more Americanized. Parts from this collection were not used later in his career. This would explain how they could have been preserved, unlike almost all other Finnish band sheet music in America, which is apparently lost. Why so active a bandmaster as Taipale was not somehow more directly involved in such national organizations as the Sibelius Club remains an unsolved mystery.

Eleven titles in the Taipale collection (numbers 72 through 82) appear to be band arrangements by Taipale himself, with a Finnish military band instrumentation similar to the British *Army Journal* published by Chappell: flute (piccolo), three clarinets, alto and tenor saxophones, three trumpets, 3 trombones, euphonium, tuba and percussion. This fifteen-part *soittokunta* score had occasional auxiliary parts for oboe, bassoon, or baritone saxophone. Most of the Taipale septet and band arrangements appear to have been played or arranged around 1910 in Hibbing, judging by notations on the music. This coincides with his earliest musical leadership activity in Minnesota. Five selections are hymn arrangements for accompanying congregational singing, one is a Christmas carol, and four are concert pieces or marches. Reflecting the breadth of social and political life in Finnish America, this collection includes both "A Mighty Fortress is Our God" and socialist workers' marches. The collection includes some incomplete pencil sketches of Taipale's arrangement efforts as well as his name listed as arranger on several parts. No published band arrangements or compositions of Taipale's appear to exist or are mentioned in any other source material.

Taipale also had salon orchestra material in this collection, which may have been intended for his family or other ensembles. Included are forty-five dance selections written out by hand, certainly enough for a complete social dance evening. They all appear to have been written down in the 1920s, which would be consistent with the family band's active period in Nashwauk. Some also appear to have been annotated in Monessen, Pennsylvania, around 1925, a time when Taipale may have left Minnesota to conduct the Louhi Band. Noteworthy is that all the dance tunes are traditional schottisches, polkas, and waltzes in an era when some of the newer tangos, foxtrots, and ragtime were possible but not included. The Taipale salon orchestra tunes, being played almost fifty years later than the brass band dance music contained in the figure 56 folio, suggest a continuation of the polka, waltz, and schottische as the preferences among immigrant Finns. For a complete list of titles, see Appendix A. This list is one of the few sources for information about what was popular in dance music among Finnish immigrants in the 1910s and 1920s. Mazurkas were still being danced, though they have since become extinct in the Finnish-American dance repertoire. Having a mazurka and a "two-step" in the same dance list represents a very wide range of tastes and the mixing of two distinct eras.

Of the pieces in the Taipale collection for the traditional seven-part brass band, only two appear to be dance tunes (*Tuulan tei* and *Kvåsar vals*). It may be that a more complete set of books of dance music for brass band was kept separately, or that Taipale did not own or control other material used. To assume from a study of this collection that brass bands under Taipale's direction did not play dance music could be an error, since there were almost no other musical groups that could play for large group Finnish dances on the Iron Range in the first decade of the twentieth century. Another possible false conclusion would be to assume that Taipale felt that a salon orchestra, rather than a brass band, should play dance music. More likely by the time he scored the dance music for salon orchestra (1920s), brass bands had generally been replaced for playing dance music. This dance or "salon" orchestra repertoire includes 41 titles: 10 waltzes, 11 polkas, 9 schottisches, 4 foxtrots, 4 mazurkas, 2 "one-steps," and one march. His brass septet material is almost all marches, patriotic music, and religious music, except for one waltz and one schottische. He separated the repertoire groupings according to function.

Remembering that many of the first Finnish brass bands in America were sponsored by temperance societies that often had close affiliation with local Finnish Lutheran churches, it might be expected that there would be few instances of temperance bands playing for social dancing. The Finnish Saturday night dance was often a rather raucous affair in which drink might readily available.[iii] However such dances frequently took place in Finnish temperance halls, and any "intemperance" would only be found outside, behind the building, or elsewhere.

Taipale's material shows that the brass band literature brought over from Finland included ceremonial music and more popular and dance music selections. Going back as far as the early 1800s, the Heinola *harmoniemusik* band books were similarly organized, so that all ceremonial music occupied the front half of each folio, the back half being lighter pieces and social dances.

Figure 58. E^b cornet part, Finnish Melodies, arr. E. Pahlman. H. N. White, 1904.

Published Finnish-American Band Material

The E-flat cornet part in Figure 57 is from a selection of popular Finnish folk songs, patriotic songs, and dance tunes arranged by Emil Pahlman. This type of medley often appears in Finnish band books both in Finland and the United States. While it seems that the American publisher, H. N. White, released this edition for general band use, it is also notable that Cleveland is very close to the northern Ohio and western Pennsylvania Finnish communities, where many bands would have been very interested in such an arrangement.

In addition to occasional publications from American houses, such as the example above, other Finnish band music published in the United States includes those by the Sibelius Club of Monessen, Pennsylvania, including works by well-known American arrangers Theodore Moses- Tobani and Karl L. King. The Club's 1917 advertisement begins with the statement "The Sibelius Club offers bands the following selections, with complete 'military band' instrumentation." Included is a march by the Finnish-American composer J. R. Kultti, an active member in the Club. There are two works by A. A. Lumme, the *Pollari* march and an *Impromptu a la Zingara*. Lumme, a Finnish name for bandmaster Aapo Liljeström, was an important Finnish military bandmaster in the pre-independence era; he was probably commissioned by the Sibelius Club to create these works for their catalogue. It is not known whether he ever came to the United States, although Wasastjerna has implied so.[iv] The *Sven Dufva* Overture, another work in the catalog, is a well-known band potpourri by H. Hedman still occasionally played in Finland. Moses-Tobani added extra woodwind parts to Hedman's original Finnish edition for the Sibelius Club edition. Other selections in that 1917 Sibelius Club catalog include the *Kesäilta* Waltz by O. Merikanto and *Savo-Karjalaisia Lauluja* by Leander. The lower half of the advertisement offers editions and arrangements for piano and other combinations of various works by Jean Sibelius, but none arranged for band.

Taipale's years as a band director in the Nashwauk–Keewatin, Minnesota, schools is quite well-documented in both the school records and the local newspapers. It is clear from the programs found that his choice of school band repertoire was entirely in keeping with standard American tastes of the time, such as seen in Table K—Hibbing Finnish Socialist Band Music Collection. The Finnish bandmasters who had experience directing public school band programs (Taipale, Hautala, Kleemola, and Ahola) all appeared to leave their ethnic roots behind them and embrace the readily available band repertoire of the time. This tendency may have been because of most school populations' ethnic diversity, most immigrant children's desire to embrace a new American way of life, and because the band repertoire of Finnish origin arranged for school band use was very limited. There are a few examples of Taipale programming Finnish music for the schools, such as Leander's *Helena Polonaise* and *Suomen laulu* for the May 23, 1917 concert, but they are unusual. A visit to the Nashwauk High School Band library in 2002 revealed that none of the musical material from the early days of the band seems to have been preserved.

A small valise found at the Immigration History Research Center turned out to contain a rare folder of music stamped "Finnish Branch #2, Hibbing Minnesota—Socialist Party." Mostly octavo-sized American band publications intended for concert (not marching) purposes, it was quite possibly overlooked and abandoned after a performance, or perhaps contained extra parts that were taken along on a concert trip. It contains only these thirteen selections and so must be only a small portion of the band's original working library: Keler-Bela, *Lustspiel* (H. Koch, J. W. Pepper, 30 parts); C.L. Barnhouse, *Evening Idylls* (C.L. Barnhouse, 19 parts); C.L. Barnhouse, *Fascination* (C.L. Barnhouse, 1890, 23 parts, solo baritone); E.W. Berry, *Operatic Mingle* (Southwell, Kansas City, 1909, 47 parts); Keler-Bela, *Son of the Puszta* (Carl Fischer, 1906, 35 parts); K. L King, *Moonlight on the Nile* waltz (C.L. Barnhouse, 27 parts); Merikanto, *Kesäilta Valssi* (K. L. King, Sibelius Club, 25 parts); W. S. Ripley, *Serenade to the One I Love* (F.

Seitz, 1911, 16 parts); George Southwell,. "No 999" Solo for Brasses (Southwell, 1887, 27 parts); O. E Swanson, *Suomi-Grand Selection of Finnish Songs and Dances* (Carl Fischer, 1913, 29 parts); E. W. Berry, *Operatic Piecework* (Southwell, 1913, 47 parts); T. B. Boyer, Overture *Tournament* (publisher, date unknown, 28 parts); Carroll & DeSilva, *Little Drop of Irish and Wee bit of Scotch* and *Oh Agnes* (one-step) (Remick, 1919, 32 parts).

The contents are quite similar to the more extensive Berkeley Finnish Socialist Band music collection housed at the Immigration History Research Center, catalogue number IHRC 167. It is contained in 21 archive boxes with somewhat over 500 titles, many with a complete set of band parts. There are only two pieces of Finnish origin in this instance, one from the 1920-era publications of the Sibelius Club of Pennsylvania, the other published by Carl Fischer.

Ameriikan poijat presented a lecture/concert in August 2002 at the University of Minnesota as a part of a Finnish-American summer festival and conference. At that event we presented live performances of a series of works created or published by Finnish-American band composers in the early twentieth century. These performances were of creditable band repertoire that has been left dormant and unheard for many decades. No recordings of these pieces have been found. The sets of sheet music were found primarily in the IHRC collection, except one that was from a set of military band books at the University of Helsinki Library. The performed pieces included:

Figure 59. Solo cornet part, Comrade's Club by Oscar Suojanen, 1914. Courtesy IHRC.

Hoolihiiveri Hopsikko, a march by Charles Kleemola, self-published in Ely, Minnesota (see figure 39).

Comrade's Club March by Oscar Suojanen, self-published in Berkeley California (Figure 58). Suojanen was mostly associated with the West Berkeley Socialist Band, but also was a musical leader in the Red Lodge Montana Finnish community for a time. There he led, among other things, an all-girls' Finnish youth brass band.

Savo March, by Lauri Koski, published by the Sibelius Club (Figure 59). Louis (Lauri) Koski was active during the formation of the Sibelius Club and led the Louhi Band of Monessen for a period of time. Not much more is known of his biography. This march is said to have been included in the John Philip Sousa concert repertoire.

Hoh! Hoh! Two-step, by Martti Nisonen, reconstructed from an incomplete set of parts.

Live performances of these compositions involved some adaptation, since they were originally for full concert-band scorings with woodwind parts that needed to be reassigned. Yet they commonly had an E^b soprano cornet part, suggesting that the composers expected that the works might be occasionally performed by the traditional Finnish brass band. Of the pieces we selected to perform, it was clear that the composers had no intention of composing along Finnish stylistic models, but reflected more universal tastes in march-composition. Suojanen's *Comrade's March* sounded Russian, and both Kleemola's and Koski's marches sounded American in style.

Figure 60. Solo cornet part, Savo March, by Louis (Lauri) Koski, 1918. Courtesy IHRC.

Instruments

Information about what brass instruments were played in Finnish bands and where they were obtained is available through a few preserved examples, some historical references and photographs. All evidence suggests that the instruments played by the Finns in Northern Minnesota were acquired in the United States from well-known domestic makers such as Conn, Holton, Lyon & Healy, and Pan-American. While a cornet or alto horn could be expected in a steamer trunk belonging to an arriving immigrant musician from Finland, no such instruments have thus far been located. Most brass band instruments in Finland were owned by sponsoring organizations, and apparently only loaned to those players who were active band members. This institutional ownership of instruments was also the normal pattern with Finnish bands in America.[v] This was further confirmed in several instances where, as a band disbanded, all its instruments were sold to another musical group as a complete set, with none kept in the hands of individual players. Because of this, it is now difficult to know which of the many older American-made instruments that might turn up in antique shops or garage sales on the Iron Range might actually have been played in the Finnish bands.

Early Finnish brass bands normally used the following instrumentations:[vi]

Swedish "Navy" Sextet (*Messingsextette*): Eb cornet, Bb cornet, Eb alto, Bb tenor valved trombone (2), bass tuba

Septet (*Seitsikko*): Eb cornet, Bb cornet (2), Eb alto, Bb tenor, Bb euphonium, Eb or BBb tuba

Dectet (*Kymmenikkö*): Eb-Cornet Bb-1 Cornet Bb-2 Cornet Eb—1 Alto Eb-2 Alto (ad lib) Bb-1 Tenor Bb -2 Tenor (ad lib) Bb-Euphonium Eb-Tuba BBb tuba (ad lib)

Nineteenth-century Finnish brass band (*Torvisoittokunta* or *Normaalivanha*): Eb cornet, Bb cornet (2), Bb trumpet (2), Eb alto (2), F trumpet (low; 2), F horn (2), Bb tenor (2), Bb euphonium, Eb tuba, BBb tuba, percussion

The earliest Finnish-American bands were usually of the *seitsikko* or septet instrumentation. Bands with more than seven players would have extra players doubling one or more of the seven parts. If a clarinet were added, it would play the E-flat soprano cornet line. The later bands included some woodwinds and adopted a more standard mixed instrumentation in order to play the available American arrangements. Those bands also played primarily American repertoire. The *Helsingin torvisoittokunta* of the early 1900s was similar to the nineteenth-century Finnish Brass Band mentioned above, but had eliminated the low F trumpets and F horns.

In the traditional Finnish brass septet the physical setup of the group says something about the musical function of the instruments. Imitating the image of the musical fermata, the euphonium player was situated as the dot in the middle and often served as the rhythmic leader, if not the director. The first B-flat soprano cornet was seated on one edge of the arc, and the E-flat soprano cornet on the other (see Figure 2). The first B-flat cornet had the primary melodic line, although it might be supported by the E-flat cornet in unison or octave, as well as the euphonium supporting an octave below. In many arrangements, however, the euphonium played an obbligato or descant part. The remaining parts, second B-flat cornet, alto, tenor, and tuba, functioned as background harmony and rhythm. It seems that the level of technical difficulty of the seven parts assumed that the more accomplished players would be assigned to the E-flat cornet, first B-flat cornet and euphonium parts. The less technically proficient musicians often played the alto, tenor, or second B-flat cornet parts. In modern-day septet arrangements, the functions assigned to the parts are usually more egalitarian, with an alto or tenor horn player more often delighted to see technically demanding passages and solo lines.

Music for Dancing

In late nineteenth-century Finland, except for the more intimate fiddle, the brass band was the only instrumental music available in many regions and so was expected to fill whatever public musical needs the community presented, including dance music. By about 1910, the accordion became widely available in Finland as well as among the American immigrants, and it proved to be a very audible, cheap, and simple alternative to the more cumbersome brass bands of large dance halls.[vii]

The early wind band in Finland was serving multiple functions in the community already in the early 1800s, decades prior to the invention of valved brass instruments. This is evidenced by the repertoire found in the Heinola Battalion Books, discussed in Chapter 1, that were organized into two sections, one of dance music and one of ceremonial and concert music. Later, the role of the Finnish brass band to provide social dance music in the late nineteenth century is well established through many repertoire lists and other historical records. This continued into the 1930s in some settings, even after jazz bands and dance orchestras were established in the larger cities. This continuation was partly due to the important military and patriotic services the brass bands offered during the fight for Finnish independence and later, during conflicts with the Soviet Union, when dance music was vital to what the military brass bands provided for the field and in the bunker.

In Finland, the early twentieth-century role of brass bands in popular culture can be seen as a factor in the nation's industrialization, urbanization, its adoption of foreign cultural influences, and its rise to nationhood during the years leading to independence. Helsinki was the center of activity, where the salon music of Central Europe was heard in restaurants and theaters, and music for public entertainment and dance was provided by military and amateur brass bands. Folk fiddlers and accordion players were featured at dances and social events in the outskirts of the city. However, by 1926, the taste in social dance and popular music had mostly left the brass band behind in favor of the new jazz band medium in urban centers. As evidenced by brass-band books used at the time, septets in Finland struggled to stay abreast of modern musical fads into the 1930s.[viii]

Finnish Social Dance Traditions

In 1995, when visiting the Swedo-Finnish village of Kronoby (*Kruunupyy* in Finnish) the members of the *Ameriikan poijat* septet were invited to participate with the local brass band in a rather formalized "entertainment" that began with a short concert, followed by an elaborate dance event (*potpourri/purpurri*). This is a very old social dance tradition in western Finland, and was the basis upon which Finnish immigrant dances were built. *Potpourri* arrived in Finland very likely from Russia in the early 1800s, where French salon dancing was very popular. This *potpourri* was a continuous series of dance segments that moved in segue from one to the next, following a preplanned order. It included all the traditional steps such as polonaise, mazurka, waltz, quadrille, schottische, and polka.

With a very large gathering of dancers (such as at a wedding), a *potpourri* could take many hours to dance. In the *potpourri* that we played, it appeared that every dancer was a partner for every other possible dancer of the opposite gender for sixteen to thirty-two bars of every dance step segment. Thus, a polka would last for however many repetitions it took until everyone had completed the possible cycle of partners, at which point the band would immediately begin the next dance step, and the routine would be repeated. I do not recall any intermissions, but I remember we brass players taking turns to give embouchures a rest. Our order of dances that year was:

1. Entry Promenade March
2. Polonaise
3. Hopptakt (Galop)
4. Waltz
5. Hopptakt II (Galop)
6. Figuré
7. Långdans (March)

Hans Erik Andtbacks, the leader of the Kronoby Hornkapell brass band says this dance order has become a strict *purpurri* tradition in the region: "As late as the 1950s, *purpurri* was played at every wedding in Kronoby, and the Hornkapell always played."

The *potpourri* dance format was apparently very popular among Ostrobothnian Finns who left for America, although this ritual didn't seem to survive the trip west in its original form. Simpler partner-dances like the polka, waltz, and schottische survived the voyage, while some of the more intricate formal dances, such as polonaise, mazurka, quadrille, and polka, didn't, at least not among Finnish-speaking immigrants. I don't recall the more rigorous Ostrobothnian *potpourri* format being mentioned among the writings or memories of any North American Finns, but other things may have influenced how the order of dance steps was selected by Finnish-American dance bands, possibly even politics. Among most Finnish-Americans today *potpourri* means a selection of dances with brief pauses, but with much shorter renditions than the original that we experienced in Kronoby.

In the very earliest immigrant days, there were no social halls yet built for dancing, especially in the smaller villages. In summer, dancing would take place on wooden bridge decks, and in the winter, in the living rooms of the community's larger farmhouses.

> If there were dances anywhere in the area, young people always managed to get there, often by walking long distances. John Mäki and Bill Hendricksen once took a horse team and logging sled and left Toivola at 3:00 p.m. for a dance in Cedar Valley. On board were (*nine names listed*) . . . (T)his group arrived in Cedar Valley by 7:00 p.m. Bill stabled the horses in Hill's barn and the young people danced into the night, returning home in time for the morning farm chores.[ix]

In a countryside setting, social opportunities seemed to be no less than they were in larger towns. However, the Finnish farm youth had to work a little harder to make it to the event. In the urban settings, Finn hall dances had a rather sophisticated result. "Finn hall dances started at 9:00 on Saturdays," In conversations and correspondence with Helvi Impola in May 2003, she recounted her experiences in New England. Admission to the dance was fifty cents. "Viola and Bill (accordion and drums) sat on the stage toward the left side of the hall." Impola was an avid social dancer and recalled many of the dance hall traditions because "my friends and I usually sat right in front of them (the band) so that, over the years, we became quite friendly with them. It may have been that the dance started with a waltz. Each dance set consisted of three dances in the same tempo. Between dance sets there was a short break– no more than 5 minutes, and the sequence went from vigorous to calmer to vigorous again. The only time I remember a set having a different dance was in the foxtrot set, which often included a Lindy. Maybe the rhumba and tango were in the foxtrot set too, but they certainly were danced."

Some of the Finnish dance bands that played in the urban Finnish halls introduced the popular American dance steps as well as the latest dances from Finalnd. Impola remembered "Bill and Viola also introduced dances they had seen in other places and taught them to us—pas d'Espagne, Boomps-a-Daisy, and Spin-Spin. Sometime in the late 1940s Bill first announced the 'humppa.'"

An intermission in the Finnish dance occurred about two hours into the evening, often preceded by dancing the three distinctly Finnish-American steps—the *Raatikko,* the *Kerenski,* and the *Kymmenen kynttä*—after which everyone would go down to the lower floor or outdoors for coffee and refreshments. Dancing usually ended by 1:00. These three dance steps, *Raatikko, Kerenski, Kymmenen kynttä,* are still known among older Finnish-Americans, but are unknown in Finland.

Musical tastes for dancing among most Finnish immigrant communities in the United States appeared not to have tried to keep current with the most popular trends in Helsinki. Even in today's Finnish-American social dances, expected tunes are mostly waltzes, schottisches, and polkas. Tangos and foxtrots (*humppa*), although introduced to Finnish society in the 1920s, are still not considered a part of immigrant culture. The young dancing American Finns did not associate ragtime-tango-foxtrot culture with the Finland they knew but perhaps searched for those dancing experiences in other dance halls outside their immigrant community.

Iltamat, the Finnish-American Entertainment

The Finnish-American evening entertainment, called *iltamat,* was the common format known during the early decades of the 1900s. It had its roots in the Finnish communities from where the immigrants came. However, the *iltamat* appears to have taken on a broader palate of content in its American immigrant version. A typical *iltamat* would be divided into three segments: a mixture of music and other performance elements followed by an intermission with refreshments, and finally a dance. The first part could often include poetry, instrumental and vocal music, an inspirational or political speech, a dramatic scene, humor, or synchronized gymnastics. Within that first segment, a brass band might play concert pieces or patriotic songs. During the intermission, which often lasted an hour, the chairs would be removed from the hall floor while attendees retired to the basement for coffee, cardamom rolls and other treats. With the hall floor cleared, attendees would then resume dancing to a brass band, accordions, or fiddles. A 1922 poster for an *iltamat* sponsored by the Virginia Finnish Socialist Gymnastics and Athletic Club ("*Tarmo*"), the primary presenters, included band music, string music, poetry, community singing, and featured synchronized gymnastics demonstrations.

This "*iltamat*"(evening entertainment) format has been the model used by many current Finnish-American groups, including the *Ameriikan Poijat* brass septet. Whenever our group performed for Finnish-American audiences, we have sensed that the audience is accustomed to an evening's entertainment unfolding in a particular order. We always await the arrival of the inevitable avid dancer, who appears after the chairs have been removed at intermission, and throws dancing powder on the floor with an eager grin of anticipation.

Performance Settings

The most common Minnesota Finnish band performance settings were the "Finn Halls" described in chapter 6 and park pavilions, many of which still exist today. In addition, summer festival band performances took place as street parades or at lakeshore picnic sites. The seating formations shown in available photographs do not suggest any great departure from that of any usual American town band. While most of the photographs were posed and may perhaps be a bit artificial with their formations, the few candid shots that have been found do not suggest any special Finnish immigrant notions about how a band should be seated.

Midsummer Festivals

The important KVS midsummer festival in Tampere, Finland, in 1888 was described in chapter 1. It can be suggested that immigrant summer festivals, be they local, regional or national, were major catalysts in maintaining and promoting Finnish cultural activity in America. Even in modern times, the annual "Finnfest USA" has become a contemporary version of the old festivals. In both the older and newer versions, the festivals have functioned as a showcase for arts and crafts, a literary conference, a sporting event, a commercial marketplace for Finnish goods and handcrafts, a concert series, a place to meet new and old friends, and a place to dance.

Figure 61 is from a published program for the 1909 Midsummer festival held in Eveleth for the second time in one decade. During these years the Northern Minnesota Finnish midsummer festivals would be hosted in rotation among the larger communities of Hibbing, Virginia, Ely, Chisholm, Duluth, Cloquet, and Eveleth. The program includes advertisements on the left and top for the often-mentioned bandmaster Victor Taipale, "Poppimies," or pop-man, advertising his bottling works business. The other advertisements are for a men's clothing store and an apartment residence. On the right is part of the festival program, starting with an announcement of the band competition *(Soittokilpailut)*, the gymnastics competition (*Voimistelukilpailut*), and the individual competitions (*Yksityskilpailut*). This is followed by a concert program that includes performances of bands, choirs, soloists, poetry, and some speeches. This particular program page is typical of such festival offerings. It also presents an example of a Finnish *iltamat*, or evening entertainment, with all the variety usually offered.

VICTOR TAIPALE, 

POPPIMIES.

Valmistaa ja myy kaikkia pehmeitä juomia.
Aineet ovat puhtaimmat. :..:..:..:..:..:

Erityinen huoli annetaan juhla- ja ulosmeneville tavaroille. :..:..:..:..:....:..:

EVELETH, PUHELIN 214. MINN.

Miksi maksatte

Enemmän puvusta kuin $15.00 tai $20.00? Miesten räätälin tekemiä vaatteita. Meillä on suuri varasto kankaita, parhaat työntekijät ja annamme puhtaan villavaatteen. Työ on parasta. Meidän hintamme on

$15.00 JA $20.00,

ei enempi eikä vähempi.

HARRY MITCHELL, 18 E. Superior st. DULUTH, MINN.

Miesten ja Lasten **VAATEKAUPPA,**

varustettu täydellisellä vaate- ja kenkävarastolla.

Suomea puhutaan.

MAX SHOPERIO,

EVELETH, MINN.

...Suomalainen Majatalo...

Varustettu nykyaikaisten vaatimusten mukaan. Suositetaan matkustajille.

Wm. Talkkari, Eveleth, Minn.

SOITTOKILPAILUT

—o—

VOIMISTELUKILPAILUT

—o—

YKSITYISKILPAILUT

—o—

IV. KONSERTTI-OHJELMA WALON LÄHDE RAITTIUSSEURAN TALOLLA KELLO 8 TÄSMÄLLEEN

—o—

1. SOITTOA . . Red Lodgen soittokunta

—o—

2. LAULUA . . . . Evelethin sekakööri

—o—

3. PUHE . . . . F. Mattson

—o—

4. SOOLOKILPAILU . . . . . Korneteilla

—o—

5. LAULUA . . . . Elyn sekakööri

—o—

6. PUHE . . . . Ivar Ahonen

—o—

7. SOITTOA . . . Evelethin soittokunta

—o—

8. RUNO . . . . . . Neiti Hanna Mattson

—o—

9. OKKESTERI . Evelethin suom. orkesteri

—o—

10. PUHE . . . . J. H. Jasberg

—o—

11. PIANO DUETTO . . . . Pastori ja pastorska Wargelin

—o—

12. ISOILLA TORVILLA KILPAILLAAN . . . . Soolo kilpailu

Figure 61. A page from the 1909 Northern Minnesota Finnish Midsummer Festival, held in Eveleth. Courtesy the Iron Range Research Center.

Parks

Mesaba Park, near Chisholm, was one of several sites in Finnish America that were developed as festival and meeting grounds primarily for socialist and co-operative organizations. The Mesaba Park Co-operative Association continues to exist today, and the park site is still in occasional use, though the Finnish leftist organizations that founded it are no longer active. The recollections of Ernest Koski describe the day when the park was first opened in 1929, and the band from Sturgeon Township came playing and parading through nearby towns on the back of a truck on its way to participate in the first gathering in the new park. This period was at the height of leftist political activity among Iron Range Finns, when almost every Finnish community had a Socialist hall, and some had two. The halls however, only served local community functions, and Alanen suggested "they could not accommodate large regional events, such as the traditional Midsummer (*Juhannus*) festivals." The 150-acre site with a lake was equipped with a large pavilion, cabins, camping sites, saunas, and open spaces for meetings and rallies. While Ernest Koski's writings are the only detailed documentation found, it is likely that many regional Finnish bands participated in the many Mesaba Park gatherings during the decades after 1930.[x]

Thoughts on Musical Performance Style

When *Ameriikan poijat* first visited Finland in 1992, one of our first stops was in the southern town of Salo, where the Fire Brigade Band hosted us. The Salo band had roots deep in the Finnish brass septet tradition, being founded around 1906 and operating continuously since. Part of the visit was an evening during which the two bands played for each other and together. The impression that our playing created among Salo band members was that of a group of trained orchestral brass players reading folk dance music as though it were concert literature. We apparently executed well-rounded note lengths and rich sonorities well within the frame of classical good taste. After our performance, they presented us with gutsy interpretations, offering an almost raucous energy with an edgy brassiness and an abrupt staccattissimo that we initially disliked as being far outside our sense of proper brass style. During that evening *Ameriikan Poijat* had the rare chance, not since repeated, to learn about the old brass traditions of Finland through listening, imitating, and conversing. Our group often refers to that Salo visit when we make interpretative decisions regarding traditional Finnish music. Since that visit in 1992, the situation has changed for many Finnish brass music participants. The Salo Band players are still playing today with old gusto, but they are a part of an increasingly smaller group who try to maintain old musical traditions. Young Finnish brass players are now growing up in a musical environment where current teachers introduce a considerable amount of American and other international influences, demonstrating a playing style that is appealing to the modern ear. *Ameriikan Poijat*, at the same time, has been working to adopt some elements of the old gutsy style whenever we play the old dance hall music and marches, in an effort to understand and recreate older tastes.

The military brass bands of the late 1800s are one influence on the development of the older Finnish brass performance style, as described above. The descriptive terms above—gutsy, abrupt, brassy, raucous—have sometimes been used by Americans to describe the older German tradition in brass band playing. In Finland, from the influence of German-born brass players and musical leaders who functioned in the Imperial Russian Army Bands as well as from many German musicians who held positions of leadership in Finnish society, the Germanic style was prevalent for several generations. Because of the availability of recordings, guest teachers, and study abroad, younger Finnish brass players today who might wish to recreate old playing styles will have to work hard at it, since it is no longer as commonly heard.

There is a robust style of playing that we heard in Salo and in other septets in Finland that may have its roots in the military tradition from which so many of the players, even in more modern groups, received their main musical training. These players used a heavier articulation, a harsher tone color, and a notably short and accented staccato. Yet the sounds heard on the earliest Helsinki Brass Band recordings, which reveal a more refined playing style with a sweeter tone color and an emphasis on virtuosity rather than sound projection, contradict the notion that this robustness has been a long-term characteristic.

There have been several modern bands in Finland who performed and recorded in a traditional style. In 1980, the Hyvinkää Railway Band (*Hyvinkään Rautatiesoittajat*), produced a typical 33.3-rpm long-playing record entitled *Asemamiehen jenkka* (*Stationmaster's schottische*).[xi] The *Hyvinkään Rautatiesoittajat* (HRS) has been known for many years as one of the better amateur Finnish bands that specialize in performances of dance music and traditional band music. The recording discussed here demonstrates a playing style typical of most Finnish bands in the 1900s, which seems to incorporate influences from Berlin cabaret orchestras, jazz bands, and the then new effects of mixing and reverberation during the recording process. Yet, old traditional mannerisms are discernable in the elements of note length, accent, note cut-off, tone, and vibrato. The HRS recording presents a mixture of instrumental choices, revealing that the band itself was in a transition between eras. Two euphoniums, a tuba, a tenor horn and an alto horn represent the old tradition. Two trumpets replace the traditional cornets. Two clarinets, a french horn, and a set of drums all reflect an interest in more modern sounds and a step away from the older bands. The HRS, and many other contemporary Finnish wind bands, has produced a large number of Lp recordings and CDs, providing a rich resource for the listener.

It is fortunate that a few recordings of very early Finnish brass bands have been accessible for listening. There is no known list of recordings that still exist from the 89 sides produced by the *Helsingin torvisoittokunta* (HTS) between 1904 and 1912. Many have been archived by the Finnish Broadcasting Company, but few are available to the public. Copies of the original 78-rpms of Finnish-American band recordings have appeared in private collections and archives, but no effort has yet been made to reproduce them for the public.

Much of the recorded material done by the HTS had more of an international flavor than one might expect from a Finnish band. Toivo Tamminen said in his 2002 correspondence that "during that time (1904-1912), there were fewer Finnish compositions recorded by HTS because of the Tsar's influence (*keisarin vallan aika*), and so the band recorded more Russian, French, and Scandinavian music" [translation by the author]. The suggestion here is that the HTS was obliged to avoid Finnish patriotic music during that contentious period just before Finland's independence, when such Finnish music would be unwelcome to official Russian ears. Printed programs for concerts performed by HTS at the Helsinki Esplanade band shell in 1906 and 1908 list many transcriptions of works by Beethoven, Verdi, Grieg, Tchaikovsky, and Smetana. Neither program lists any compositions by Finnish composers. All HTS recording stopped in 1912, although the band continued until 1918. In that year, the HTS bandmaster Apostol became Finland's chief military band conductor after independence was declared. The HTS band was reconstituted after World War II, and exists today with the name *Annantalon puhallinorkesteri* (the Anna Street Concert Band), named after the old city building where the band now rehearses.

To help understand the performance style of the time, I analyzed two recordings of the same composition: one done by the HTS in 1904 and one done by the Columbia Band in 1917. Tamminen's correspondence adds little to solving the mystery of how the Columbia Band came to be involved in recording Finnish music in New York: "I have learned nothing of the Columbia Band or its players, but it seems obvious there was some Finnish connection." The comparison is also of two arrangements. The HTS version was arranged by Apostol or the composer Merikanto himself, for the band's traditional brass instrumentation. The Columbia Band arrangement was for mixed instrumentation and is probably the same edition K. L King arranged for the Sibelius Club.

The level of technical ability in both bands was very high. Florid writing was assigned to either the clarinets in the Columbia Band or to cornets and euphoniums in the HTS band with similar expectations. The recording quality for the 1904 example might be expected to be less clear, but, excepting some distortions in louder passages, the sound was listenable in all ranges. The Columbia Band's recording quality was better, reflecting thirteen years of technological development. Both bands took quite fast tempi, but in the 1904 recording of *Summer Evening Waltz*, Apostol also chose to accelerate within each section. Without woodwinds, the entire band of brass players was obliged to play the composer's obbligato and rapid-scale passages. For instance, what was assigned to clarinets and flutes in the opening waltz section of the 1917 recording was assigned to tenor horns and euphoniums in 1904. The brass playing was brilliant, with courageous tempi and very clean rhythmic unity. The Otava Music Dictionary refers to the performance level of HTS as being very high and these recordings confirm that to modern ears.[xii]

While the performance of the same work by the Columbia Band cannot be construed as a comparison between two Finnish groups, the differences still provide interesting information. K. L. King's arrangement includes Merikanto's extended coda, which is absent from the HTS recording. It may have been that the earlier 1904 recording could only contain shorter pieces. Having conducted and performed the Merikanto waltz several times with Finnish bands in Finland, I recognize the K. L. King arrangement as being true to the original and merely adding parts to the score to accommodate all of the American band instruments. With more repeats and the coda, the waltz became 3 minutes long in the 1917 recording. To compare the quality of playing between the two recordings might be a bit unfair, considering that members of the HTS band probably had played the waltz every week for many years, whereas the Columbia Band may have been doing little more than sight-reading. Some rhythmic discrepancies and occasional missed notes in the 1917 recording suggest this possibility.

I did not hear any of the "gusty brassiness" in the HTS recording that I heard live with the Salo Fire Brigade Band. A similar energy was evident in the old recording, but the effect was also quite polished. Perhaps a recording of a traditional march, an example of which I have not been able to hear, might reveal the HTS band being more "raucous." My sense from all the recordings I've heard is that the HTS band was an elegant and professionally prepared ensemble.

Comments on recordings by two other older bands add some information to this discussion of style. The Finnish folk song recorded by the Arthur Pryor Band in 1918 is of a well-known melody. The arrangement was done for American bands, with extensive sections given over to woodwinds. Frederick Pacius composed the original work in the late 1800s, about the same time that he composed the Finnish National Anthem. The Sibelius Club does not list this folk song in its band catalogue, and no other arrangements have surfaced anywhere. The Finnish Broadcasting archives lists the Pryor Band recording as the only one ever made of this piece. Musicologists comment on how successful German-born Frederick Pacius was in capturing elements of Finnish folk music in his compositions, as this example demonstrates. The recording of this lyrical piece includes excellent playing, with especially solid flute and first cornet renditions. The brass playing in general is fine, with clearly audible tuba lines. Searching the archives for concert programs of the Pryor Band that might have included this piece has thus far yielded nothing.

The final older recording to be considered is the only one thus far that was actually performed by the Finnish-American band *Louhi*. I have not yet been able to listen to the *Louhi* Band of *Pois rannoilta Suomen*—New York label number 764—but did access their performance of the Finnish National Anthem-Victor 72203. Early recordings of *Maamme* ("Our Homeland") are rare. There were a small number done by vocalists on wax cylinders before 1905. The most successful were by the HTS in Helsinki in 1912, by the Finnish-American Elite Choir of Duluth in 1913, and this *Louhi* Band in 1918. The recording by the Helsinki brass band took place in the year they stopped recording entirely. Offering such a patriotic piece to the public in such volatile times was a brave gesture on conductor Apostol's part. The *Louhi* Band recording was made in the year Finland declared independence and just before the band left for a Finnish tour. The performance is well executed, although the tempo is excessively grandiose, even ponderous, compared to how it is performed today. The style is convincingly fervent and is from an arrangement done especially for the *Louhi* Band. It's not clear if Louis Koski, George Wahlström, or possibly other arrangers did the arrangement. An edition of *Maamme* was available at that time from the Sibelius Club, but it is not known who made that arrangement for publication, or if it was the one recorded. This arrangement often has the theme given to alto and tenor lines in the band, which differs from the versions now played in Finland. A copy of the 1912 recording of *Maamme* rendered by the HTS has not been found.

After listening repeatedly to the ten older recordings that have become available, I conclude that the level of brass band playing in Finland, among Finnish-Americans, and in the New York sound studios, was of a high level. It has taken repeated listenings to develop an ability to filter out the hissing and distortions, but eventually the sounds produced by the musicians become dominant in the listener's ear. Common to all the recordings is a romantic rubato approach to the tempo, and a tendency to prefer staccato to tenuto whenever possible. Considering that the American musical circles were also populated with many German immigrants, including brass players and teachers, it could be anticipated that brass players who came from Finland might have found their playing tastes in common with the musicians they met in New York. It would be difficult to determine which was recorded in a New York studio or in a Helsinki studio, based on an evaluation of style or technique.

This study of the style of Finnish brass bands should continue with further analyses of more amateur recordings and live performances done in Finland and in the United States. I feel it is more useful to move away from recordings of professional players to discover the local playing mannerisms and those hometown stylistic regions where brass playing becomes a kind of folk music as when I experienced a septuagenarian tuba player playing tunes for which he hasn't bothered to look at the music in years.

---

[i]Hans R. Wasastjerna, ed. "History of the Finns in Minnesota." trans. Toivo Rosvall, *Minnesotan suomalaisten historia* (Duluth, MN: Finnish-American Historical Society, 1959), 232.

[ii]Anthony C. Schulzenberge, "Life on the Vermilion Range before 1900," (Typewritten manuscript, Minnesota History Center, 1963), 22.

[iii]Sorvari Saralampi, *Echoing Footsteps* (Toivola: Little Swan, 1987), 113.

[iv]Wasastjerna, "History," 299.

[v]Ibid., 51, 69.

[vi]Kauko Karjalainen, Suomalainen Torviseitsikko–Historia ja perinteen jatkuminen (The Finnish Brass Septet—History and Living Tradition) (Tampere, Finland: Tampere University Press, 1995).

[vii]Pekka Jalkanen, Alaska, Bombay, ja Billy Boy Jazz kulturin murros Helsingissä 1920–luvulla (The rise of jazz music culture in Helsinki) (Helsinki: Jyväskylän yliopiston musiikkitieteen laitos, 1980), 69.

[viii]Ibid., 389.

[ix]Saralampi, *Echoing Footsteps*, 111.

[x]Ernest Koski, "Tune of the First Festival," *Fifty Years of Progressive Cooperation, 1929–1979* (Superior, WI: Työmies Society, 1979; Arnold Alanen, *A Field Guide to Architecture and Landscapes of Northern Minnesota* (Madison, WI: the author, 2000), 31.

[xi]*Hyvinkään Rautatiesoittajat*: *Asemamiehen jenkka*, JP Musiikki Oy, long-play catalogue number JPLP 2014, 1980.

[xii]Otavan Musiikkitietosanakirja, Helsinki, 2: 592. "jonka taiteellinen taso oli eritäin korkea." ("When the artistic level was very high.")

Chapter Seven
Where Are the Finnish-American Bands Today?

Band Culture on the Iron Range

If there is any continued Finnish presence in northern Minnesota today from the brass band activity of bygone years, it is minimal. Several players in the municipal bands for such towns as Two Harbors, Virginia, Eveleth, Hibbing, and Proctor have Finnish surnames and maybe had grandfathers who played in the old bands. The ”Ely Clown Band”, with several Finnish American members, will occasionally get together in the summers for parades and festivals. School bands still include significant numbers of young players with Finnish last names, but the importance that characteristic, musically, should not be overstated. It is merely a reflection that Finnish-Americans, though more blended into general society with each generation, are continuing to contribute to cultural life in their hometowns in the normal way. No ethnocentric case can be made for modern Finnish-Americans on the Iron Range doing any more than their proportional share in community-wide cultural activity. If their contribution to local ethnic music seems large today, it is only because Finns are still a significant percentage of the Iron Range population, to the extent that Finnish-American music is a large part of the regional folk music that shares it.

The immigrant musicians of previous generations have all contributed to the development of the well-known high quality of instrumental music on the Iron Range. Other than the examples discussed below, no one is playing the old Finnish marches in North America anymore. Yet, visits to the existing remnants of the past, such as to the old Hibbing Municipal Band music library, or the ”Kaleva Hall” in Virginia, evokes a spirit of those old bands that seem to still echo in many parks, halls, and streets.

Finnish-American Popular Music after the Brass Bands

The contemporary effort to preserve and appreciate Finnish music culture today is a process that appears to involve a much wider constituency than merely those with specific ethnic roots. Within the Finnish-American community, ethnic event organizers are often surprised by the number of people who have no family ties to Finland but who come to sing, dance, listen, and play, adopting Finnish culture as their own. Finnish folk and dance music constitute the main regional folk musical styles of the Northern Great Lakes area. Many such participants who have adopted Finnish culture grew up in or near Finnish communities on the Iron Range or elsewhere where the Finnish elements of language, food, traditions, and music were naturally present in everyday life. Americans whose ethnic identity might be obscured by many generations in the melting pot often become interested in a cultural group whose characteristics are easier to define and who present a vibrant and successful program of activity. If one dances to the music, tastes the food, and hears the language in the neighborhood for a time, such circumstances seem adequate to begin wearing that ethnic cloak.

The history of the Finnish-American bands has not always been parallel with that of Finnish-American music in general on the Iron Range. There have been other significant chapters in Finnish-American music history that were contemporaneous with the brass bands at first but then continued into the present day, as the bands disappeared. As previously stated, the disappearance of the bands coincided with the rise of other kinds of Finnish-American music-making, especially surrounding the accordion band, the Finnish-American dance hall staple by the 1920s. An Iron Range Finnish accordion "orchestra" would minimally have an accordion, a set drummer, and possibly a string bass, maybe a fiddle or a trumpet. Additions might include more accordions a mandolin, guitar, or banjo. Viola Turpeinen (accordion) and William Syrjälä (trumpet and drum set) managed as a duo for hundreds of dances for more than two decades.

Following the popular dance craze of the interwar era, and with the influence of the phonograph, Finnish-American music was more danced to and more listened to than ever before. The enthusiasm for the local accordion dance bands and for the 78-rpm discs of Kosola, Turpeinen, Salomaa, Kylander, the Maki Trio and many others sustained a Finnish-American dance hall culture that continued for the next three decades. The period from about 1920 until about 1950 constitutes the most significant era in Finnish-American popular music, for which there is an intense nostalgia that continues today. There has been no detailed study of Finnish-American popular and folk music activity into the modern era, but it can be said that the many veteran dance bands as well as more recently formed groups still draw upon the music first played and recorded during those intensely active three decades. The inspiration continues into the future with the modern Finnish dance bands that have recorded CDs and traveled more widely, such as *Conga se mene* and the *Oulu Hotshots. These bands contributed significantly to modern day interest in Finnish-American popular and dance music, and have inspired many other such bands to continue or to be newly formed. Unfortunately, these two bands that were very active into the 1990s have been victims of the unfortunate march of time. Both groups have lost members to the inevitable intervention of age, health, and death. The Oulu Hotshots* (Wisconsin) is no longer active, but *Conga se mene* (primarily from the Marquette Michigan area) is still occasionally performing. The Finnish-American community now looks with hope and some anxiety to the next generation. Will it continue?

Finnish folk music in Minnesota enjoyed some bursts of energy in the late 1900s. The first of these was a family band from the Iron Range called the

"Fifth Generation", which kept active as long as there were enough younger players to cover the parts. The Santa family yielded a number of professional musicians who went on to have successful careers, and the band inspired others to take up the Finnish folk cause. Another was Helena Pakola's "Singing Strings", an intense Finnish folk fiddling workshop for young players, which continues today.

Because they are inspired by older musical experiences and memories within Finnish-American communities in Minnesota that are almost a century old, many of the performances by local Finnish accordion bands heard today are almost aural museum pieces. The best example of such a modern day traditional Finnish-American dance band is the "*Finn Hall Band*", known in earlier versions as the *Minnesota pelimannit,* or *Keskiläänen pelimannit,* a six-piece band with accordions, drums, mandolin/guitar, string bass, and singers. This group is located in Minneapolis-St. Paul and plays regularly for dances in several venues. They can be thought of as a musical revival, as they strive for a continuation of old traditions.

The musicians in the contemporary Finnish groups are often from several generations in one family and their music is founded on elements of musical performance and style transmitted by repetition and imitation from mixed models many generations old. This can be compared to what happens to immigrant language, where living second generation Finns still speak with a dialect and vocabulary that hasn't been heard in Finland since before 1900. Neither do such Finnish-American musicians reflect much of the evolutions in folk and popular dance music that have taken place in Finland during the passage of the twentieth century.

If any modern examples of Finnish-American music reflect outside influences, they usually are from the American musical melting pot from where the Finnish musicians have borrowed country and western, Wisconsin polka, folk-rock and Latin styles in an effort to modernize their music. Each of the recently active examples of Finnish-American musicians such as Diane Jarvi, Kip Peltoniemi, *Conga se mene*, and the *Oulu Hotshots* has a stylistic flavor that shows influences from contemporary American popular music. Such musicians usually have a listening audience well beyond the ethnic community. Unique examples, such as the folk duo *Kaivamaa,* present folk traditions directly from modern Finnish sources learned through study with active practitioners in Finland. *Kaivamaa,* fiddle and harmonium, is quite unique today but may foretell the future of Finnish music performance in America, where the popularity of traveling Finnish groups such as *JPP* and *Tallari* are exciting the attention of many American folk musicians and enthusiasts, who adopt these exciting new forms.

Because Finland itself is no longer an agrarian society, many native Finns who perform folk music have not grown up in the context from which Finnish folk music traditions emanated, being perhaps even more removed than are the Iron Range Finnish-Americans. Many American Finns fear that the practice of folk culture will soon be lost, since it apparently is in the hands of a dwindling and aging group. Considerable energy is being invested in efforts to motivate and educate younger Finnish-Americans through language villages, summer camps, Finnish exchanges, and language classes. The world is now a smaller place, and we can anticipate that future demonstrations of Finnish music culture in the United States may have less to do with the music of grandparents and may start reflecting more contemporary American tastes and the contemporary native Finnish musical output, which is increasingly international. I hear more Irish and Balkan mannerisms in the Finnish folk music of today than a decade ago.

As much as anywhere in North America, there has been continued robust cultural activity in the Finnish communities on the present-day Minnesota Iron Range. During the 1990s, Finns have sponsored a local Iron Range summer festival called Festival Finlandia, which had been held at the Ironworld Center in Chisholm. This regional event attracted many musicians, dancers, artisans, food preparers, souvenir stands and booksellers for a two-day outdoor fair. That festival, while no longer active, did promote Finnish culture on the Range for a decade. Now we await the next opportunity to gather and share. The village of Embarrass, one of many that suffered hard economic times following the closing of large Iron Range mining operations, has recently developed a community-wide tourism project that presents its heritage in architecture, food, entertainment, hospitality, and scenery, with significant volunteer community participation. Since its start during the Depression Era, the town of Palo has continued to celebrate a February *Laskiainen* festival, which features winter sports contests, folk arts, music, and dancing rooted in Finnish traditions. Other Northern Minnesota communities like Nisswa, Wadena, and Walker have multi-ethnic festivals that usually include Finnish participation. Many Finnish-Americans residing in Minneapolis-St. Paul are originally from Northern Minnesota and contribute to a lively calendar of events involving music, dance, holiday celebration, and cultural programs, recently energized by an immigrant population of contemporary Finns working in Minnesota's technical and academic sectors.

Finnish-American Musical Activity Outside Minnesota

The Lake Superior region, including northern Minnesota, northern Wisconsin, the Upper Peninsula of Michigan, and the Canadian shore of Lake Superior, has recently shown considerable success in developing local music festivals that highlight Finnish-American folk and dance music. In addition to the Minnesota examples already noted, the cases of the Covington (Michigan) Finnish Music Festival held on July 4 each year, and the Aura (Michigan) Jamboree on the third weekend each July, are the most notable examples. The planning and management of these festivals are done entirely by local volunteers, with some financial support from regional and state cultural agencies. They invite many local dance bands, fiddlers, accordion players, spoon players and singers, which always means that the music played includes Finnish material. In both cases, activities are divided between the formal published program on a main stage, and a considerable amount of "jamming" by impromptu groups, sharing tunes with each other on the festival grounds. Having attended these newer Finnish-American village music festivals, my biggest surprise is that they appeal to a large number of younger musicians as well as to the older, tradition-bearers. The audience in attendance, often in the thousands on a nice summer day, is a mixture of Finnish-Americans and others who have come to understand that Finnish music is a part of their local folk music.

The grandest of these Finnish American gatherings is Finnfest-USA, an annual gathering that is a movable feast, having been held in Florida, Washington State, Northern Michigan, Arizona, and many other places. It is a comprehensive showcase of Finnish American musical activity, and a wonderful mixing ground for native Finnish and American musicians.

Finnish-American Bands Today

Other than *Ameriikan poijat*, and the Red Lodge Band of Montana, a brass band organized in Fitchburg, Massachusetts, a vintage brass band in Florida, and the old Finnish Band of Thunder Bay, Ontario are all of the known groups that play the old Finnish repertoire. An "old-time" band from the North Suburban Community Band of Minnesota occasionally mixed a few Finnish tunes in with their primarily German dance-band repertoire, while Finnish American tuba player Marvin Loff was active.

A very important example of a currently functioning band that plays Finnish music is the Red Lodge Band of Montana (see figure 12 for an historical photograph of the band). The Red Lodge Band has Finnish roots and has existed without interruption since 1900. The Finnish community in Red Lodge has always been somewhat isolated due to its remote location, and that seems to have affected the band as being more able to faithfully preserve a playing style and repertoire that goes back to its origins. The Red Lodge Band continued to play after all others had ceased. *Ameriikan poijat* and the Red Lodge Band met in Minneapolis for the first time in 2002 during Finnfest USA, and it was the first time either group had direct contact with any sister organization in North America. Current members of the Red Lodge Band have been developing plans for the publication and distribution of performance material from their old repertoire. The live recordings that the Red Lodge Band has released are exceptional examples of bygone playing styles and repertoire.

Evidence of two other known examples of Finnish style bands that have existed in recent decades include a band seen in a book of community photographs from Tower/Soudan in the 1980s and a newspaper photograph of a small brass band in Fitchburg, Massachusetts in the 1990s. This band has appeared at the local Saima Park since about 1992 and was organized by local musician Armas Kaukoranta. It was first formed to play for the annual Finnish Independence day celebration. The Fitchburg Finnish-American newspaper *Raivaaja* has recorded the band's musical activities in the region. Jonathan Ratila from *Raivaaja* noted that the most recent appearance of this band was on November 30, 2003, and a picture of the group appeared in the December 10, 2003, issue of *Raivaaja*.

> It looks like there are two trombones, one baritone, four trumpets and a bass horn. Of these eight, I'm aware that five have Finnish ancestry. The instrumentation has varied over the year. Armas Kaukoranta usually recruits the musicians during summer band concerts that are held in Fitchburg and surrounding towns. The Independence Day "brass band" is a volunteer effort.[i]

The Florida example is the 3rd Florida Regimental Band, a confederate revival brass ensemble, whose director, John Joline, has Finnish-American heritage. Through his family connection, he became interested in the brass band music of Finland. As previously noted, the Finnish septet and the American civil war ensemble have very similar instrumentation. Joline has collected a substantial repertoire of Finnish music that the 3rd Florida Regimental Band regularly performs. As with most Civil War bands, the Florida band plays on antique instruments from the mid-1800s, such as shown in the Minnesota band photograph in figure 41.[ii] The "over the shoulder" instruments apparently were not played in Finland or anywhere else in Europe.

I have received correspondence from many players who would like to form a Finnish style wind band, but often the problems of finding performance materials and assembling a balanced instrumentation discourages them from going forward. *Ameriikan poijat* have recently published the sheet music for twenty five Finnish American band repertoire, found in the archives in Hancock, Fitchburg, Conneaut and elsewhere. *Poijat* wants to offer workshops at future Finnish festivals to encourage new groups to get started.

Although there are several municipal bands active on the Minnesota Iron Range today, none of them have any Finnish music in their repertoire, regardless of the fact that there are Finnish-American musicians playing in the bands, and that some Finnish-Americans are conducting. Access to repertoire is certainly a primary problem. There is a good deal of attractive and modern band music being written in Finland today. I hope to get this modern material to the interested municipal and school bands in Minnesota's Iron Range and other areas with Finnish populations. If Finnish band music, either traditional or modern, has any broad attraction, it would seem that Iron Range bands would present the likeliest situations for performances in America.

Ameriikan poijat—a Finnish Brass Band Revival

The brass ensemble *Ameriikan poijat* started casually with a group of players from Minnesota meeting for the first time in 1990 to play through some old Finnish brass band books and test the group's level of interest in forming a more permanent organization. This collection of old Finnish septet music given to me in the 1980s was our first material. Within this collection were some works written for the Finnish KVS festivals, which sponsored composition contests and also commissioned works for brass. In the 1880s and 1890s these festivals spurred such notable Finnish composers as Toivo Kuula, the young Sibelius, Leevi Madetoja and others to write important brass band repertoire for each annual midsummer celebration. These works, plus some interesting modern compositions, were part of the attraction for getting the Minnesota brass players to peruse this unknown repertoire.

I had hoped from our first performances that *Ameriikan poijat* would be well received by Finnish-American audiences, even though our initial repertoire list included very little of what the schottische dancers might hope we would play. Because we have never seen ourselves primarily as a Finnish dance band, there are still many standard Finnish-American "favorites" for which we do not as yet have arrangements. As trained musicians are apt to do, we have continued to cultivate the more serious repertoire that was meant for festival events and concert performances, while still trying to have the schottisches and waltzes available to meet audience demands.

For the most part, *Ameriikan poijat* has performed and recorded music that was written in Finland. However, the most recent findings from my research for this study have included a surprising amount of band music that was composed or arranged for Finnish-American bands of the early twentieth century. Following our initial presentation of some of these works in 2002, members of the *Ameriikan poijat* ensemble became interested in editing more of this Finnish-American material for future performances and recordings. We have also arranged many of the Finnish-American favorites to be part of our dance repertoire. Our effort to reintroduce the original immigrant band music, and adapting some of the old popular music, has been our recent work, following many years of preoccupation with known Finnish brass septet music.

Ameriikan poijat never initially intended to be a re-enactment of brass band culture from the early twentieth century in Minnesota. Although we have often played for Finnish-American audiences, it was only in 2002, with the performance of the Finnish-American marches at the lecture/recital at Finnfest USA, that we first started to pay attention to preserving the musical elements of the immigrant music heritage. The group's repertoire was almost entirely derived from sources in Finland, including Finnish arrangements of international pieces. Through the septet's numerous performances in Northern Minnesota and other Finnish-American centers, we have confirmed that our repertoire contains many works that are well known here. Two such pieces, *March of the*

Finnish Infantry by Jean Sibelius and *Präludium* by Armas Järnefeldt, were performed by *Ameriikan Poijat* at an evening entertainment held in October 2002 at the Kaleva (*Valon tuote*) Hall in Virginia, Minnesota. The Finnish influence was most clearly felt in the hour or so of dancing at the end of the concert performance, as can be seen from the following dance sequence:

Odottava Waltz
Life in the Finnish Woods/Waltz
Heilani Jenkka /Schottische
Nikkelimarkka / Schottische
Karjalan Polkka/ Polka
Säkkijärven polkka/ Polka
Kuningaskobra-/Tango
Sä kaunenin oot-/Humppa/Fox
La Cumparsita/Tango
Femme Fatale/Tango
Taikayö/Waltz
Äänisen Aallot/Waltz
Joko uuvuit sa uneen? / Tango
Ei Toista Kertaa/ Tango
Kun Yössä kuljin/ Humppa/Fox
Tuntuitaival/ Humppa/Fax
Väliaikainen/ Tango
Lenna mun lempeni laulu/ Waltz
Akseli ja Elina Häävalssi/ Waltz
Josef, Josef/ Humppa/Fox
Kengät kuluu/ Polka
Sysmån Polkka/ Polka
Kulkurin/ Waltz
Laura Waltz/Waltz
Tango Illusion/Tango
Taikarenkaat/Tango
Unelma/ Slow Waltz

Sound recordings and videotapes of the group have been available since 1992. The sheet music publishing project offers many works with score and parts, edited for American musical groups interested in performing the music. Until now, the lack of availability of such musical material in the United States has thwarted the likelihood of finding anyone to play old Finnish band music. The editions include alternate parts for instruments to substitute for the E^b cornet, alto and tenor horns that are usually unavailable.

Conclusions

The early Finnish immigrant brass bands became the pioneering community musicians on Minnesota's Iron Range. Many immigrant players and bandmasters arrived having had considerable experience with brass bands in Finland and so became the catalysts for drawing more new musicians to join in. The circle in which they moved quickly grew to be much wider than just the Finnish settlements. The international nature of their band music became not only the musicians' door into the larger American community, but it also eventually compromised their original function within the ethnic circle. That process of cultural transformation took place over a couple of decades as the importance of the ethnic brass band within the Finnish community gradually diminished. Both the bandsmen and the Finnish communities had transformations in their musical tastes. The bandsmen became more interested in the American music of the municipal bands, and the Finnish communities preferred dancing to the accordion orchestras.

By the 1930s, some Iron Range school and municipal bands had become among the most successful programs in the United States. It is not easy to measure the impact of the Finnish bands in a scientific way, but the fact that they provided a "ready-made" band music culture at that very moment when the communities were being formed suggests that they developed an expectation for cultural life which an early Iron Ranger never remembers being without. The Finnish brass bands' unique musical characteristics were received in the multicultural Iron Range setting of that time, and the very fact of their existence in such a remote unsettled region were compelling motivations for this study. The Finnish bands' fate is an indicator of how much of the newly arrived immigrant culture ultimately fared later in twentieth century America.

Since the brass band tradition dissipated among Finnish Americans after just a few years in America, the question may arise: how ethnically Finnish were those Finnish brass bands? There seem to be two answers, responding to what the brass band genre was, or to what role they played in the ethnic community. The international roots of European brass band music refute that the Finnish brass band culture had particularly Finnish ethnic origins to begin with. The Finns certainly played some music that seemed identifiably Finnish to their listeners, although their instruments were quite interchangeable with those of bands of other nations. Many communities in Finland today are interested in their old band histories because, over many decades, the Finnish brass bands developed a unique repertoire and historical function within their local circles. The Finnish town fire brigade band or workers' band had a significance that was noted in local history books and was not diluted by any other musical groups or styles in the community at that time. Such direct community identification was far less traceable in the multi-ethnic immigrant communities of the Minnesota Iron Range.

So, why couldn't there have been a modern band revival in Finnish-America? Perhaps their "American" era was too short to leave a strong impact on community histories. A big challenge to the Finnish brass bandsmen when they first came to America was that, unless they sang, there was very little discernibly "Finnish" about their music, especially if the listener didn't have any previous experience with Finnish music. The instruments the Finns played in America were usually piston models newly and locally purchased, and though they played with the same fingerings, there was a cultural difference compared to the rotary-valved cornets they left back home. Perhaps that difference was enough to remind them each time they picked up their shiny new "C. G. Conn" piston cornet, "I'm in America now." The original Finnish band music included examples the military march and opera repertoire, material played by bands all over the western world and its colonies. Even the best-known Finnish dance music had international roots. The brass band playing style was imbued with Russian and German traditions, and was not unique for many listeners on the Iron Range or in other regions with large numbers of European immigrants. In fact, the mixed ethnic communities immediately identified with and embraced the music of the Finnish bands because of its universality, as well as because they were the only bands in town. Other than occasionally accompanying the singing of a patriotic song or a folk song, the Finnish brass band's music had no connection to the language. Band music was probably the most international cultural contribution the immigrant Finns made to the communities in their new homeland. The Finnish bandsmen were delighted to find that they could immediately sit down in municipal bands, play the music of Sousa, and only worry about speaking English later. The more they embraced the American band medium, the more they were accepted into the wider community.

The international roots of the bands explain why the Finnish immigrant music and musicians were quickly absorbed into local community culture. Yet, the instruments in an Iron Range Serbian brass band and in a Finnish brass band are of similar physical design but it does not mean that they performed with the same musical results. There is a case for the uniqueness of musical style and tradition even though the sounds are emanating from a universal musical medium. As I sat in with the brass band in Lieksa in 1982, I experienced the connection between traditional Finnish music and the worldwide brass band tradition. Yet my senses were attentive to the "Finnishness" of those schottisches and waltzes I was playing, and I was not thinking of myself at that moment as participating in an international brass brotherhood, but with Finns.

In the late nineteenth century, Finns had embraced the brass band medium, assigned it an important function in their cultural history, and created their own repertoire, all of which apparently still has validity even in today's Finnish community life. The Finnish brass bands in America could have maintained an ethnically identifiable playing style, if that was their choice. Some bands were slower to adapt to American band music than others, but the trend was to blend in, and not to maintain the ethnic separation.

The numerous Finnish bandsmen across the region had a lasting effect on the musical life of the Iron Range for many years, even after the Finnish-American bands eventually disappeared. The rapid changes in musical tastes and the push to culturally integrate community life influenced all ethnic bands. However, the individual contributions of immigrants, as musical pioneers and as dedicated community musicians, are clear. Thus, the measure of the impact of ethnic musicians on community culture must be taken on the individual as much as on the group level.

There may seem the implication that some great tragedy of neglect had taken place as the ethnically Finnish bands disappeared. If there was any tragedy, it may only have been felt at the time by those Finns who valued the old traditions as they disappeared. If they had regrets, we don't know; the record is silent on the matter. Most seem to have been content to move on into the modern era. One tragedy is that the opportunity better to understand the connection between ethnic bands and community life that was so vibrant a century ago was lost to later generations of Finnish Americans. The recent revival of such bands in Finland, however, has been heartening. Perhaps a revisiting of old cultural institutions could eventually happen among Finnish Americans.

After the Finnish-American bands disappeared, Finnish festivals, dramatic presentations, political and benevolent movements, churches, agricultural cooperatives, newspapers, and other activities continued to involve and inspire many of the aging first generation immigrants and their children. The bands, with their romantic sounding names like *Kaiku* and *Sampo*, had disappeared, overrun by the new trends in dance music, the evolution toward the modern American concert band in schools and communities, and new media of radio and phonograph. By 1930, almost all of the pioneer Finnish bandmasters were old men, had left the Iron Range, or had passed away: Hemming Hautala had left for South Dakota, Victor Taipale for Detroit, Charles Kleemola was deceased and William Ahola had retreated from Hibbing to the small village of Brimson. None of the younger generation of Finnish musicians seemed interested in continuing the tradition.

Not many elements of the old musical traditions well known in the 1890s survived intact into the next century, including the tastes of American-born citizens on the Iron Range. Today, if you stopped by the American Legion Hall in Virginia on a Saturday night to hear the accordion bands play, it would be a challenge to separate out from the stylistic mixture you hear which elements are specifically Finnish, Slovenian, or Italian. The dance tunes alternate freely between the three heritages and reflect the same mixture of those dancers in attendance.

Today, most Iron Range Finnish American communities have had only limited resources available to them to learn about the history of bands that were active in their past. That lack of information has made it difficult for students of community history or ethnic history to include band music in their historical profiles. The many anniversary books previously published by Iron Range communities pay differing degrees of attention to musical heritage, but often the subject is either neglected or omitted. Because old music happened "in real time" and only exists afterward as a memory for the witnesses, efforts to find those rare physical artifacts about community music of the past are often not successful. However, such efforts are the only way to keep musical heritage in the written history books. The hope of possible discoveries should spur researchers to dig more deeply for more cultural information that is waiting to be discovered.

During *Ameriikan poijat's* existence, the ensemble has played to thousands of listeners in concerts and dances, has distributed thousands of recordings, and has made many radio broadcasts. The story of this one musical group does not however indicate the revival of an old tradition. Yet, *Ameriikan poijat* can say that it has a community of listeners, Finnish–American or otherwise, and people know that *"poijat"* is perpetuating an old musical model. Whenever it might occur that another seven-part Finnish-American brass group has been successfully formed, there will be hope for declaring a possible revival of Finnish brass bands in America.

In the 1960's, when University of Minnesota Professors Berman, Chambers and Smith saw their basic research about labor history in Minnesota develop into a large collection of materials on immigrant life on the Iron Range, the Finnish-Americans suddenly took on a more prominent place in the cultural history of the state. As that collection became the Immigration History Research Center at the University and continued to grow, the musical collection within it gathered enough material to provide researchers with a view of how music functioned in Finnish immigrant life. The process of cataloguing the collections of Finnish American musical material has just begun, and still has very far to go.

Because the volume of collected material exceeds archivists' ability or budget to process, the collections of musical material in various Finnish-American archives has not yet had much impact on the general community. We cannot appreciate what we cannot easily find. It is heartening to note that, during the last three decades, the amount of new musical material submitted to archives has grown substantially. Archives continue to receive materials that document the immigrant experience, but no clear solution is in sight for funding the costly process of having these collections properly organized.

Seppo Tirronen from Joensuu, Finland, recorded audiotapes of his grandfather speaking about band life among American immigrants. These tapes were created in the 1960s. In correspondence in 2004 Tirronen shared this story about grandfather Heikki, who arrived in New York in 1912. An active bandsman back in Finland, very soon he was

> "invited to lead brass band in Virginia, Minnesota. There was also a train ticket in the mail. He didn't understand how it was

possible. So he traveled soon and there were the players of the band waiting for him in the Virginia railway station. It was the brass band of the Finnish Workers' Association. They had two weeks time to practice for the competition arranged in Virginia. They won the first prize. I am not sure, when this exactly happened, in 1912 or 1913."

Tirronen's father eventually returned to Finland after a rather short stay in Minnesota, and some additional time in New England. Heikki Tirronen's name does not appear in any Virginia Finnish band records, however, or in the records of any bands in New England. This is only one example of many bandsmen whose experiences with Finnish-American bands were somehow disappointing, and who soon returned to Finland. Much information of such musical encounters is still remaining to be gathered, or perhaps lost forever.

Ideally, Iron Range families and communities who may be connected with Finnish-American music will be more observant of the potential value of any old papers, photographs or other memorabilia. The most influential Minnesota Finnish bandmasters, including Miettunen, Taipale, Kleemola, Hautala, and Ahola have been discussed here. Because they were better known musical pioneers and because they appeared in the historical records with sufficient detail, their importance could be more easily measured. Because of the unevenness of available information, their stories may now overshadow other possibly important contributors such as Haapasaari, Koivunen, Lindroos, or Matara. There are indications that these other Finnish bandsmen were also significant contributors, but their histories are, for now, undiscovered.

As the Iron Range schools developed their comprehensive programs to include instrumental music, several Finnish-American bandmasters in the region were called upon to lead school band programs, but not always easily. Ely, for example, had some standards for teacher training were established quite early, thus disqualifying those initially willing immigrant bandmasters who hadn't yet received pedagogical instruction according to American standards. We know that Hautala went to Chicago for such courses, and it appears that Taipale also achieved a teaching license of some sort fairly early after arriving in Minnesota. It would be valuable to learn more about how such credentials were gained and what sort of instruction these men received. No documentation on this has thus far been found about the early years of music education licensure in northern Minnesota. The entire milieu of music the Iron Range schools in the early twentieth century, with mixed cultures and languages, fast-paced growth, and unusually generous financial resources, poses a fascinating subject for further study.

Very little is known about how Finnish bandsmen were recruited by the Finnish Americans to immigrate. Perhaps they didn't need much encouragement after the dissolution of the Finnish Army Bands, but the musicians still had to find out about playing or directing opportunities that were available in the immigrant communities. Reino Kero notes that a few advertisements did appear in Finnish newspapers at the turn of the century, announcing vacant positions for bandmasters to lead Finnish-American bands.[iii]

The fate of the Finnish-American brass band, playing in a medium that seemed to travel easily, was short-lived. The original ethnic brass music suffered in the transition, but the individual musicians seemed well equipped to move into new circles. The young Severus Ruuhela, pictured with the cornet and boutonniere in the Finnish Bovey Socialist Band (see figure 2, chapter 1), went on to play in bands in the area for another thirty years. Even with the passing changes in band traditions, political winds, and economic conditions, Ruuhela and hundreds of other Finnish immigrant brass players kept showing up at rehearsals, playing the concerts and parades, and inspiring a younger generation of community musicians.

If one walks down a street in Virginia, or attends a band concert in Hibbing today, the contributions those Finnish-American bands made to Minnesota's Iron Range one hundred years ago would be hard to detect. Yet, in a region that developed a very healthy sense of community, and, for many decades enjoyed an excellent music culture, the Finn bands provided some very important early building blocks. Today many of the Iron Range communities are often economically threatened and witness only a portion of their former musical life, yet they demonstrate a vibrancy and pride reminiscent of what the immigrants generated in the old days. The Finn bands' history, as a manifestation of the cultural past, can perhaps encourage more preservation, more nostalgic music making, and be a reminder that important history is being made every day.

Many of the European immigrant groups that arrived in America a century ago, now into fourth and fifth generations, are currently experiencing a growing disconnect from the ethnic traditions of the original settlers. Each new young generation has attached itself more closely with popular American culture than with the older immigrant cultures. Yet, some of these same young people seem eventually to recall community memories and then, as adults, try to reconnect with those ethnic elements that seem to distinguish them from others. It is on the shoulders of these young adults with positive memories of their heritage that much of the older ethnic culture in America currently rides. With each succeeding generation, such as among the Finns in America, their numbers become smaller and smaller. This apparent death and rebirth of ethnic awareness is a continuous process, but vulnerable to ultimate extinction with each succeeding generation more removed from the original settlers. This creates a growing pressure among those among us who see value in the preservation and perpetuation of older ethnic traditions.

Why should there be an interest in celebrating and preserving such cultural history? It is often said that "music is a universal language," and, certainly, anyone can listen to the music of an unfamiliar culture and derive some level of meaning from the experience. The medium of musical sound, as in this case of the brass bands, immediately admits the uninitiated listener into an "ethnic" world of the Finnish culture at least at a superficial level. The early experiences of listening to such music is akin to hearing a foreign language spoken when one may hear similarities to known language sounds, and yet differences that can not be defined or explained. The meaning and effect of any ethnic music tradition depends on who is the listener. For the Finnish immigrants, the meanings they connected with sounds of their brass bands were imbued by the many earlier experiences in dance halls, public ceremonies, parades, and evening entertainments. The sound of the brass band was a vital aural element in their community life. For those Iron Range citizens outside the Finnish-American community of the time, the bands were at least an object of great interest and source of entertainment. Today, after the Finnish immigrant brass bands have been silent for generations, it may seem possible to recreate their sounds by simply reading through some of their old sheet music. While the written notation has been a way for musicians of an earlier era to communicate with us today, much of the nuance and meaning that flavored the older renditions can only partially be put down on manuscript paper. The challenge for the student of this material is to find out more about those un-notated meanings and nuances. The story of the Finnish brass players, their repertoire, audiences, and function within the Finnish American community, might spark the imagination of the generations to come.

The Finnish-American brass band tradition cannot ever have the same function and meaning it had at the turn of the century. What they created as a musical repertoire and tradition could not survive intact as the old immigrant culture dissipated. Without personal and community relevance, historical music becomes silent.

---

[i] From correspondence with Jonathan Ratila, March 2004.

[ii] More information about the 3rd. Florida Regimental Band can be found at this web site: http://www.newtonmusical.com/ensembles/band-m.htm

[iii] Reino Kero, *Migration from Finland to North American in the Years Between the United States Civil War and the First World War* (Vammala: Vammalan Kirjapaino Oy, 1974), 115.

Afterword:

The Writing of *Cornets & Pickaxes*

There are several people who had a hand in moving the writing of this book forward, and this chapter is intended in part to mention them specifically and with my deep gratitude. The push to get the research into book form has been coming recently from Raoul Camus, a noted band authority and historian who came across my research through our mutual membership in the International Society for the Preservation and Promotion of Wind Music (a lofty name for a few wind music enthusiasts that like to meet in Europe during summers and share research, and maybe drink a glass of wine.) . The following pages are supplementary to the main story of Finnish brass bands on the Iron Range but I include them here especially for the reader who wants to learn more, pick up the story from where I left off, and go forward.

Process

I completed the preparation of Cornets & Pickaxes in three stages: identifying sources, evaluating and collecting information, and, finally, determining the story and meaning from the findings. Starting by studying readily available sources such as books and personal contacts, I eventually planned this study's scope in terms of an appropriate historical period, a limited geographical region, and the range of musical activities in which brass band musicians participated. My very first plan was to study Finnish immigrant bands across the United States, since "FABBs" had existed from New York to California. Minnesota, however, soon proved to be a conveniently rich ground of Finnish immigrant band activity, with as fine archival resources as could be found anywhere.

At the beginning of my research efforts in 1991, I found most of the initial information at the Immigration History Research Center (IHRC). My contact with other libraries and archives followed. Important information was also discovered through direct contacts with older Iron Range Finnish-Americans who had memories of bands, or through descendents of the bandsmen. Early in my research, I learned about which Iron Range communities had sufficient evidence of Finnish brass band activity to warrant further investigation. I developed an agenda for field research, based on responses to regional newspaper announcements that I submitted requesting information from the readers. Direct contact with historical societies, public schools, Finnish clubs, and individuals, added new information not previously collected. All of these efforts confirmed that there was an Iron Range Finnish band culture, with its bandmasters and community involvement. Although some gaps in the whole story remain, the research efforts were encouraging.

My primary tools for collecting and keeping records included a digital camera (for recording various images), a digital scanner (for recording older photographs and other documents), a tape recorder (for recording interviews and listening to dubbed copies of old 78- RPM records), and eventully a laptop computer (for collecting information and writing text).

I approached each research opportunity with a set of general questions that framed my inquiries.

1. Who were the Finnish bandsmen and where did they come from?
2. What were the circumstances of their arrival in Minnesota?
3. How were they trained and what was their previous experience?
4. With what repertoire and in what settings did the bands play in Minnesota?
5. How did the bands and players sound?
6. How did the groups function (organization, finances, personnel)?
7. What was the relationship of these bands to the general, non-ethnic community?
8. What were the factors and circumstances of their demise?
9. Did this band or musician carry any tradition into the future generations?

While partial answers to some of these questions were known before I began this study, that limited background information only pointed to the important work that needed to be done.

Thus far, the most studied and documented aspect of Finnish immigrant cultural activity in Minnesota is that of the amateur theater, where archives are rich and writers have been several. In musical activity there has been much less. Regarding the Finnish-American bands and choirs, which were common in many Iron Range communities, the previous research and writing is almost non-existent. The Finnish-American village choirs and church choirs continued many years after the bands had disappeared, with several singing groups still existing today. The Finnish choral tradition in America would appropriately be another subject for future historical research. Finding material about Finnish community choirs would present a challenge equal to that of the bands, however churches have been more diligent in keeping archives of their choral activity than other institutions. Substantial collections of music and memorabilia about Finnish-American choral activity are found in the same repositories as for the band music material.

The Finnish bands tried to preserve their ethnicity while interacting with American musical culture. This dual effort describes the underlying conditions for the immigrant musician of the time. This study has found, however, that the cultural influence seems to have gone both ways on the Iron Range. The Finnish bandsmen played a significant role in the musical life of the region even as they were absorbed into American culture.

Limitations and challenges

Because it was almost impossible to find any living witnesses to the musical events that took place during the most important years of Iron Range Finnish bands, my research had to use the available published and unpublished written accounts, living descendants' recollections, recordings, and photographs. The photographic record of Finnish brass band activity in Minnesota is surprisingly rich, though it is not well supported with supplementary documentation. It seems that the Finnish-American brass bands, with their colorful uniforms and shiny instruments, were fascinating subjects for photographers a century ago, and they were a source of pride within the ethnic community. In many cases, memorabilia or records have been lost, yet photographs remain. For this study, I recognize the value of the photographic document as the primary, or often the only, evidentiary source.

Finnish immigration archives are not housed in one central location, but they are found in several sites. It has been necessary to travel to various locations in Minnesota and Michigan in search of the important available material. Much of this material has not been catalogued in detail perhaps because it is complicated to classify for the non-musician archivist and challenging for non-Finnish speakers. Often I was the first researcher to open the box, use and evaluate many of the document files.

Not many of the Finnish immigrant bandsmen had biographical articles written about them during their lifetime. Two "Who's Who in Finnish America" volumes were published, in 1927 and 1948, with a few musicians included. While such sources provide only a sentence or two of general information on each person, they also have been valuable leads to other sources, providing clues for further research. Documentation generated by the Finnish-American bands of their own activity is rare. The best-known exceptions were souvenir publications from concert tours to Finland, though no bands from Minnesota made such trips. A great-granddaughter of bandmaster Charles Kleemola explained to me, "Mostly, they all just wanted to play music, and didn't pay any attention to newspaper notices or keeping diaries". [1]

[1] Telephone interview with Deanne Levander, July 2002.

Regrettably, the research I did in the 1990s should have been done in the 1950s, when many participants were not only alive but also were still playing their instruments. The oldest Iron Range Finns whom I had the honor to interview were usually recalling childhood memories of the bands, often with a parent or older sibling as a playing participant. Not much detail about musical subjects could be gleaned from the interviews, but the childhood memories recalled the atmosphere and excitement associated with the old Finn Bands. My interest in the subject often surprised them: it seems that with acculturation there was often pressure to conceal or forget some elements of the old ethnic culture. Once the memories were suppressed, they often seemed hard to revive.

During my contacts with Iron Range Minnesotans, surprising new finds of material emerged. The following excerpt from an August 2003 telephone conversation reveals how the search for a certain kind of information ultimately yielded something different:

> "Hello Milli; this is Paul Niemisto calling from Northfield."
>
> "Hi; nice of you to call. I remember hearing you guys at the Kaleva Hall in Virginia last October. I play your brass band CDs all the time on the Ely Finnish radio show."
>
> "I'm calling, Milli, because Toivo Tamminen from Riihimäki mentioned your name to me as someone who may know something about the old Sampo Band in Ely."
>
> "Oh yeah, Toivo; he's the brother that doesn't speak any English, right? Well, all I really have is one picture of that band. That's about it. But I was good friends with the Bjorkman family and was able to save a lot of old papers and memoirs after Emil's daughter died. She was quite a collector."
>
> "Oh yes, Bjorkman the choir conductor. He was in Minnesota, and Michigan, and everywhere. So you probably have some of his original papers?"
>
> "Probably. Also Bjorkman was a relative of the Finnish composer Erkki Melartin. I guess there was correspondence. There sure is a lot of stuff. It almost got thrown out. I got to it at the last minute. So when are you coming up to Ely to have a look at it?"

My Role

Colleagues in Finnish-American studies have described me as the "participant observer", with tape recorder in one hand, and brass horn in the other. My earliest exposure to Finnish music began with childhood experiences as a member of a Finnish-American community in Northern Michigan, where I sang the songs and danced the dances from an early age. My interest developed

[2]See map in Figure 17

further through some undergraduate research projects at the University of Michigan, which provided my first access to good libraries. Early opportunities to visit Finland occurred in 1969 and 1973, when I began to see the potential for future musical activity and research there. Since 1981, I have been a frequent visitor to Finland as a brass teacher, performer, and band conductor. I was first invited there to share my training and background in the American wind band tradition at summer camps and festivals, but soon I was also learning about Finnish music first-hand, such as with the lakeside experience with the old Finnish brass band described earlier.

In 1990, as *Ameriikan Poijat* was formed, I also began my doctoral study program and the work on this current research at the University of Minnesota. I discovered that the Iron Range locale offered as particularly rich a ground for study, as good as anywhere in the United States.

The personal experience I have had with Finnish-American culture, with the study and performance of Finnish brass music, with travel in Finland, and with many years living in Minnesota and Michigan, have provided me a unique platform for much activity over more than two decades.

Historical and Geographical Context

The Iron Range is a region of Northeast Minnesota that lies mostly in St. Louis County, starting near Grand Rapids in Itasca County on the west, and ending at the Lake Superior shore on the east.[2] As early as 1880, Finns were the fifth-largest immigrant group in the state, preceded only by the Germans, Norwegians, Irish, and Swedes, and most of these Finns went north. Minnesota reached a population of one million at that time, with 36.5% foreign-born immigrants. Finns became the largest immigrant group on the Iron Range (Riippa in Holmquist, 1981:304.)

The period of development of brass bands in Finland (period “a”) is somewhat earlier but almost coincides with the first bandsmen arriving in North America (period “b”) around 1885. This was during the earliest wave of Finnish immigration into the Iron Range of Minnesota. The third period (period “c”) from about 1900 until about 1920, was from the time when Finnish bands began to be a part of Iron Range community life until they began disappearing as identifiable ethnic ensembles, and coincided in the middle with the development of socialist politics among the Finnish-Americans. The fourth period (“d”) was during the 1930s, when interest in community bands renewed and resulted in the formation of new bands in several Finnish villages in St. Louis County with support of the federal Works Progress Administration. This fourth period of Minnesota Finnish band history approximately parallels the Depresson Era, which spurred a surprising revival of band culture in many Northern Minnesota Finnish rural communities, and was a unique instance of the American government directly supporting ethnic and small-town culture. In the final period ("e"), Finnish-American bandsmen moved away from the ethnic ensembles to play with municipal bands. This last period was primarily during the inter-war decades but was already occurring well before 1920.

The history of the "Finn Band" in Northern Minnesota has not been previously studied in any depth, yet that term is still commonly known on the Iron Range, even after several generations. This common knowledge is evidence of how prevalent Finnish brass band activity on the Iron Range was, especially during its "Golden Era" from about 1895 to 1920.

The desire to maintain an active immigrant culture among the Finns in Northern Minnesota was, in part, a result of their small, isolated, and somewhat monocultural society. They were thrust into the large, pluralistic setting of the Minnesota mining towns. The crowded streets of Ely and Virginia were filled with the sounds of many foreign languages. The Finns, like all immigrants, tried to maintain their identity in the often-threatening new land by continuing cultural activities from their homeland. Bands were one voice of those traditions.

Methodology and Sources

In addition to work in Minneapolis-St. Paul at the Immigration History Research Center and the Minnesota History Center, I gathered information from resources in northern Minnesota and at Finlandia University (Hancock, Michigan). During research trips to northern Minnesota, I conducted interviews with several people who had experience within the Iron Range Finnish community. Some interviews with elderly Iron Rangers took place in the Twin Cities area, where several have now retired. Of equal importance was correspondence with interviewees before and following interviews. Through such correspondence I was able to glean information omitted from the live interviews, and to clarify details.

My folders of correspondence, clippings, photographs, audiotapes, and e-mail messages that had been steadily accumulating over the decades have developed into a very important resource. Much of this collected material was initially unexamined and uncatalogued, having come into my possession before I was sufficiently prepared to process and appreciate it. Much of the material was received from older immigrant descendents who had supported and encouraged me in this historical research after having read about it in the Finnish-American press. Most of them have since passed away and only their correspondence remains. As my knowledge of this subject area deepened, these letters have grown in importance, as has my regret for not being able to connect personally with them when they were alive.

Identifying how components in the large body of accumulated information were connected has been the final and most difficult stage of this work. My ability to discern the value of information only improved with experience. It had been too often that data or sources that I dismissed earlier proved ultimately to be important. One regrettable example of this was in 1991, when I had the opportunity to meet 90-year-old William Syrjälä during a concert trip to Florida with the *Ameriikan poijat* septet. At that very early stage of my research work, I had no idea who Syrjälä was, and so I declined an opportunity to meet with him. This contact might have changed the course and tempo of my research considerably. I had thought, "Why would I be interested in talking to an old dance band musician who wrote fiddle tunes? What could he possibly have to do with brass bands?"

It was not until the notice of his death two years later that I awakened to the temporal dimensions of this research, and my need to make haste with still-living witnesses. Syrjälä is included in the Chapter 4 discussion of Finnish bandmasters.

Interviews

I conducted the interviews with people who could share some personal experiences about Iron Range bands, who were descendents of bandsmen, or who were regional historians with knowledge important to this study. A list of those contacts follows here:

Robert Ahola, son of William Ahola, was keeper of several souvenirs and papers of the conductor.

Bill Haavisto, a retired farmer in Sturgeon Township, from a pioneer family and has memories of hearing and seeing the Sturgeon Finnish Band when he was a child. He was in his nineties when interviewed.

Helmer Hanka, retired engineer, was active with the Embarrass Town Band with founder Neilo Hakala in the 1920s and 1930s. He was in his nineties when interviewed.

Clarence and Eila Ivonen are active leaders in the Virginia Finnish community and are knowledgeable about the history of the *Valontuote* temperance society, which had a band.

David Kess, an active Ely historian, is from a musical family and has done research and writing about musical life in Ely.

Lyle Klein was band director in the Ely public schools for many years. He wrote on the history of bands in Ely. (Klein's master's degree paper on the band history of Ely is at the Bemidji State University Library Archives).

Gladys Koski Holmes, granddaughter of John Wilenius, Jr.
Harry Lamppa continues to be an active researcher at the Virginia Historical Society. A native of Embarrass, Minnesota, Lamppa keeps an interest in Finnish immigrant music, although he is not a band instrumentalist.

Robert and Richard Latvala of Nashwauk had relatives who played in the early bands of the town.

Mary Ellen (Kleemola) Levander, the granddaughter of Charles Kleemola. She retains most of the findable historical materials related to him.

Marvin Loff was an active tuba player. He grew up in Bovey, where he played under Hemming Hautala. Marvin had had lifelong contacts with many other Iron Range musicians.

Sally Parviainen, daughter of John Paananen, founder and bandmaster of the Eagle Lake/Cromwell Finnish Socialist Band. Sally had childhood memories of the active band life around Cromwell as well as photographs.

Milt Stenlund ,the son of a Sampo Band member who played under Charles Kleemola in Ely during the 1910s. His father also played with the Scandia Band in Ely. Milt has the only example of an Iron Range Finnish brass band uniform thus far found.

Bea Tamminen, a retired schoolteacher from Nashwauk, had memories of some of the Finnish-American band activity from the early 1900s. Ms Taminen was in her nineties when interviewed.

James Trembath, a member of the Tower-Soudan Historical Society, and had shared the Society's archives and photographs for this research. Though he had no contact with brass bands, he reminisced about life in the multi-ethnic Iron Range towns.

John Wilenius, Jr., the son of the first Sturgeon Finnish Band leader. He also played in the Sturgeon Finnish Band. He was in his eighties when interviewed.

Leo Wilenius, John's brother. He had memories of the Sturgeon band as well as some photographs and documents. He was in his eighties when interviewed.

Leo Wiljamaa, a retired schoolteacher from the Iron Range, knew many of the Finnish-American bandmasters who worked as music educators in the St. Louis County schools. He was in his nineties when interviewed.

Most of these interviews were first recorded on audiocassettes and then transcribed. Some interviews were not recorded due to technical difficulties. Some interviews were supported by the pre-and post-interview written correspondence and telephone conversations.

My work in collecting memories about Finnish bands did have precedent. In the 1980s, Alaine Pakkala conducted important interviews with older Finnish musicians, primarily from Ohio and Michigan.[3] Her interviews are collected on seven audiocassette tapes, which she labeled: "Humina Band Memories" (Ohio), May 8, 1987, and June 18, 1987; "Interviews with Mr. and Mrs. Hjerpe" (Ohio), Nov 6, 1982 and Nov 8, 1982; "Interviews with Luoma,

Paananen, Mustonen, and Lake" (Michigan), undated; "Interview with Paul Mackey" (Ohio), 1982; "Interviews with Rudy Kemppa and Ed Haapa" (Michigan), 1984; and "Interview with Ernest Koski" (Superior, Wisconsin), Dec. 29, 1983. Koski had been an active member of the Iron Range Finnish Socialist bands and his story is discussed in Chapter 3. These tapes are the only known interviews with active participants of the golden days of the Finnish-American band movement. The tapes have not been transcribed.[4]

Internet Sources

A detailed list of Internet sources used in this research can be found in the bibliography. Because the information needed for this thesis crosses over many areas of knowledge, there is no one crucial site or source. As you read this, it I scertain that the cyber world has changed since this writing and the resources will have new names and possibilities.

For general bibliography searching, OCLC for "FirstSource" with "WebCat" were the most thorough. This "Online Computer Library Center" is an international library co-operative with 45,000 member libraries in 84 countries. FirstSource is a commonly used search mechanism for browsing literature and other media about any subject. "ArticleFirst" will search periodicals. I searched FirstSource for available references on practically every category that came to mind, from brass history to Minnesota community anniversary booklets. "Webcat", one of the tools within FirstSource, yielded the most valuable summaries of the publications I needed. In specifically musical inquiries, RILM Abstracts were also a choice within FirstSource. These sites also yielded information about foreign language publications. OCLC is available only through libraries that subscribe. If a publication is on the shelf of one of the 45,000 member libraries, it is listed in OCLC. Since the Library of Congress is a member, this resource is thorough.

Regarding websites related to Minnesota history, I primarily used the Minnesota History Center and the Immigration History Research Center at the University of Minnesota. The IHRC is integrated with the University of Minnesota Library System (LUMINA). The libraries at the Ironworld Research Center, Iron Range Historical Society, the Finlandia University Heritage Center, and others, have not yet put their complete holdings in online catalogues.

I conducted Finnish and Minnesota genealogy searches primarily through the sites FinnGen, Hiski Project, and RootsWeb. These are all large websites with many features and bountiful information. They also are the starting point for chat groups that pursue specific inquiries. Searches for Finnish

[3] The tapes are in the Alaine Pakkala Collection at the Immigration History Research Center (IHRC) Archives, Elmer Anderson Library, the University of Minnesota.

[4] Alaine Pakkala collection, IHRC.

immigration history and genealogy of immigrants can also be pursued through the Institute of Migration in Turku, Finland *(Siirtolaisuus-instituuti)*.

There are numerous websites for learning about Finnish culture and history. A useful starting point is the home page of the Finnish Embassy in Washington, D.C. Information on almost any Finnish musical subject can be found starting from the comprehensive home page of the Sibelius Academy in Helsinki.

Brass band culture worldwide accounts for hundreds of websites. A starting point is the home page of the Harrowgate Brass Band (England). It has very useful links and seems to be well maintained, with the link addresses being current.

For Finnish brass band research, both the University of Helsinki Library and the Finnish War Archives can be searched online, but some knowledge of the Finnish language is very useful. Both institutions have staff that speak English and can assist with an inquiry.

Electronic mail correspondence has been a regular component of my contact with all of the institutional research sources, as well as with private contacts. That correspondence archive continues to be a valuable source of information worthy of frequent review. I have maintained an archive of all important email correspondence related to this research, and I have revisited it frequently for information or clarification.

Archives

Having much of the research archives essential to this work available in Minnesota has been a convenience. Housing many vintage books, photographs, newspaper microfilm, and primary source materials, each institution has some collections of special interest and was somewhat distinct from the others.

The **Immigration History Research Center** (IHRC), is housed at the Elmer Anderson Library, University of Minnesota, Minneapolis; The IHRC contains the largest archive of Finnish-Americana in the United States. Research materials collected over several decades, as well as consolidated collections from many sources, were of great value to this study. Rare materials, such as the papers of Kaups, Pakkala, and Riippa, are housed at the IHRC. The IHRC has an extensive collection of published literature on Finnish immigration and Finnish-American culture, including some old and rare volumes. Unique to these archives are the sheet music collections of Finnish bands from Northern Minnesota and elsewhere in the United States. Photographs, correspondence, society minutes, and ledgers are examples of primary material found here. The IHRC has one of the only inventories of early Finnish-American newspapers on microfilm.

Minnesota History Center, the archive of the Minnesota Historical Society **(MHS)**, St. Paul, provides access to statewide microfilm of newspapers, death indices, alien registrations, and immigration documents. The document archives had material on Iron Range activity including biographical information, old books, and the minutes and archives of various Finnish social organizations. The History Center houses nearly all books, videos, and sound recordings that have been published in Minnesota, or have content about Minnesota subjects. Some older publications, such as Eugene Van Cleef's "The Finn in America" (Duluth, 1918), cannot be found in any other collections.

The **Ironworld Research Center (IRRC),** is located in Chisholm, Minnesota, and has been the destination for much older, historical material from Iron Range communities of all ethnic orientations. The photograph collection at IRC is substantial, but it is often difficult to use since much of the identification and source data is incomplete. It houses early drafts (written in Finnish) of Hans Wasastjerna's "History of Finns in Minnesota," in addition to most of the original material from the Minnesota Finnish-American Historical Society used in the compilation of his text. That collection of papers has many personal letters and other documents that are of unique value to immigrant historians. Not all of the material collected was included in the published history.

Unfortunately, very few of the Wasastjerna book's photographic originals are included in the IRRC's collection. It may be that the author borrowed most of the photographs, subsequently returning them to personal family collections. The IRRC also has a nearly complete inventory of early Iron Range English language newspapers on microfilm (although some important early Hibbing papers are absent). I noted that IRRC has a more convenient viewing facility than the far more heavily used microfilm library at the Minnesota History Center in St. Paul.

The Northeast Minnesota History Center (NMHC), is located at the University of Minnesota-Duluth. It has a useful collection of published books, periodicals, and monographs about Iron Range history. Much of its material is duplicated in other institutions, but the NMHC is a very convenient and easy-to-use facility. I was able to access older books on Iron Range history (including Polk directories) and some important papers, such as Syrjämäki's thesis on Iron Range social conditions.

The Iron Range Historical Society (IRHS), is located in the old town hall in Gilbert. It is particularly rich in material about the towns east of Virginia, such as Eveleth, Biwabik, Palo, Gilbert, and Aurora. It is also the repository for the extensive Lee Brownell Collection of old photographs from Ely and other Iron Range towns. Brownell was an avid historian, collector, and son of a town musician who also had been a photographer. That collection is primarily of photographs taken by his father. Occasionally, however, Brownell the younger, or others, speculated incorrectly on a photograph's identification, so interpretation of his material must be done carefully. The IRHS archive was most helpful with its information about Victor Taipale and his early activity in Eveleth. It houses a large collection of books, newspapers, a complete set of Polk Directories, and other memorabilia.

Virginia Area Historical Society Archives, primarily contain information about the City of Virginia and nearby villages. Harry Lamppa, a local resource, has also research interests in homesteading, labor history, Americanization of Finns, and has collected material about these subjects from all over Northern Minnesota. The Society's photograph collection is of great interest. These archives helped with documentation about the relationship between Finnish bandsmen in Virginia and the municipal band.

The Ely-Winton Historical Society Archives, is located at the Vermilion Community College in Ely. It has a large collection of photographs, although many of them are not well identified. Information about musical groups and Finnish communities is not as extensive as it is in other archives, but the facility is nonetheless important for learning about Ely, the first community with Finnish musical groups on Minnesota's Iron Range. Most of the important paper documents about musical life in early Ely appear to still be in private collections.

The Hibbing Historical Society, is located in the Hibbing Community Center. It houses a very large collection of material in the process of being re-shelved and re-catalogued. It is rich with information about Hibbing musical groups, especially the Hibbing City Band. Housed in the same building is the old Hibbing City Band music library, one of the very few old Iron Range band libraries still intact. These resources helped to clarify information about William Ahola, and to identify Finns who played in the Hibbing City Band.

Finlandia University (formerly Suomi College) houses the **Finnish-American Heritage Center and Historical Archives** in Hancock, Michigan. This is a major archive of older books and documents about Finnish immigrant life and culture. Between the Finnish Heritage Center in Hancock and the Immigration Research Center in Minneapolis, copies of most existing vintage publications on Finnish-American subjects can be found. I found most books and periodicals cited in the earliest bibliographies of Ilmonen and Kolehmainen on Heritage Center shelves. This facility holds the very oldest music manuscript books for brass bands to be found in North America. It contains such unique items as a press-clipping scrapbook from the Louhi Band (Pennsylvania) tour of Finland in 1920. Their photographic collection is quite large, but does not include Minnesota to the extent of facilities mentioned here. The Heritage Center's photographic collection is not well documented as to source and subject.

Recordings

There are no known recordings made of the Finnish brass bands from Minnesota in the early 1900's.[5] The *Louhi* Band in Pennsylvania did make a small number of early 78- RPM discs, perhaps because they were located closer to recording studios and had made contacts more easily. These recordings, as do the others made at the same time by the *Helsinki torvisoittokunta* (Helsinki Brass Band), give us rare audio samples of the Finnish brass band sound. They are contemporary with the early John Philip Sousa and Arthur Pryor band recordings. Since the Minnesota Finnish bands were often prizewinners in national contests, they probably played at a similar level of skill as the Finnish bands that made recordings.

Much of the Finnish popular music recorded in the early years featured a vocalist accompanied by a wind band. Because of the directional clarity and intensity that brass and woodwind instruments gave to recordings in the pre-electronic "Victrola" era, they were favored over strings, piano, and other soft-toned instruments. In listening to an early Finnish recording standard such as Juho Koskelo's *"Porilaisten marssi"*[6] from 1911, the background ensemble is clearly a brass band. These vocal recordings present a reliable resource for understanding brass band performance style, even though they are not exclusively band recordings.[7]

The band instruments are in the background of many early Finnish-language vocal solo recordings made both in Finland and in the U.S. Although some of the 78-RPM discs that feature singers were recorded somewhat later than the 78s of the early Louhi Band, or the *Helsinki Torvisoittokunta*, the playing style and quality seem consistent. After World War I, the popularity of sound recordings expanded, and post-World War I is a rich source of information about Finnish-American popular music. However, recordings of strictly band music are not found in Finnish or Finnish-American 78-RPM catalogues much after 1920. That is also the time when the accordion became favored for vocal recordings, and technology improved to allow for better fidelity recordings of violins, guitars, and other softer instruments.

Listening to the many village brass bands in Finland today provides a sense of how early Finnish bands sounded as they arrived in Minnesota. The traditions of such bands in Finland are treasured and preserved. In many cases, the basic repertoire has hardly changed.

Although portable recording equipment was known to be used around the Midwest in the early 1900s, little was done with Finnish immigrant music in Minnesota until the 1930s, by which time the brass bands were mostly extinct.[8] It is not known why the great Finnish bands of Ely, Virginia, Eveleth, or Hibbing were never recorded. The Louhi Band of Pennsylvania that recorded in 1918 was thought to be the premier Finnish band in America at the time, well connected with the Sibelius Club, and about to go on tour to Finland. Yet, the level of playing of many Finnish-American bands, based on testimonials of witnesses and on contest results, suggests that there were other excellent groups that certainly would normally have been recorded.

---

[5]However, the "Finnish-American Elite Choir" from Duluth recorded three two-sided discs on June 16, 1913 (Victor disc numbers 65418, 65419, and 65420). The recording location is not known. Information is from the Finnish Archives of Recorded Sound, Helsinki.

[6]March of the Pori Brigade is a well-known march in Finland, anonymous and probably 18th Century.

[7]Koskelo, Juho: 78-RPM (Edison 11555), *Porilaisten marssi*, Finnish Archives of Recorded Sound, Helsinki. Recorded June 1, 1911 (probably in New York).

[8]Personal conversations in January 2003, with William Shaman, sound recording historian and archivist, Bemidji State University Libraries.

The following table identifies all known early recordings of Finnish music performed by Finnish-American or American bands. "Early" is defined here as "before 1920".

Table A. List of Known Early Finnish-American Band Recordings (chronological)

78-RPM Disc Artist Name	Contents	Record Label and Number	Location and Date
Columbia Orkester	Side 1: *Hedersvakten* Side 2: *Finska rytteriets marsch*	Columbia E392	Berlin, 1904
The Columbia Band	Side 1: *Itkevä huilu* (Juho Koskelo, Tenor) Side 2: unknown, but probably band piece *Elomme Päivät*	Columbia E708	12/12/1910
Military Band	Side 1: *The Royal Gotta Military Band," Eisngraber* (?) Side 2: *The March of the Björneborgs*	Columbia 2862	1916
Juho Koskelo Tenor, and the Columbia Band	Side 1: *Merellä* (Juho Koskelo, tenor) Side 2: *Kesäilta valssi* (Columbia Band)	Columbia E3433	1917
The Columbia Band	Side 1: *Finnish Polka* Side 2: *Finnish scotch* (Schottisch?)	Columbia E3376	1917
Soittokunta Louhi, Pennsylvania (Louhi Band, Pennsylvania)	Side 1: E pluribus Unum March (composer Lauri Koski) Side 2 *Kesäpäivä kangasalla* (popular Finnish folk song)	New York No. 764	1918
Soittokunta Louhi, Pennsylvania Soittokunta Pryor (Arthur Pryor Band)	Side 1: *Maamme* (Finnish National Anthem) Side 2 *Pois rannoilta Suomen* (Finnish national song)	Victor 72203 Victor 72203	7/5/1918 11/20/1918[9]
The Columbia Band	Side 1: *Rakastetuni polkka* Side 2: *Äidin ja isän valssi*	Columbia E4351	1919-1920
The Columbia Band	Side 1: *Joosepin häät polkka* Side 2: *Suununtai iltapäivän valssi*	Columbia E4525	1920

The Juho Koskelo vocal recording found at IHRC (E3433) has the Columbia Band performing Merikanto's *Kesäilta valssi* on the second side (see Figure 37). Most of Koskelo's recordings have *"orkesteri säästy"*, or ensemble accompaniment. The size and instrumentation of the accompaniment may have varied, but these recordings sound like a wind band. His first use of accordion accompaniment appears to be in 1923. It is not known what the Finnish connection to the Columbia Band was, or if the Columbia Band was merely a group of American musicians doing session reading for that day's production.[10] The Columbia Band is also the named group for several other recordings of Swedish music in the "E" series of ethnic recordings on the same label.

[9] From Finnish Broadcasting Archives (http://www.yle.fi/aanilevysto), Gronow has July 1919 listed as the recording date.
[10] Columbia's "E" series were just one example of the recording industry's interest in producing "ethnic" recordings for the American and European markets.

The reverse side of the second Victor disc (see Table A) was performed by "*Soittokunta Pryor*", which would seem to be the famous Arthur Pryor Band[11] This is certainly possible, for the Pryor Band was called upon to record many works. It is not known why they recorded a Finnish folk song, and why the Louhi Band was not doing it in this instance. Record companies would often reissue recordings in various languages, for the foreign and immigrant markets. That, however, would be expected of a musical selection that the Pryor Band had already released to the English-speaking American market, which is not true for this case. Why they made a recording that apparently was not intended for the broader American market remains a mystery. Thus far, queries of the Library of Congress and the Finnish Broadcasting Archives suggest that all copies of this recording seem to be lost, and no data from sound recording historians has resulted in any further information.

Bands were in some of the very earliest commercial recordings. The many recordings of early brass bands made in Finland are valuable and accurate representations of the original Finnish brass band sound, although only a small number of them are available to the public today. The most extensive recording activity by any Finnish style brass band in the early 1900s was by the *Helsinki torvisoittokunta* (Helsinki Brass Band), conducted by former military bandmaster Alexei Apostol, and populated by former military musicians.[12] The recordings included some players who were in this band and then later emigrated to America. Between 1904 and 1912, the *Helsinki torvisoittokunta* recorded 121 sides with 89 titles. Appendix H is an index of those recordings. The larger Finnish brass band instrumentation ceased to exist after Apostol's *Helsinki torvisoittokunta.* The more standard band of mixed instrumentation then became popular in Finland. Unfortunately, no one has thus far tried to revive the original Finnish brass band instrumentation, even if only to experience the sonorities these old scores would produce. This old brass instrumentation, called "*normaalivanha*" or "regular old fashioned' by Finnish researchers, is discussed in more detail in Chapters 1 and 5.

Later in the 20th Century, other Finnish brass septets continued to record. *Otava*, a Finnish brass septet that was active in recording and broadcasting for Finnish Radio in the 1930s, produced some 78 RPM discs that can be found in collections such as those in the Folk Music Institute in Kaustinen, private collections, and at Finnish Broadcasting (YLE). Such groups had members from among the professionals in Helsinki at the time: members of the Helsinki Philharmonic, Opera Orchestra, and other such ensembles. Olavi Lampinen, trombonist with the Helsinki Philharmonic and professor at the Sibelius Academy, formed a septet in the 1960s and produced a 33.3-RPM long-

[11]The Arthur Pryor Band, performing mostly in Philadelphia, was formed in 1903 and continued regular touring until 1909. After that, The Pryor Band continued to play the various summer seasons in Philadelphia, with winters in Miami. In the off-season, the band was busily engaged with enlarging Victor's growing record catalogue. The band continued until 1933, when Pryor retired (from notes by Daniel F. Frizane and Frederick P. Williams of Crystal Records).
[12]See Appendix X, a complete list of *Helsinki Torvisoittokunta* recordings.

playing album. I bought a used copy at a Finnish festival in Florida in 1991, although the LP had been out of print for more than twenty years.[13] The Lampinen group played on conventional orchestral instruments, and the sonority is more like an expanded modern brass quintet than of the old "cornet family" sound heard on earlier recordings.

Since 1980, many groups in Finland have released septet recordings, usually privately produced. An index of these recordings is an appendix to Kauko Karjalainen's book on the Finnish brass septet (Karjalainen, 1995:144). If still available, these recordings are usually obtained from the performers directly, often through Internet web sites. Additional information about recordings of Finnish bands can be found in the section on performance style in Chapter 5.

Newspaper Archives

Older newspapers, both on microfilm and on paper, have been important sources of information for many aspects of this research. Information about musical activity and about how Finnish musicians and bandmasters came in and out of communities has been difficult to find from any other sources. Because these newspapers, both in English and Finnish, began publishing at about the same time or just after musical groups were formed, there is often no press record of some band's very earliest years. These newspapers often also reported on activities in other regional communities, causing the same events to be noted in several regional papers. Finnish-American papers would often report on activities across the entire Lake Superior region, into Michigan and Ontario, and across the nation.

Table B includes the names of important local and regional papers that covered Finnish immigrant musical and cultural activity, and the date when paper started publishing. The comparisons of the dates when newspaper publication started, with the dates when communities were formed, and with the starting dates of Finnish and municipal bands, it is revealed that a rapid pace of development in Iron Range culture was occurring just before 1900. This table is organized from earliest to the latest start date of publication. None of these Finnish papers is published today,[14] and some of the English papers have stopped publishing, or combined with other papers under new names.

[13] Olavi Lampinen Septet: 14200 *Grams of Brass,* Blue Master LP, (BLU-LP 103), 1967.
[14] However, there are currently several Finnish-American newspapers published in North America, including one in Minnesota (the *New World Finn*)

Table B. Early Finnish and American newspapers that provided information

Newspaper	Lang.	Location	Start Date
Vermilion Iron Journal	E	Tower	1887
Ely Iron Home	E	Ely	1888
Amerikan Suometar (the American Finn)	F	Hancock, MI	1889
Työmies (Workingman)	F	Ishpeming, MI	1889
Ely Times	E	Ely	1890
Duluth News Tribune	E	Duluth	1892
Siirtolainen (Immigrant)	F	Duluth	1893
Virginia Enterprise	E	Virginia	1893
Hibbing News	E	Hibbing	1894
Ely Miner	E	Ely	1895
Eveleth Star	E	Eveleth	1895
Virginian	E	Virginia	1895
Uusi Kotimaa (New Homeland)	F	New York Mills	1897
Hibbing Daily Tribune	E	Hibbing	1898
Eveleth News	E	Eveleth	1902
Pâivälehti (Daily Journal)	F	Duluth & Calumet MI	1903
Chisholm Tribune	E	Chisholm	1904
Itasca Iron News	E	Bovey	1905
Amerikan Kaiku (American Echo)	F	Duluth	1906
Eastern Itascan (Nashwauk Herald)	E	Nashwauk	1910
Biwabik Times	E	Biwabik	1907

Avallarie is a complete index of newspaper articles that specifically relate to the research for this thesis. In general, the English language newspapers can be found on microfilm at the Minnesota History Center and the Iron Range Research Center. The most complete collection of Finnish language microfilms is now at the Immigration History Research Center. Finnish newspaper microfilms are also at the Finnish-American Heritage Center in Hancock, at the University of Michigan, and at the Migration Institute in Turku, Finland. The Minnesota History Center has a microfilm collection of all the Finnish language papers ever published in Minnesota, as well as all English language papers.

Literature Sources

Books, articles, and other written resources for this study mostly fall into the following general classifications:

- Finnish music history and general history. The bibliography for this thesis shows a particular eye for sources on Finnish music culture and Finnish brass bands. A related area of reading has been brass band history throughout continental Europe, especially in Germany, Imperial Russia, and Sweden as well as in Finland.

- Immigrants and immigrant culture, especially Finns in Minnesota.
- Minnesota Iron Range history, with a particular emphasis on musical, educational and cultural issues.

There is currently very little published research regarding Finnish music in America, whether about bands or choirs or otherwise.[15] In fact, there is only a "handful" of published works on the general subject of immigrant band music from any culture. Two useful starting points are Victor Greene's *"Passion for Polka" Old Time Ethnic Music in America*, and Margaret and Robert Hazen's *The Music Men, an Illustrated History of Brass Bands in America,* both of which have some passages about immigrant brass bands.

A landmark event for enthusiasts of Minnesota Finnish cultural history was the publication of "*History of the Finns in Minnesota*" by Hans Wasastjerna, published by the Minnesota Finnish-American Historical Society, in both Finnish (1957) and English (1959) versions. This important book, even with its many serious flaws, has been both a starting point and sometimes 'the final and only word' for various elements of this thesis. The information Wasastjerna presented was uneven in detail and was very dependent on the quality of whatever the local community sources provided him. He was chosen by the Minnesota Finnish-American Historical Society to assemble a book on the history of Finns in the state. His book is organized mostly by the geographical regions, although it includes some sections about general subjects such as "temperance" or "the co-operative movement". There are many references to musical activity, but these usually omit much of the kind of detail that would be helpful to this research. Musicians or their descendents were apparently not generous in their contributions of information for the Wasastjerna book. In addition, a Finnish band's political or social affiliations could easily have influenced whether its story was either submitted or included in any such a community history. In the midst of the McCarthy era it was a delicate a time for Finnish socialist or communist groups on the Iron Range to bring attention to themselves in print, even for a functioning band, or even if any such band was no longer in existence. Many of the Finnish bands in Minnesota that still existed by mid century had socialist affiliations. Since most of the Finnish bands were long gone by the 1950's, not many people remembered the historical details or kept any records. For many bands, my research has been dependant on whatever information the Wasastjerna text provided.

15Joyce Hakala's book about the Kantele (plucked zither) is one notable example:" Memento of Finland: A Musical Legacy", St. Paul, Minn.: Pikebone Music, 1997. The other is Kenneth A Swanson's monograph about Laestadian Lutheran church music: "Music of two Finnish-Apostolic Lutheran Groups in Minnesota: the Heidemanians and the Pollarites" Minneapolis: University of Minnesota, Dept. of Music, 1971.

Wayne State University press published a new English translation of Armas Holmio's *History of Finns in Michigan* in 2001. This book, written originally in Finnish in the early 1960s, was inspired by the earlier publication of the Wasatjerna Minnesota history. Holmio organized his book around historical themes, such as "temperance" or "socialism", and he documented a far broader geographic scope than merely Michigan. The text contains many elements of value to this study, and includes frequent references to Minnesota. I particularly recommend this book because of Dr. William Hoglund's extensive preface. Hoglund's essay is the most important modern-day overview of Finnish-American historical scholarship and would be a necessary first-read for any scholar wishing to approach the subject.

The only study previously done on the specific subject of Finnish band music in America is Alaine Pakkala's paper presented at the University of Michigan as a part of a Music Education degree in 1984. *The Instrumental Music of the Finnish-American Community in the Great Lakes Region, 1880-1930* is, in part, a general history of the role that wind bands played in Finnish-American communities and in organizations from New York to Montana. Its emphasis, however, is more on bands from the Ohio and Pennsylvania regions. At the time of writing, in the 1980s, it is probable that information that is more primary was available from those communities than from other regions. Pakkala includes some background information about several bandmasters and players, though only a few of those are connected to Minnesota. The Pakkala bibliography has some parallels to John Kolehmainen's Finnish-American music bibliography, which is mentioned below. A good deal of the latter half of the text is a general Finnish-American discography along with other elements, though interesting, not directly related to the subject suggested by the title.

Other important books about Finnish-American history include William Hoglund's *History of Finnish Immigrants in America-1880-1920*, a summary of the Finnish immigrant experience from coast to coast, with a few references to music culture. Salomon Ilmonen's "*Suomalais-Amerikan historia*" (The History of Finnish-Americans) is a multi-volume history in Finnish, completed in installments during the years between 1910 and 1930. Timothy Laitala Vincent has been translating some portions of Ilmonen's work into English. The volume on community histories is now complete (Ilmonen, Salomon: *The History of Finnish-Americans,* Volume III: 1998, Salt Lake City, UT.) Ilmonen compiled his historical writing during the decades when older Finnish cultural activity (such as bands) was still very widespread. Nevertheless, he admits in this early book that a lot of information was already lost and forgotten at the time he wrote, because so few records were kept. If Ilmonen was finding only incomplete information as early as 1910, it seems a rather formidable task for me to attempt to gather much new information now! It appears that all these Finnish-American historians relied upon good citizenry for information. The result is that, with musicians not very forthcoming, the detailed information about music and bands is all too rarely included in any of the histories.

The Finns in America, a bibliographical guide to their history by John Kolehmainen, (Hancock, MI, 1947.) is the best of the bibliographies that cover the eras of my study. Kolehmainen was the most prolific and respected Finnish immigration historian of his day, and he gives us a very comprehensive list, with an entire section devoted to musical materials. Almost all the texts and papers that he cites can still be found at the Finnish-American Archives at Finlandia University, and at the Immigration History Research Center at the University of Minnesota.

Judy Johnson's "A selected bibliography of primary and secondary sources about the Finnish experience on the Iron Range" (Chisholm, 1989) reviews the Finnish archival holdings of the Ironworld Center. The IRRC collection includes numerous unpublished transcripts, interviews, and papers, but it also includes periodicals, a pamphlet index, and a list of Iron Range communities with historical files at the Center. Ironworld's extensive library of published works and dissertations on Finnish subjects is not included in the Johnson bibliography, but would be a useful addition.

There are numerous community histories and anniversary books done by Minnesota's Iron Range towns and other American communities with Finnish heritage (such as Calumet, Michigan; Astoria. Oregon; Ashtabula Heights, Ohio; Monessen, Pennsylvania; Fitchburg, Massachusetts; and Finntown-Brooklyn, NY). These books occasionally provide information about Finnish immigrants who may have known about or played brass band music. The Bibliographical Information section includes a list of such community booklets from Minnesota.

Some academic research papers have been very valuable sources, often telling the histories of school bands or community bands of the Iron Range. Mark Widstrand's "Biwabik City Band," a Master's paper at the University of Minnesota, has yielded some information about Victor Taipale. Three Masters' degree students attending Bemidji State University during the 1970s produced similar papers: "A History of Bands in Buhl Minnesota," by John Pustover (1972), "A History of the Hibbing Municipal Band," (1972) by Arthur M Hill, and "A History of Instrumental Music in Ely Minnesota" (1977) by Lyle Klein.

Clayton Tiede's doctoral thesis, *The* ***Development of Minnesota Community Bands during the Nineteenth Century,*** Ph.D., Musicology, University of Minnesota, 1970, does not discuss band activity in Northern Minnesota. It does not offer much information about ethnic brass bands in Minnesota other than the numerous German bands. However, it is an excellent and detailed history of brass bands in Minnesota during the decades after the Civil War, with particular emphasis on Mankato, St. Peter, Minneapolis, and St. Paul. These 19th Century Minnesota bands preceded the Finnish migration by several decades, so the Tiede study's period is too early to have a direct connection with Iron Range bands. Yet these older brass bands, some connected with Fort Snelling, laid traditions in band music that were felt by all Minnesotans including the immigrants and their bands in later decades.

When the Finns arrived in the north, brass bands had already been an ongoing activity in most southern Minnesota cities, as well as in other American communities from which the many American-born newcomers to the Iron Range came. Tiede's thoughts on the connection between the old Minnesota brass bands and their communities is a very detailed explanation of an interaction and interdependency.

Scholars of Finnish America have been, for a century, prolific writers about immigration issues. No doubt, it has been the favorite subject for research and publication for numerous Finnish-American social scientists. John Syrjämäki's earlier doctoral thesis: *Mesabi Communities-a study in their development,* (Yale, 1940) is an important early study for learning the background of immigrant group interaction, the role of public schools, and ethnic organizations on the Iron Range. The *Finnish Experience in the Western Great Lakes Region: New Perspectives* is a series of papers presented at the first conference on Finnish Migration Studies, (Turku Finland, 1975) and indicates the start of a research revival in the subject. *They Chose Minnesota: A Survey of the State's Ethnic Groups*, edited by June Drenning Holmquist, 1981, includes Timo Riippa's excellent article on the Finns and Swedo-Finns. Arthur Puotinen's book *Finnish Radicals and Religion in Midwestern mining towns, 1865-1914* (NY, 1979), and Carl Ross' *The Finn Factor in American Labor, Culture and Society* (New York Mills, MN, 1977) help explain the sociopolitical turmoil that characterized Finnish immigrant life in the newly forming communities. The social conditions had a direct effect on the function and form of the brass bands in those communities. The subject most often written about, "literally tons of articles, too numerous to mention"[16] is that of Finnish political radicalism. This topic is directly connected with the Finn Bands, but it is also part of an important chapter in greater Minnesota political history, including a contribution to the formation of the Democratic-Farm-Labor Party.

Minnesota in a century of change: the state and its people since 1900, edited by Clifford E. Clark, Jr. (1989) includes Arnold Alanen's informative essay, "Change on the Iron Range." William E Lass *Minnesota: A Bicentennial History* (1977) also discusses the position of the Iron Range within the state's history. Contemporary materials from the era in question, such as Walter Van Brunt's "Duluth and St. Louis County Minnesota, Their Story and People" (1921) and Leggett and Chipman's "*Duluth and Environs: Historical, Biographical, Commercial and Statistical Record* (1895)," and Hodges' "Report on immigrant life and institutions" (1909) give us interesting views of the place and the time.

Public school education on the Iron Range developed extremely quickly and has been a subject of some study. Berman, Smith, and Chambers, University of Minnesota professors, wrote a series of studies in the 1960s on social wel-

[16]Karni, Michael, personal correspondence, 1996.

fare and education issues on the Iron Range. See the bibliography for citations of these mostly unpublished works. The important research about the Iron Range done by these scholars precipitated a large collection of material that eventually became the Immigration History Research Center.

A series of papers called *"Scandinavian immigrants and eduction in North America"* edited by Philip Anderson, Dag Blanck and Peter Kivisto (1995) includes two papers on Finnish immigrant education. They have little to say about musical topics but they describe the Finns' efforts to educate their own children in language and religious values, and they also describe the challenges of public education for immigrant children.

Photographic Evidence

In the course of this research I have viewed many hundreds of photographs, and have collected about 250 digital images about Minnesota Finnish bands, and another 150 about Finnish bands from other regions in the United States. They were collected initially as background study material but have become a vital component. Because the bands were visible in festive and ceremonial settings, with their shiny instruments and splendid uniforms, the brass bands were often photographed. Other artifacts and documents, such as newspaper clippings, correspondence, and sheet music, have not done as well in surviving into the 21st century. Photographs have remained in comparatively fine condition, being more durable than other paper material, and perhaps they have been stored more carefully in the closets and attics. It seems that photographic images retain an importance among descendents that is often not extended to other artifacts.

Photographs always present important information and impressions, although too often photographic images may be the *only* physical object documenting a band or a musician. While some brass band photographs may have information about the date, location, occasion, and personnel, it is equally likely that no such additional supporting information can be found anywhere. Also unfortunate is that sometimes, incorrect or speculative information was added to the back of a photograph later, and has since been found to be inaccurate.[90] Therefore, the use of photographs as historical evidence is not without its problems.

Print media has convinced us that photographs can be evidence of authenticity, making a powerful contribution to what the critic Roland Barthes (1969:141) has called the 'reality effect.' The photographer's predisposition will influence the image, possibly skewing its relationship with reality. Hodges' report (1909) on immigrants in the Iron Range includes many of his own photographs of working and living conditions in that year though they seem

[90] For example, several subsequent citations added to original photos in the Brownell Photo Collection from Ely, now kept at the Iron Range Historical Society in Gilbert, have proven to be erroneous.

to dwell on negative or critical scenes that reinforce his pre-concepts. These images were not falsified, however, but were merely focused on certain scenarios that interested him, surprised him, or fulfilled his predetermined mission as an Immigration Inspector. Burke (2001:25) defends photography as "evidence of the material culture of the past." a position that supports this study's use of photography to give good evidence about clothing, instruments, performance sites, personnel, and other relevant details about the bands. Wasastjerna's text has numerous photographs of bands, usually supported with very little textual information. These omissions may have been because either the author did not have access to further information or, because his editorial tendency was to tacitly admit, "images often show material culture that people at the time would have taken for granted and so failed to mention it." (Burke, 2001:99) Wasastjerna's judgment may have been that the photograph spoke clearly and needed no further elaboration. If he had more information, he chose not to include it.

The creator of a photographic image or other representational art usually has an agenda to project to the viewer. What may also be revealed, unintentionally, are some important subtleties that may or may not have been observed by the photographer: "So far as the history of material culture is concerned, the testimony of images seems to be most reliable in the small details. It is particularly valuable as evidence of the arrangement of objects and of the social uses of objects, not so much the spear or fork or book in itself but the way to hold it"(Burke, 2001:103). It is notable that Burke makes no distinction between photography and the other graphic arts as vessels of cultural information, but puts them all on the same plane. Alan Trachtenberg (1989: 251-252) supports this idea that photographic imagery comes from the beholder, in the same way as a painting: "A photographer has no need to persuade a viewer to adopt his or her point of view, because the reader has no choice: in the picture we see the world from the angle of the camera's partial vision, from the position it had at the moment of the release of the shutter."

My research led me quickly to the study of old Finnish-American band photographs because few sources were as rich with information. Not all the material culture data to be gleaned from such images may be obvious upon the initial examination. With repeated study, the images seemed to grow in informational value. I have never yet felt completely done with the study of any band photograph. Going back always reveals new things for me. The discovery of newly revealed photographs has had an influence on how previously studied examples are interpreted. Burke (2001:185) states what has become obvious to me, that "The testimonies of the past offered by images are of real value, supplementing as well as supporting the evidence of written documents. Their testimony is particularly valuable in cases where texts are few and thin."

The use of a digital scanner has not only been very helpful for collecting and preserving photographic images, but has also assisted with information gathering through various editorial modifications. For example, by enlarging the view or by enhancing image contrasts I have found new data, such as an obscure band logo on a hat from a blurred image in the photograph's corner, or an instrument brand name. My collection of digital photo images for this study will continue to be a resource for new information as I examine them further with an increasingly more learned scrutiny.

Recognizing faces in band photographs has been useful for classifying an unidentified photograph, for such information as date, location, occasion, as well as personnel. A set of photos from the Virginia Finnish Socialist Workers' Band, taken a couple years apart with slightly different personnel, still helps me to identify those players who appear in both.

Figure 61: Virginia Finnish Workers' Band, ca. 1907. Antti Tiikkainen, in center with baton, is the bandmaster. No other members are identified here. Photograph courtesy IRRC-Chisholm.

Wasastjerna writes that the Virginia band pictured in Figure 61 started out as a Finnish band at the same time as the Virginia City Band, and was made up mostly of Finns who were not members of the City Band. The band's name was "Jyrinä" ('rumble' or 'roar') and was, at first, a politically independent group that played for both socialist and temperance activities in the Virginia Finnish community, and sometimes the occasional Slovenian funeral. Note the unusual percussion mallets in the bass drummer's hands: he holds a bass drum wooden mallet (right hand) and a hoop-like device that makes a suspended cymbal sound, much like a crash cymbal (left hand). While these percussion tools do not appear in instrument dictionaries, Raoul Camus notes that such cymbal clashers were common in marching bands in the early 1900s. Such solutions were necessary when one drummer was obliged to sound like a full percussion section, with snare drum, bass drum, and cymbals.

[17]From correspondence with band historian Raoul Camus, May 2003.

It is likely that the trophy cup (in foreground) is from a Finnish-American summer festival of that year.

Figure 62: Virginia Finnish Workers' Band in 1910. Photo courtesy IRRC

Figure 62 also shows the Virginia Workers' Band. This photo has a roster, which was useful in identifying some of the players in Figure 61 through facial comparisons. This later photograph clearly shows the trend toward enlarging bands with woodwinds. Nevertheless, this 1910 photograph shows the band keeping Finnish traditions rather strongly, and remaining a FABB (defined earlier). Antti Tiikkainen again sits in the middle with his baton (and euphonium). The group is larger than the one shown in the 1907 photo, although it has many of the same members. Available name lists designate the clarinetist and drummer as two "unknowns". My speculation is that the two men are Virginians of other ethnic backgrounds. Known names in this photographs are: Front row: Sulo Löyvä, Isak Wälmä, unknown, Alfred Tasti, John Nykänen. Second row: Yrjö Helin, John Forsman, Antti Tiikkainen (the bandmaster), Tuomas Pakarinen, and Konstu Sarell. Top row: William Mäki, Mikko Koski, Hjalmar Linstrom, unknown, Julius Jalkanen, John Markkonen, and unknown (but apparently Italian) drummer. It is not known why the band was not dressed in uniform in other photographs. Although a "Finnish Workers' Band," the participation of an occasional Italian or Slovenian seemed normal.

Both of these Virginia Finnish Workers' Band photographs are from a collection of Virginia photographs at the Iron Range Research Center in Chisholm. Although the pictures' original source is obscure, they were thought to have been collected at the time of the compilation of the Wasastjerna history in the 1950s. Figure 61 appears in his book, where the names were found.

Modes of dress, instrumentation, and background settings help clarify the otherwise incomplete information from a photo. A Virginia City Band photograph at the Olcott Park Bandstand shows two important Finnish-American bandsmen, Victor Taipale and Charles Kleemola, as playing members. In Figure 63, their faces are easily identifiable, though no name list accompanies it. Even though this photograph (from the Kleemola family collection) has no text on the front or back, we know it is the Virginia City Band because of the easily recognizable band shell. Olcott Park today has a bandstand in the same location, a newer model that looks very much like the original.

Figure 63: Virginia City Band ca. 1910, Frank Meehan, Director. Taipale, as a cornetist, is in the top row (fifth from the right); Kleemola is a cornetist in the second row (second cornetist from the right). Kleemola's brother, a trombonist, is also in this photo, as are several other Finnish players. Photograph courtesy of Kleemola family collection.

The playing style and tastes of the musicians and their leaders also become clearer through the photographs. One photograph of the Raju Athletic Club Band from the early 30s shows an obvious effort to revert to an older, traditional Finnish brass band model with exclusively brass band instrumentation. Yet, another photo of the same band taken earlier shows a younger group with modern American band instruments.[18] Such a curious juxtaposition of instrumentations and dates is confusing.

Figure 64: The Raju Hall Athletic Club Band in 1926. Photograph courtesy IRRC.

In Figure 64, the man in the center with the baton appears to be the bandmaster, John Anderson, but the other persons in this photo are not identified. However, we can try to compare the faces and instruments in Figure 64 with those in Figure 65, with some duplication. While the passage of a couple of years between photographs makes facial matches less than definite, the Finnish music community in Cromwell was so small that a reasonably close match is quite enough. A comparison with Figure 12, the Cromwell-Eagle Lake Band, seems to also yield some important matches with several of the same people.

On first glance, one might identify Figure 8 as the older of the two photographs, with the all-male and nearly all-brass instrumentation common to the old-style Finnish septet. Figure 7 seems newer, or more modern, with woodwinds, a French horn, and women musicians. The Cromwell Raju Athletic Club Band's history during those four to six years is not well-recorded, but the photographs reveal some significant changes: the band seems, surprisingly, to be moving away from the American band model and toward the 19th-Century Finnish brass septet format. We do not know how long the "Raju" band continued, but it is certain that it stopped by the beginning of World War II. The sponsoring Raju Club disbanded in 1953, at about the same time that the House of Representatives' Un-American Activities Subcommittee began to study such left-leaning groups with more scrutiny.

[18] Figure 63 shows slide trombones, a mellophone, and a clarinet, none common to the FABB. The number of women players is also notable.

Figure 65. The Raju Hall Athletic Club Band in early 1930s. Bandmaster John Anderson does not appear in this photograph. Names from the back of photograph: (from left to right, standing) John "H". Peter Peterson, John "R". Wäinö Koskinen, Abel Laine, Arvid Kastell; (from left to right, sitting) John Korpi, Matt Paananen, Mike Mononen, Sulo Väsinoja. Photograph courtesy Parviainen family collection.

While most of the collected photos for this study have come from larger public archives, private family collections have also yielded important finds, especially photos from the descendents of Stenlund, Kleemola, Paananen, and Ahola. A collection of memorabilia from the family of William Ahola included the unique photograph of William as a young bandsman in Hibbing. Together with the photograph was a packet of other material, including some newspaper clippings, a lease certificate for a cornet from the C.G. Conn Company, and the actual cornet itself in its case. This is one of only four instruments preserved from the Finn band era in Minnesota I have found. The C.G. Conn Company's lease arrangement may have been typical for the time, although no such documents have surfaced for other Iron Range musicians thus far.

In many of the archives, material has been stored and catalogued in whatever organizational format it was received in. Seeing material in its original condition is very valuable to the researcher because a collection's organization (even in a randomness) can reveal information about the internal relationship of the contents. Unfortunately, photographs and documents have often been separated from other materials and catalogued in a different manner from the original configuration. This leaves many photographic subjects unidentified, or potentially mis-identified. IRRC, for instance, has a very large collection of photographs, and negatives that were donated by regional communities, historical societies, or individuals and often with limited supporting documentation. Two other examples show how original, "archeological" information becomes lost and unavailable to the researcher for learning about the material: both the University of Helsinki Library and the Immigration History Research Center at the University of Minnesota received collections of old band music in their original storage cases. The music was removed from the cases and reorganized in archival boxes. Not only the organization of the musical material, but also the old containers themselves, offer important information about the contemporary status of the material. Having studied the materials in Helsinki and Minneapolis at first in their original state with the original containers, and then later in standard archive boxes, I can say that such archeology is an element of this research process that archivists sadly seem to be ignoring.

The photograph in Figure 66, donated by the Lehto family of Virginia, shows an interesting but anonymous Finnish baritone horn player. Knowing the likely source of this photograph, it would be easy to assume this player was with some Virginia Finnish band. However, an enlargement of the image reveals that the musician was a member of the Monessen, Pennsylvania Louhi Band (see chapter 3). Nothing is known about him, such as if he traveled between Pennsylvania and Minnesota. How the original materials were organized, what any other photographs may have been associated, and the order in which they were received with other material (such as paper documents), may have revealed more information on his identity or his connection with Monessen. All of this associated information is probably lost. One ray of hope is that numerous donations to the archives remain on shelves as received, and have not yet been processed. Perhaps future efforts to process such historical material can keep in mind this important archeological organization as a factor when it is formally processed.

Figure 66: Photo of euphonium player from the Lehto/Virginia collection. Player and date unknown. Photograph courtesy IRRC, Chisholm.

Such portraits as in Figure 66 were often made as gifts and souvenirs for friends, and should not be interpreted as necessarily representing the image of a solo musical artist, or representing the idea that the fellow would ever play his euphonium in any other setting but with a band.

The photograph in Figure 68 was accompanied by limited documentation. The design of the uniform conforms to that shown in other group photographs of the Cloquet band. This was the only clue in the photograph about Jokela's band affiliation. No other information about this photograph has been found thus far. However, it is tempting to compare this photograph with Figures 32 and 33 and speculate if Anton Jokela is posing in either.

Figure 67: Enlargement shows the Louhi name on the hat

It is unfortunate that photographs are often stowed away for decades, brought out for examination only "immediately after the death of a close relative, usually the person who could have answered the question you face upon discovering the photos"(Frisch-Ripley, 1991:6). I have regularly shared my photograph collections with those I interview in the course of this research. In several cases, my photographs have triggered others' memories or led to other contacts and discoveries. I have found it useful to inform my sources and colleagues about what I have found and what shape the research is taking, and remind them that their contributions are important and need to be acknowledged. There has been a danger, however, of soliciting responses from interviewees that they felt might be more satisfying to me. That concern, combined with my need to inform my sources about my line of inquiry, may have at times been in conflict. However, the photographs have been, in general, powerful conversation pieces in arousing memories during interviews.

Figure 68: Anton Jokela, a cornetist with the Cloquet Finnish Temperance Band. Undated. Photograph courtesy of IRRC, Chisholm.

The application of iconography and graphics for musicology and ethnomusicology is not a new idea, but it has traditionally been more focused on the pre-photographic era (Slobin in *Imago Musicae*, 1989:129). While it would seem that photographs of music-making in pre-recording eras would be the most valuable, Slobin points out that picture artifacts of immigrant music from any era are of great value, in that "they serve as a gateway into the internal ethnic world that groups construct as a part of their self-conception." This position may be partly true for the early Finnish-American bands, but many of their photographs seem to indicate a desire to present an American, or at least international, model of the brass band. No Finnish brass bands on either side of the Atlantic ever wore traditional folk costumes, or played anything other than quite standard instruments. Their image, in both uniforms and formations, is in keeping with an international style that could be found in almost any country. It would need a trained eye to spot any ethnic peculiarities in such a brass band, and such determinations might well be based as much on the surroundings as on the subjects of such a photograph. What little we know of the photographers who took these Iron Range pictures is that some were Finnish immigrants and some were not.[19] Perhaps the most telling photographs of Finnish ethnic bands are the rarely found informal shots taken spontaneously, such as in Figures 71-73.

Figure 69: Cromwell-Eagle Lake Finnish Socialist Band, ca. 1930. Seated from left to right: Sulo Väsinoja, Oscar Hill, John Korpi, John Paananen, and bandmaster. Standing from left to right: John Oberg, Hjalmar Hoglund, Mike Mononen, Abel Laine, and John Anderson. Photo courtesy Toivo Tamminen.

A richly charactered example of a posed shot is the photograph of the Cromwell-Eagle Lake Socialist Band, which elicits a different impression for the observer than the more formal, posed photos.

Figure 69 shows the old traditional Finnish band septet instrumentation and a model from before 1900, but here being played in the 1930s. By this time, most Minnesota Finnish bands had adopted the American-style mixed instrumentation. It seems that the players are political leftists with a taste for old Finnish tradition. Yet, musical skills always took precedence over society affiliation when the membership for the bands in smaller communities was determined. These were farmers, forest workers, and businessmen whose faces appeared in pictures of various bands that formed in a community. Thi photograph shows a group with pride, seriousness and yet a casual bucolic demeanor quite opposite the formal poses of, for example, the Virginia Finnish Socialist Band.[20]

Old photographs of the Finnish immigrant bands, along with those of choirs, theater groups, and dance groups, are important indicators of the community's cultural values at that time. Slobin's (1989:129) observation, that immigrant ethnicity is a two-part process, is confirmed by our example, and there is constant tension between "maintaining ethnic boundaries or choosing to tear them down in the face of mainstream pressure."

Hodges' candid photograph of the Virginia Socialist Band on foot (Figure 70) is a contrast to the posed pictures of the same group, and more closely resembling the Cromwell band's casual image. Hodges had a non-ethnic eye with a possible prejudice toward creating a negative impression[21] , and avoiding any idealism in the shot. It is one of the very few un-posed band photographs I have found. It is one of twelve photographs taken on a day when Hodges attended a Finnish Socialist rally in Virginia. In his immigration report, he includes no text about this, or about any other bands.

These bandsmen apparently are just starting to assemble for an event. Because the coats are still buttoned and ties tied, I speculate that they have not marched or performed yet. It is probable that at least some of the musicians shown here were also posing in the other photographs of this band.

[19] A particularly well-known Iron Range Finnish photographer from the early 1900s, Erick Anttila traveled from Virginia around the region making family portraits, photographs of farmsteads, and groups. It is not known if any collection of his photographic negatives or prints still exists. It is likely but not certain that many of the Minnesota photographs referred to in this thesis were made by Anttila.

[20] See Figure 58

[21] My opinion based on the text of his Immigration report

Figure 70: Hodges' own caption: "Members of the Band, Socialist Meeting Grounds, June 24th, 1909". Names are unknown, but Antti Tiikkainen could be on the left. From Hodges, 1909, p. 127.

Information confirmed or revealed by a photograph can be quite convincing, even though that picture may raise as many new questions as it answers. An example under study often is an image posed in an artificial setting. There is value in studying both the posed photograph under controlled conditions and the candid photograph with random results, although they should be approached differently. We must try to understand the mindset of both the photographer and the photographed. This study's use of photography has been very valuable, but it has not always been a very direct or clean process for gathering information. The photographic medium traditionally tends to foster a posed presentation of an ideal. For the era in question, those accidental, candid exposures of bands are extremely rare. Three notable examples, from Ellen Niemi's family album, are shown below (Figures 14, 15, and 16). All photographs show the Hibbing Socialist Band at a Midsummer picnic concert, and were taken informally, probably with an old Kodak box camera. They show bandsmen on a day of celebration, when their participation is clearly valued and when their music making is an integral and expected part of the day's activities.

Figure 71: Hibbing Socialist band midsummer concert. Photograph courtesy Ellen Niemi collection.

Figure 72: Hibbing Socialist band midsummer concert. Photograph courtesy Ellen Niemi collection.

Figure 73: Hibbing Socialist band midsummer concert. Photograph courtesy Ellen Niemi collection.

These photographs are candid snapshots from a family album sent to me as the family was clearing out old boxes. Knowing the source, I am certain they were taken at one or more midsummer Finnish festivals in the Hibbing area, but the year or years, are unknown. These rare and pleasant candid images say much about the happy atmosphere that was often associated with the Finnish bands playing for festivals. Figure 71 shows some smiling Finnish musicians holding American-style trumpets, a slide trombone, a bass drum, and a mellophone.[22] Figure 72 is more difficult to understand, partly because the image is a bit unclear. While the seated drummer is discernable, other musical instruments are not easily seen. I imagine that the row of three men with their backs to the camera is a row of trumpet or cornet players. I also surmise that the man in the white jacket facing the camera is the bandmaster, probably the same Antti Tiikkainen pictured earlier. Figure 73, and probably taken following the Midsummer performance, showing the young musician father with his tie unfurled and jacket unbuttoned. Mother and child look ready to end the festivities and head home. There are unanswered questions, such as, "Who was wearing the uniform hats?" "Who was not?" and "Why?" Perhaps the three photographs really are from different years. They are nevertheless full of thought-provoking imagery, suggesting much about the joy of music making and the status of bandsmen in the community.

Research in Finland

The contact I had with Finnish research sources was indispensable in the completion of this work. Three active Finnish researchers in brass band history that I have known for many years are Kauko Karjalainen, Simo Westerholm, and Jukka Vuolio. Karjalainen's (1995) book is cited. His approach has been as a musicologist who also is a brass player. He was the first to compile general information on Finnish brass band history and have it published. Westerholm, from the Kaustinen Folk Arts Institute, is primarily an ethnomusicologist but sees the Finnish brass septet as a legitimate part of Finnish folk culture. Vuolio is a Finnish military music historian and writes primarily about the military bands, their instrumentation, personnel, and leaders. Together, the work of these three give the scholar a broad view of brass band history in Finland.

Musicologist Pekka Jalkanen's book *"Alaska, Bombay, ja Billy Boy"* (1989) about the rise of jazz culture in metropolitan Helsinki, traces the brass band's early participation in Finland's popular culture and social dance music, and then the negative effect of the emergence of jazz orchestras on that old brass culture.

[22] A mellophone was often used in American amateur bands as a close cousin to the French horn, but less expensive and easier to play. As for the "American-ness" of having trumpets, an older-style Finnish band would have only cornets instead.

Several conferences on the general theme of "Changes in Finnish Music Culture" were presented in the 1980's with many papers then published in anthologies as the first modern scholarship about old Finnish brass bands (Leisiö 1985 and Kurkela/Valkeila 1982). Many of the scholars contributing to those early conferences (Vuolio, Kurkela, Karjalainen, Leisiö) have continued to do research and publishing on the subject. All of the material is in Finnish.

The Department of Musical Anthropology at the University of Tampere has recently been the host for a large national research project about 19th and 20th century Finnish music history. Current knowledge about brass bands and folk music culture has been included in the project's purview.

Paavo Talvio's pamphlet on Finnish military band history was the first work of its kind containing some information about the Finnish bands of the earliest years. However, the pamphlet focuses mostly on the era after 1917 independence, and therefore does not have direct value to my research except the first few pages.

During my travels to Finland over the past twenty years, I have found extensive material on Finnish brass band history in the archives listed below. These holdings are rich collections of original music manuscripts, with both scores and parts, in addition to other paper archives.

- The Finnish Military Archives in Helsinki (Suomen Sota arkisto)
- The University of Helsinki Library Music Manuscript Collection
- The Sibelius Museum archives (the music archives of the University of Turku-Åbo Akatemie) in Turku. The Sibelius Museum is the musicology library of the University of Turku (Åbo Akatemie)
- Finnish Broadcasting Archives-Helsinki.
- The Finnish Folk Institute and Instrument Museum in Kaustinen
- University of Tampere (National Folk Culture Research Center)

These Finnish visits have also taken me to many communities who have their own band archives and music collections. These included the larger cities of Turku, Tampere, Kuopio, Jyväskylä, Helsinki, Rauma, and several smaller villages. Information from these collections has been useful for my understanding of the earlier military music and village brass band activity experienced by the Finnish bandsmen who later came to America.

Individual band libraries and archives that I visited included:

Mänttä Village Band, Mänttä
Turku Workers' Band, Turku
Tampere Workers' Band, Tampere
Center for Musical Anthropology, University of Tampere
Finnish Folk Arts Center, Kaustinen
Helsinki Brass Band-*Helsinki Torvisoittokunta-*

Kronoby Hornkappelle, Kronoby
Jyväskylä Brass Band, Jyväskylä
Hyvinkääkylä Brass Band, Hyvinkää
Kuopio City Museum, Kuopio

The music catalogues of the Finnish Guards Band of the late 1800s were a project that I completed in 1999. These catalogues have provided valuable information about the repertoire available to Finnish brass bands during the years just before and during their emigration to the United States. These indices are available on line.

Organization of this Work

This study has focused on several specific goals: (1) describing music and culture among the newly arrived Finnish immigrants to the United States, (2) putting this musical activity into the context of the economic, social, and geographical setting of the ethnic communities, (3) describing the intermingling of music cultures within and among new immigrant groups and with the American-born community, (4) tracing the evolution of immigrant instrumental music from its arrival as a relatively intact cultural entity to its ultimate diffusion into the plural American community, and (5) describing the integral role of Finnish bandmasters and players in the development of instrumental music programs in Iron Range schools and towns.

Learning about the musical training of the players and bandmasters has been an important element of this study. Many important contemporary examples of the sheet music and the teaching materials are included here to help illustrate the resources of the era. As both teachers and students, many of the Finnish immigrant brass players were a part of the music education process that evolved on the Minnesota Iron Range. Their participation, both in the schools and in the wider community, is described in several sections with the most detail in Chapters 3 and 4.

I initially hoped that the presentation of this material would follow a neat, chronological flow in which all events and characters fit in their proper place. There have been some exceptions to this hoped for model. Discussed in detail later, these exceptions include the band leaders who emigrated here decades earlier than the main migration, as children, and were completely integrated into the American band movement in spite of a Finnish heritage; the players who arrived in America and immediately joined non-Finnish community bands; and the bands who formed as late as the 1930s, using the older Finnish septet instrumentation rather than the prevalent American model adopted by most FABs at that time.

In spite of these exceptions, the general organization of the historical portion (Chapters 1 through 3) follows a chronological format that fits most bands under consideration, starting from “the brass band in Finland” to the “brass bands among Finnish immigrants in America,” and the ”Finnish bands and bandsmen in Minnesota". The concluding chapters review social, political, and educational roles within their communities and the bands’ repertoire and performance practices.

Because so much of the Iron Range social environment was newly formed and still evolving as the Finns settled, the communities in question were rapidly changing and pushing the bands to adapt to new needs and tastes. This basic material in this study examines the more important communities and personalities that played a part in the Finn Band legacy, and how these social groups affected the community at large.

APPENDIXES

Appendix A: A Catalogue of the Victor Taipale Collection in the Helsinki University Library

An octavo-sized leather case was found at the Helsinki University Library (MMus 98) in March 1999. It contained an assortment of scores and parts that were the property of Victor Taipale during his years in America. The leather case was American-made ("MW" trademark). The contents have since been repackaged in an archive box. The contents of that case is listed below.

A letter from the Consulate Office in New York to the University (1959)
New York Pääkonsulinvirasto 14 Loka, 1959

Pääkonsulinvirasto lähetää kunniotivasti Ulkoasianministeriölle tämän mukana jäljenöksen kunsuli Harri Virjon 9.10.1959 päivystä kirjeestä, josta käy selville, että suurin osa Victor Taipaleen kirjastosta on hävitetty, mutta ovat perilliset luvanneet luovutta jäljellä olenav materiaalin Detroitissa olevalle Suomen kunniakonsulille. Pääkonsulinvirasto palaa asiaan. Seppo Pietinen

A letter to the Consulate Office in New York (1959), from Detroit Consul Harri Varjo.
Pääkonsulaati- New York:
Re: No 4550/J 30765–Victor Taipale

Olen puhunut uesampaan otteeseen Taipale-veljestan kanssa. Suurin kirjastosta on havitetty.

Jack Taipale on kuitenkin luvannut lahitulevaisuudessa tuoda toimistooni mita on jäljellä. Niinpakuin saan jaamiston haltuuni lähetän sen teille.
Kuulema mitä in jäjellä on arvokkain osa kirjastosta. Harri Virjo, Konsuli. Detroit, Lokakuu 9, 1959

Parts found for the **salon orchestra** include Violin 1,2, Cornet A (B), Trombone treble clef, and piano.

ID #	Scoring	Description/Title	Composer	Arr	Dates	Comments
01		Muistoja Pispalasta valssi 9				
02	?? Cornet	30 vuotisen sodan marssi	X	x	x	Single march-size sheet (back of above)
03	?? Cornet	Kirkas Tähti	X	x	x	Single march-size sheet (back of above)
04	Band Carl Fischer band edition	Swedish Guard March	Lovander	x	x	March-size edition, six parts found
05	Band Carl Fischer band edition	Björnaborgaren March	X	x	x	March-size edition, six parts found
06	Band: Solo Cornet/Cond	Lyric Overture	Mackie (Mäki) Beyer	(JW Pepper, pub)	1935	No other parts
07	Band? Basso B	Rotsing Marssi!	X	X	x	Single march-size sheet
08	Salon Orchestra	Sun Haltuus rakas isäni valssi	?	Taipale	?	4 parts found
09	Salon ork	Unkarin valssi 1	X	x	1926?	Newspaper date in folder
10	Salon ork	Mandolin polkka 2	X	x	1926?	Newspaper date in folder
11	Salon ork	Fanny Schottis 3	X	x	1926?	Newspaper date in folder
12	Salon ork	Mazurkka 4	X	x	1926?	Newspaper date in folder
13	Salon ork	Mabel valssi 5	X	x	1926?	Newspaper date in folder
14	Salon ork	Kengät kuluu polkka 6	X	x	1926?	Newspaper date in folder
15	Salon ork	Meren rannalla sottis 7	X	x	1926?	Newspaper date in folder
16	Salon ork	Sanna mazurka 8	X	x	1926?	Newspaper date in folder
17	Salon ork	Polkka 10	X	x	1926?	Newspaper date in folder
18	Salon ork	Mustalais schottis 11	X	x	1926?	Newspaper date in folder
19	Salon ork	Mazurkka 12	X	x	1926?	Newspaper date in folder
20	Salon ork	Kvåsar valssen 13	X	x	1926?	Newspaper date in folder
21	Salon ork	Iso Polkka 14	X	x	1926?	Newspaper date in folder
22	Salon ork	Schottis 15	X	x	1926?	Newspaper date in folder
23	Salon ork	Elsi Mazurkka 16	X	x	1926?	Newspaper date in folder
24	Salon ork	Älä unhoita minua valssi 17	X	x	1926?	Newspaper date in folder
25	Salon ork	Pariisi polkka 18	X	x	1926?	Newspaper date in folder
26	Salon ork	Schottis 19	X	x	1926?	Newspaper date in folder
27	Salon ork	Krakoviak polkka 20	X	x	1926?	Newspaper date in folder
28	Salon ork	Fox trot 21	X	x	1926?	Newspaper date in folder
29	Salon ork	Augusta two/One step 22	X	x	1926?	Newspaper date in folder
30	Salon ork	Betjaari marssi 23	X	x	1926?	Newspaper date in folder
31	Salon ork	Zuzu Two One Steo 24	X	x	1926?	Newspaper date in folder
32	Salon ork	Kulkurin valssi 25	X	x	1926?	Newspaper date in folder
33	Salon ork	Ibla Two One Step 26	X	x	1926?	Newspaper date in folder
34	Salon ork	Fox trot 27	X	x	1926?	Newspaper date in folder
35	Salon ork	He lei no Kailuni Valtz 28	X	x	1926?	Newspaper date in folder

ID #	Scoring	Description/Title	Composer	Arr	Dates	Comments
36	Salon ork	Porzueona Vals 29	X	x	1926?	Newspaper date in folder
37	Salon ork	Suru valssi 30	X	x	1926?	Newspaper date in folder
38	Salon Orkesteri, 5 pts include piano, vln	Härmän Polkka 1	X	x	Monessen Pa, 5.5.1925	Octavo MS, in large black folder, 10 pieces
39	Salon Orkesteri, 5 pts include piano, vln	Vanha Saksan Polkka 2	X	x	Monessen Pa, 5.5.1925	Octavo MS, in large black folder, 10 pieces
40	Salon Orkesteri, 5 pts include piano, vln	Ylipään Schottische 3	X	x	Monessen Pa, 5.5.1925	Octavo MS, in large black folder, 10 pieces
41	Salon Orkesteri, 5 pts include piano, vln	Talitit Tattit 4	X	x	Monessen Pa, 5.5.1925	Octavo MS, in large black folder, 10 pieces
42	Salon Orkesteri, 5 pts include piano, vln	Mustalaispojan Polkka 5	X	x	Monessen Pa, 5.5.1925	Octavo MS, in large black folder, 10 pieces Note name: Elis Ranta
43	Salon Orkesteri, 5 pts include piano, vln	Nurmon Polkka 6	X	x	Monessen Pa, 5.5.1925	Octavo MS, in large black folder, 10 pieces
44	Salon Orkesteri, 5 pts include piano, vln	Polkka Mazurka 7	X	x	Monessen Pa, 5.5.1925	Octavo MS, in large black folder, 10 pieces
45	Salon Orkesteri, 5 pts include piano, vln	Elimäen Polkka 8	X	x	Monessen Pa, 5.5.1925	Octavo MS, in large black folder, 10 pieces
46	Salon Orkesteri, 5 pts include piano, vln	Isoo Antti Rannanjärvi Schottisch 9	X	x	Detroit Mi, 15.3.1926	Octavo MS, in large black folder, 10 pieces
47	Salon Orkesteri, 5 pts include piano, vln	Mä Meripojast' iloisesta laulun tein 10	X	x	Detroit Mi, 15.3.1926	Octavo MS, in large black folder, 10 pieces
48	Salon Orkesteri, 8 pts include piano, vln	Nujulan Talkoopolkka	X	x	X	In salmon folder
49	Salon Orkesteri, 8 pts include piano, vln	Pikku poika schottische	X	x	X	In salmon folder
50	Salon Orkesteri, 8 pts include piano, vln	Kulkurin valssi	X	x	X	In salmon folder
51	Salon Orkesteri, 8 pts include piano, vln	Orpopojan valssi	X	x	X	In salmon folder
52	seitsikko	Kvåsar Vals	X	x	X	MS loose sheets in black folder
53	seitsikko	Saetergjentens Söntag	Bull	x	X	MS loose sheets in black folder
54	seitsikko	untitled march	X	x	X	MS loose sheets in black folder
55	Seitsikko (all parts found)	Raatikkon Marssi	X	x	X	John Wirkkala small black folder: small sheets
56	Seitsikko (complete)	Kirkkomessut, Päätösmessut	X	x	X	Small sheets

ID #	Scoring	Description/Title	Composer	Arr	Dates	Comments
57	Seitsikko- 11parts	Suomen laulu	Pacius	Taipale	31.3.1903	March-size, MS, all parts found.
58	Seitsikko I Kor B	Yli maiden ja merien march	X	x	X	Single sheet, in paper folder
59	Seitsikko II Kor B	Yli maiden ja merien march	X	x	X	Single sheet, in paper folder
60	Seitsikko- parts only	Parad Marsch	W, P. ?	x	X	March-size, MS, all parts found.
61	Seitsikko, all parts	Porilaisten marssi	Wegelius??	Taipale	Hibbing, Mn 17.5.1905	Octavo size paper
62	Seitsikko, all parts	Tuulan Tei		Taipale	Hibbing, Mn 17.5.1905	Octavo size paper
63	Seitsikko, all parts	Koraali No 310		Taipale	Hibbing, Mn 17.5.1905	Octavo size paper
64	Seitsikko, score and parts	Zigeunerlied	X	Hedman	1901	Oulu, written out by K A Sarviranta in larger black folder
65	Seitsikko, with extra parts	Reppurin Laulu	Merikanto			Small sheets, in large black folder
66	Seitsikko: Album of Finnish pieces	Häämarssi, Maame laulu, etc	Five books found: Kornetti B I, Baritone B, Kornetti Ess, Basso Ess, Altto Ess		1904	Tästä kirjasa soitettu entinen 7nen H L Tarkk'ampuja Pataljoonan 4nen Komppanian 3nen Plutonan Torven soittaja pääsy pois pataljonasta Tammuk 31 päivä 1896, ja se oli iloinen Hetki. Entinen B Basson soittaja ja nykyään 1 Kornetin soittaja Frivlightissa, Tammikuu 14 pv 1904, Emil Mäki
67	Seitsikko: KVS stemmat seitsikkolle	1897 Mikkeli ohjelma, stemma vihkot	3 books complete: Tenori B II, Tnori B I, Altoo Ess		1904?	Kornetti B 2- "Tästä kirjasta soitelee entinen 7nen H.L Tarkk'ampujan Patal. 4 kompp. 3 patal. Torven soittaja päässy pois Tammik 31 Pv 1896.ja se on iloinen hetki. ENTINEN BBASSON SOITTAJA JA NYKY¨AN 1 KORNETTIN SOITTAJA FRIVILIGHTISSA, Tammikuu 1904
68	Seitsikko: MS score	Saksan polkka	?	?	?	No watermarks on paper, two sheets, loose
69	Seitsikko: one Ess bass part	Sotilaspoika, Karjalaisen laulu, Jumala ompi linnamme, Suomen laulu, Maame	Pacius etc	??	X	GW signature at bottom, large format sheet. Wahlstrom?

ID #	Scoring	Description/Title	Composer	Arr	Dates	Comments
70	Seitsikko: Tenor B	Yli maiden ja merien march	X	x	X	Single sheet, in paper folder
71	sketch	unidentified (a march?)	X	x	X	Arranging sketch, pencil and ink.
72	Soittokunta (13 pts found)	Mustalaispojan polkka	X	x	X	Loose pages, many cut to very small size
73	Soittokunta (17 pt)	Työväen Marssi	Merikanto/	Taipale	1910	Ashtabula harbor Aug 15 1910
74	Soittokunta (17 pt)	La Marseillaise		Taipale	1910	Ashtabula harbor Aug 15 1910
75	Soittokunta (extra parts for clarinets	Saetergjentens Söntag	Bull	x	X	Four extra loose sheets, Kvåsar vals not included
76	Soittokunta- 13 pts found, clarinets	Ruusu laaksonen	W.B.	x		Small sheets, found in large black folder
77	Soittokunta 14 pts	Rukous	x	Taipale	2.7.1910	Three church pieces on one sheet
78	Soittokunta 14 pts	Koraali no 21	x	Taipale	2.7.1910	Three church pieces on one sheet
79	Soittokunta 14 pts	Jumala ompi linnamme 153	x	Taipale	2.7.1910	Three church pieces on one sheet
80	Soittokunta 8 pts	Jo Joutin Arma Aika 472	x	Taipale	16.8.1938	Single piece on school music paper
81	Soittokunta incomplete pts	Koraali nos 12,21,100, 349	x	x	X	Scoring list on cover sheet
82	Soittokunta, 18 parts, include clarinets	Kirkas Tähti	x	Taipale	1904, Hibbing	Single march-size sheet, found in large black folder

Appendix B: Index of Finnish-American Bandsmen in Minnesota

If a Finnish immigrant bandsman came from a Finnish military band, that information is noted in column three. Sources for the information gathered below are abbreviated in column seven as follows: "W"= Wasastjerna's *History of Finns in Minnesota*, "Lager"= correspondence with the late Dr. Finny Lager, "Carlton"= the Carlton County Historical Society, "Toivo" = Toivo Tamminen, "Shirley" = Shirley Parviainen, "MEL" = Mary Ellen Levander, "IRRC"= Ironworld, "IRHS"= Iron Range Historical Society, "Hibb"= Hibbing Historical Society, EMN, "MDN"= Mesaba Daily News. Some names are repeated, if they had multiple affiliations.

Last	First	Military	Minnesota	Info date	Immigration date	Source	L.P
Anderson	Mary		Aurora Finnish Socialist Band	1910		W	P
Arvinen	Victor		Aurora Finnish Socialist Band	1910		W	P
Hendrickson	Yrjö		Aurora Finnish Socialist Band	1910		W	P
Korpela	Wallace		Aurora Finnish Socialist Band	1910		W	P
Korpela	Isaac		Aurora Finnish Socialist Band	1910		W	P
Lahti	John		Aurora Finnish Socialist Band	1910		W	P
Laukkonen	Nestor		Aurora Finnish Socialist Band	1910		W	P
Manner	Victor		Aurora Finnish Socialist Band	1910		W	P
Mattila	Frank		Aurora Finnish Socialist Band	1910		W	P
Mononen	Esa		Aurora Finnish Socialist Band	1910		W	P
Niemi	David		Aurora Finnish Socialist Band	1910		W	P
Niemi	Matt		Aurora Finnish Socialist Band	1910		W,	P
Oja	Hilma		Aurora Finnish Socialist Band	1910		W	P
Oja	Andrew		Aurora Finnish Socialist Band	1910		W	P
Rengo	Matt		Aurora Finnish Socialist Band	1910		W	P
Wainio	August		Aurora Finnish Socialist Band	1910		W	P
Viitanen	Antti		Aurora temperance band, Minn.			W	P
Walma	Isaac		Aurora temperance band, Minn.			W	P

Last	First	Military	Minnesota	Info date	Immigration date	Source	L.P
Laupiainen	Jalmar		Aurora temperance band, Mn			W,	P
Niemi	Matt		Aurora temperance Minn. 1910		1906	W	L, P
Ahola	Oskar		Bovey Finnish Band	1909		Lager	P
Koski	Martti		Bovey Finnish Band	1909		Lager	P
Mottonen	Victor		Bovey Finnish Band	1909		Lager	P
Ruuhela	Severus		Bovey Finnish Band	1909		Lager	P
Miettinen	August		Buhl Town Band			IRRC	L
Haapanen	Henry		Calumet 1886 Finnish Band			W	L
Hulme	JG		Chisholm Finn Socialist		1913?	W	P
Hermanson	Helmer		Chisholm Finn Temperance			W	P
Koivunen	Alex		Chisholm Finn Temperance		1913	W	L
Hautala	Hemming		Chisholm, Hibbing,		1909	W	L P
Hoffren	Aksel		Cloquet Finnish Band	1910		Carlton	P
Jukola	Anton		Cloquet Finnish Band	1910?		Carlton	P
Laaksonen	Carl		Cloquet Finnish Band	1910		Carlton	P
Lukkonen	R Cornel		Cloquet Finnish Band	1910		Carlton	P
Luukkonen	Emil		Cloquet Finnish Band	1910		Carlton	P
Wikstrom	Erik		Cloquet Finnish Band	1910		Carlton	P
Kastel	Arvid	Oulu-Raahe	Cromwell Eagle Lake Band		Passport 1899 #435	W	L
Aho	John		Cromwell Eagle Lake Soc Band	1920s	0	W	L
Paananen	John		Cromwell Eagle Lake Soc Band	1920s		Toivo	L P
Anderson	John		Cromwell Eagle Lake Soc.Band	1920s		Toivo	P
Hill	Oscar		Cromwell Eagle Lake Soc.Band	1920s		Toivo	P
Höglund	Hjalmar		Cromwell Eagle Lake Soc.Band	1920s		Toivo	P
Korpi	John		Cromwell Eagle Lake Soc.Band	1920s		Toivo	P
Laine	Abel		Cromwell Eagle Lake Soc.Band	1920s		Toivo	P
Mononen	Mike		Cromwell Eagle Lake Soc.Band	1920s		Toivo	P
Oberg	John		Cromwell Eagle Lake Soc.Band	1920s		Toivo	P
Vasanoja	Sulo		Cromwell Eagle Lake Soc.Band	1920s		Toivo	P
Anderson	John		Cromwell Raju Ath Club Band	1930s		Shirley	L, P
Kastel	Arvid	Oulu-Raahe	Cromwell Raju Ath Club Band	1930s		Shirley	P
Korpi	John		Cromwell Raju Ath Club Band	1930s		Shirley	P
Koskinen	Wäinö		Cromwell Raju Ath Club Band	1930s		Shirley	P
Laine	Abel		Cromwell Raju Ath Club Band	1930s		Shirley	P
Mononen	Mike		Cromwell Raju Ath Club Band	1930s		Shirley	P
Mononen	Mike		Cromwell Raju Ath Club Band	1930s		Shirley	P
Paananen	Matt		Cromwell Raju Ath Club Band	1930s		Shirley	P
Peterson	Peter		Cromwell Raju Ath Club Band	1930s		Shirley	P

Last	First	Military	Minnesota	Info date	Immigration date	Source	L.P
Vasanoja	Sulo		Cromwell Raju Ath Club Band	1930s		Shirley	P
Laine	William		Crosby Ahti Band	@1917		W	P
Lehto	Frank		Crosby Ahti Band	@ 1917		W	P
Pelto	Arne		Crosby Ahti Band	@ 1917		W	P
Suvanto	Matti		Crosby Ahti Band	@ 1917		W	P
Talvitie	Isaac		Crosby Ahti Band	@ 1917		W	P
Ulvinen	August		Crosby Ahti Band	@ 1917		W	P
Matara	Eero		Crosby, Rice River		1906?	W	P
Lindroos	Frans	Kaarti	Duluth		1902? 1905.	W	L
Vehviläinen	Gust		Duluth Finn Socialist band	1905		W	L
Wahlberg	Matti		Duluth Finn Socialist band	1905		W	P
Mäki	John		Duluth Soc. Finn Band	@ 1913		W	P
Seppälä	Richard		Duluth Soc. Finn Band	@ 1913		W	P
Sihvola	Toivo		Duluth Soc. Finn Band	@ 1913		W	P
Vanhala	Armas		Duluth Soc. Finn Band	@ 1913		W	P
Yrjölä	Yrjö		Duluth Soc. Finn Band 1913	@1913	1902? unsure	W	P
Kellosalmi	Alfred	Lappeenranta	Duluth Socialist			W	P
Holopainen	Kalle		Duluth Socialist 1905		1913 (wrong)	W	P
Beckman	Emil	Lappeenranta	Duluth Socialist Finnish Band		1900.1902	W	P
Louhi	Joseppi		Duluth Socialist Finnish Band		1907	W	P
Castren	Oskar		Ely /Hibbing	1895		W	P
Bäckstrom	Hjalmar		Ely 1890			W	L
Farihoff	John		Ely Finnish Band	1904		W	L
Laitila	Erkki		Ely Finnish Band	1904		W	L
Liimatainen			Ely Finnish Band	?		W	L
Pyylampi	Matti		Ely Finnish Band	1904		W	L
Hendrickson	Charles		Ely Sampo Band	1907		MEL	P
Herranen	Matt		Ely Sampo Band	1907		MEL	P
Huossa	Jack		Ely Sampo Band	1907		MEL	P
Johnson	John		Ely Sampo Band	1907		MEL	P
Jylhä	William		Ely Sampo Band	1907		MEL	P
Kanniainen	Ben		Ely Sampo Band	1907		MEL	P
Koivunen	Onni		Ely Sampo Band	1907		MEL	P
Lampinen	Ed		Ely Sampo Band	1907		MEL	P
Mäenpää	John		Ely Sampo Band	1907		MEL	P
Mäki (Hulme)	John		Ely Sampo Band	1907		MEL	P
Martell	Toivo		Ely Sampo Band	1907		MEL	P

Last	First	Military	Minnesota	Info date	Immigration date	Source	L.P
Marttila	Eric		Ely Sampo Band	1907		MEL	P
Niemi (Sirppi)	Henry		Ely Sampo Band	1907		MEL	P
Paavola	Nels		Ely Sampo Band	1907		MEL	P
Partti	Toivo		Ely Sampo Band	1907		MEL	P
Partti	Theodore		Ely Sampo Band	1907		MEL	P
Pete (Perttula)	John		Ely Sampo Band	1907		MEL	P
Pietila	Henry		Ely Sampo Band	1907		MEL	P
Slogar	Anton		Ely Sampo Band	1907		MEL	P
Stenlund	Amalius		Ely Sampo Band	1907		MEL	P
Watilo	Andrew		Ely Sampo Band	1907		MEL	P
Miettunen	Nikolai		Ely, Chisholm, Duluth	1887	1888	W/obit	L
Kleemola	Kalle		Ely, Chisholm, Eveleth			W/L	L, P
Aho	John		Eveleth Finnish Band	1904		EMN	P
Härmäla	Eric		Eveleth Finnish Band	1904		EMN	P
Harris	William		Eveleth Finnish Band	1904		EMN	P
Henrickson	Toimi		Eveleth Finnish Band	1904		EMN	P
Jacobson	Filemon		Eveleth Finnish Band	1900?		W	L
Kala	Fred		Eveleth Finnish Band	1904		EMN	P
Kleemola	Matti		Eveleth Finnish Band	1904		EMN	P
Koivunen	Alex		Eveleth Finnish Band	1895		W	L
Lindberg	Herman		Eveleth Finnish Band	1900?		W	L
Maijala	Salomon		Eveleth Finnish Band	1904		EMN	P
Mäntynen	Nicolai		Eveleth Finnish Band	1904		EMN	P
Palda	Henry		Eveleth Finnish Band	1904		EMN	P
Saari	John		Eveleth Finnish Band	1904		EMN	P
Sillanpää	Nestor		Eveleth Finnish Band	1904		EMN	P
Toppila	Antti		Eveleth Finnish Band	1904		EMN	P
Toppila	Eric		Eveleth Finnish Band	1904		EMN	P
Collander	John	Häme	Eveleth Kaiku Band	1901	1899	W	L
Huru	Matti	Oulu	Eveleth Kaiku Band	1901	0	W	P
Husgafvel	Lauri	Uusimaa	Eveleth Kaiku Band	1901		W	P
Ikola	Emil		Eveleth Kaiku Band	1912	Born in U.S.	MDN	L
Kajander	Kalle		Eveleth Kaiku Band	1901	1902	W	P
Kalliolahti	Matti		Eveleth Kaiku Band	After 1912		W	P
Kauppinen	Emil		Eveleth Kaiku Band	1901	1902	W	P
Kyllönen,	A	Kaarti	Eveleth Kaiku Band	1901	1893?	W	P
Mäkivirta	Vik (Mrs)		Eveleth Kaiku Band	After 1912		MDN	P
Mäkivirta	Vik		Eveleth Kaiku Band	After 1912		MDN	P

Last	First	Military	Minnesota	Info date	Immigration date	Source	L.P
Mattson	Rikka		Eveleth Kaiku Band	After 1912		MDN	P
Öhman	Knut F	Kaarti	Eveleth Kaiku Band	1901	0	W	P
Paavola	John		Eveleth Kaiku Band	1901	1902	W	P
Parkkonen	Victor		Eveleth Kaiku Band	1901		W	P
Pehkonen	Jacob	Vaasa	Eveleth Kaiku Band	1901	1902	W	P
Penttilä	Ville	Oulu	Eveleth Kaiku Band	1901	1902	W	P
Potti	August		Eveleth Kaiku Band	1901		W	P
Rehnström	Arthur	Viipuri	Eveleth Kaiku Band	1901	1904	W	P
Ruski	Matti		Eveleth Kaiku Band	After 1912		MDN	P
Ruuhela	Henry		Eveleth Kaiku Band	After 1912			P
Saari	-- (Mrs)		Eveleth Kaiku Band	After 1912		MDN	P
Sarviranta			Eveleth Kaiku Band	1901	0	W	P
Sholund	Hilding		Eveleth Kaiku Band	1901		W	P
Sholund	Peter		Eveleth Kaiku Band	1901		W	P
Toivola	John	Häme	Eveleth Kaiku Band	1901	1903 passport # 690	W	P
Valma	Ike		Eveleth Kaiku Band	After 1912		MDN	L, P
Yrjölä	Oscar		Eveleth Kaiku Band	1901		W	P
Miettinen	August		Eveleth Kaiku, Aurora		1911?	W	L, P
Eklund	Waldemar	Kaarti	Eveleth Kaiku, Hibbing		1902 pass. (Boston)	W	P
Taipale	Victor	Kaarti	Eveleth, Hibbing, etc	1901 to MN	1900 to Worcester	Hibb, W	L P
Erkkilä	Walter		Fayal (Eveleth) Finnish Band	1906		IRHS	P
Forsman	John		Fayal (Eveleth) Finnish Band	1906		IRHS	P
Hämäla	Erik		Fayal (Eveleth) Finnish Band	1906		IRHS	P
Hauru	Matti		Fayal (Eveleth) Finnish Band	1906		IRHS	P
Hendrickson	Henry		Fayal (Eveleth) Finnish Band	1906		IRHS	P
Hytönen	Tykö		Fayal (Eveleth) Finnish Band	1906		IRHS	P
Mäkipaaso	August		Fayal (Eveleth) Finnish Band	1906		IRHS	P
Miettinen	August		Fayal (Eveleth) Finnish Band	1906		IRHS	P
Mikkilä	John		Fayal (Eveleth) Finnish Band	1906		IRHS	P
Parkkonen	Victor		Fayal (Eveleth) Finnish Band	1906		IRHS	P
Potti	August		Fayal (Eveleth) Finnish Band	1906		IRHS	P
Raski	Matti		Fayal (Eveleth) Finnish Band	1906		IRHS	P
Saari	Gust		Fayal (Eveleth) Finnish Band	1906		IRHS	P
Sholund	Hilding		Fayal (Eveleth) Finnish Band	1906		IRHS	P
Sivula	Matti		Fayal (Eveleth) Finnish Band	1906		IRHS	P
Topari	Erik		Fayal (Eveleth) Finnish Band	1906		IRHS	P
Yrjölä	Oscar		Fayal (Eveleth) Finnish Band	1906		IRHS	P

Last	First	Military	Minnesota	Info date	Immigration date	Source	L.P
Frankson	Helmer		Hibbing City Band		0	W	L,P
Haapasaari	John		Hibbing Finn Temperance Band	1895		W	L
Laitinen	Aapeli	Kuopio	Hibbing Finnish Workers Band		1906	W	P
Laitinen	Aapeli		Hibbing Finnish Workers Band			W	?
Rosendahl	Hugo		Hibbing Finnish Workers Band			W	P, L
Bay	Emil		Hibbing Finnish Workers' Band	1912		W	P
Blomberg	Paul		Hibbing Finnish Workers' Band	1912		W	P
Gröndahl	Edward		Hibbing Finnish Workers' Band	1912		W	P
Hermanson	Jeremias		Hibbing Finnish Workers' Band	1912		W	P
Hongel	Alfred		Hibbing Finnish Workers' Band				
Karhu	Adolph		Hibbing Finnish Workers' Band	1912		W	P
Laine	John		Hibbing Finnish Workers' Band	1912		W	L, P
Miettunen	Otto		Hibbing Finnish Workers' Band	1912		W	P
Mikkola	Victor		Hibbing Finnish Workers' Band	1912		W	P
Nurmi			Hibbing Finnish Workers' Band	1912		W	P
Nurmio			Hibbing Finnish Workers' Band	1905			L, P
Ruotsala			Hibbing Finnish Workers' Band	1912		W	P
Gröndahl	Edward		Hibbing Kaiku Band	1913		W	L, P
Murto	Toivo		Hibbing Kaiku Band			W	P
Rahko	Wilho		Hibbing Kaiku Band			W	p
Rajanen	John		Hibbing Kaiku Band			W	P
Rajanen	John		Hibbing Kaiku Band			W	P
Aho	Emil		Hibbing Tapio Temperance band	1913		W	L, P
Carlson	H		Hibbing Tapio Temperance band	1903		Hibb	P
Ekstrom	A		Hibbing Tapio Temperance band	1903		Hibb	P
Ekstrom	E		Hibbing Tapio Temperance band	1903		Hibb	P
Frantila	M		Hibbing Tapio Temperance band	1903		Hibb	P
Harris	W		Hibbing Tapio Temperance band	1903		Hibb	P
Karkkainen	S		Hibbing Tapio Temperance band	1903		Hibb	P
Kleffman	E		Hibbing Tapio Temperance band	1903		Hibb	P
Kontio	J		Hibbing Tapio Temperance band	1903		Hibb	P
Lundquist	C		Hibbing Tapio Temperance band	1903		Hibb	P
Martin	Geo		Hibbing Tapio Temperance band	1903		Hibb	P
Mattson	Alex		Hibbing Tapio Temperance band	1903	1911?	Hibb, W	P
Murto	Toivo		Hibbing Tapio Temperance band	1913		W	L, P
Newman	Al		Hibbing Tapio Temperance band	1903		Hibb	P
Ojala	O		Hibbing Tapio Temperance band	1903		Hibb	P
Perry	J		Hibbing Tapio Temperance band	1903		Hibb	P

Last	First	Military	Minnesota	Info date	Immigration date	Source	L.P
Rahko	Wilho		Hibbing Tapio Temperance band	1913		W	L, P
Rajanen	John		Hibbing Tapio Temperance band	1913		W	L, P
Salminen	C		Hibbing Tapio Temperance band	1903		Hibb	P
Smith	F		Hibbing Tapio Temperance band	1903		Hibb	P
Ahola	William		Hibbing Tapio Temperance band,	1903		Hibb	P
Gröndahl	Edward		Hibbing Tapio Temperance band,	1913		W	L, P
Ahola	William		Hibbing, Bassett bands		0	W	L P
De Petro	*B*		Nashwauk Town Band	1910		W	P
DePetro	*Raymond*		Nashwauk Town Band	1910		W	P
Kaminen	Charles		Nashwauk Town Band	1910		W	P
Kokko	George		Nashwauk Town Band	1910		W	P
Korhonen	David		Nashwauk Town Band	1910		W	P
Larro	*Peter*		Nashwauk Town Band	1910		W	P
Lilja	Hugo		Nashwauk Town Band	1910		W	P
Lindevall	Arvo		Nashwauk Town Band	1910		W	P
Lindevall	Elmer		Nashwauk Town Band	1910		W	P
Lindfors	Frank		Nashwauk Town Band	1910		W	P
Matara	Eero		Nashwauk Town Band	1910		W	P
Miettinen	August		Nashwauk Town Band	1910		W	L, P
Rakala	John		Nashwauk Town Band	1910		W	P
Saccoman	Louis		Nashwauk Town Band	1910		W	P
Sulonen	Charles		Nashwauk Town Band	1910		W	P
Toivola	John		Nashwauk Town Band	1910		W	P
Varonen	Hemming		Nashwauk Town Band	1910		W	P
Matara	Eero		Rice River			W	L
Koivunen	Alex		Soudan Temperance Band	1889?		W	L
Westerinen	Pekka		Soudan Temperance Band	1888	0	W	L
Nordquist	Toivo		Sturgeon-Alango Band-		0	W	L P
Wilenius	John		Sturgeon-Alango Band-		1904? unsure	W	L P
Haapasaari	John		Virginia Finn Temperance Band	1895		W	L
Forsman	John		Virginia Finnish Workers Band	1910		W	P
Hetlin	Yrjö		Virginia Finnish Workers Band	1910		W	P
Jalkanen	Julius		Virginia Finnish Workers Band	1910		W	P
Koski	Mikko		Virginia Finnish Workers Band	1910		W	P
Löyvä	Sulo		Virginia Finnish Workers Band	1910		W	P
Lundström	Hjalmar		Virginia Finnish Workers Band	1910		W	P
Mäki	William		Virginia Finnish Workers Band	1910		W	P
Nykänen	John		Virginia Finnish Workers Band	1910		W, L	P

Last	First	Military	Minnesota	Info date	Immigration date	Source	L.P
Pakarinen	Tuomas		Virginia Finnish Workers Band	1910		W	P
Sarell	Konstu		Virginia Finnish Workers Band	1910		W	P
Tasti	Alfred		Virginia Finnish Workers Band	1910		W	P
Tiikkainen	Antti		Virginia Finnish Workers Band	1910	Passport 1901	W	L, P
Tiikkainen	Antti		Virginia Valon Tuote Band		Passport 1901	W	L, P
Hietala	***Frank***		***Virginia?***			***MDN?***	***P***

Appendix C:
Index of Finnish-American Bands in Minnesota

Community	Name	Affiliation	Conductor(s)	Dates/ Notes
Aurora	Aurora Band		Miettinen/Matti Niemi/Jalmar Laupiainen/ Isaac Walma/Antti Viitanen.	1910
Biwabik	Biwabik School Band	public school	Victor Taipale	1902
Chisholm	unknown	Temperance	Helmer Hermanson/ Miettunen/ Kalle Kleemola/ Victor Taipale	1904?
Hibbing	unknown		Matthew Walter Lehtinen	letter from daughter
Chisholm	unknown	Socialist	Kalle Kleemola/Victor Taipale/Alex Koivunen/Hemming Hautala, Roy Järneström (2nd generation)	St. Louis County Rural Band Association?
Crosby	Ahti	Independent	Eero Matara	?
St Louis County	School bands		Royal Järneström (2nd generation), Hemming Hautala	
Crosby	"Independent"	Independent	Matara	After 1917
Cromwell	Eagle Lake Band		Aho, John Paananen	
Duluth	SSO Osasto			Photo 1913
Duluth	Nuija Youth Society	Nuorisoseura	Kalle Holpainen/ Louhi/ Kellosalmi/ Beckman/ Yrjölä	1905
Duluth	DSS	Socialist	Frank Lindroos (1913–18)	(1913–18)
Ely	Sampo	Temperance	Kalle Kleemola, Emil Bjorkman	Wiljamaa letter
Ely	Not sure; some indication Ely had two Finnish bands	Socialist? rehearsed in hall	Oskar Castren/ Miettunen/ Farihoff/ Erkki Laitala/Jack Castren/ Kalle Kleemola/ Liimatainen/ Pyylampi	1890
Eveleth	Kaiku	Temperance	Alex Koivunen/Herman Lindberg/ Filemon Jacobson	1895
Eveleth	Fayal	Temperance	Victor Taipale, Emil Ikola	1901?
Hibbing	Kaiku	Temperance (Tapio)	Alex Mattson/Oscar Castren/William Ahola/Hemming Hautala	photo 1913
Nashwauk	City Band		August Miettinen	Photo 1914
Nashwauk	School band		Victor Taipale	
Hibbing	Lake Superior Cornet Band	Temperance (Tapio)	Victor Taipale (1901)	Became town band
Hibbing	Workers Club Band	Socialist	Ed Grondahl	Photo 1912
Moose Lake	Raju Athletic Club Band	Vellamo Society		
Nashwauk	Town Band		John Colander/August Miettinen/Victor Taipale	Photo 1912
Soudan	Finnish Band	Temperance	Oscar Castren, Alex Koivunen	1887 newspaper
Virginia	Workers Band	Socialist		Photo 1910
Virginia	Temperance Band, Valon Tuote	Temperance	John Haapasaari, Antti Tiikkainen (1920-30)	1895
Virginia	Yrinä	Independent/ Socialist		Photo 1910

Appendix D: Index of Newspaper Articles

This compilation of newspaper citations comes from those English- and Finnish- language newspapers in which reports on Northern Minnesota Finnish cultural activity have been found. The index is organized as follows:

Column 1: Newspaper and date/page (where possible). The Finnish paper Työmies (TM) was published from several locations in its history. The cities are noted in each citation.

Column 2: Brief summary of article subject.

Column 3: Minnesota community about which the article reports (abbreviations are Au=Aurora, Biw=Biwabik, V=Virginia, H=Hibbing, Ch=Chisholm, C=Cloquet, E=Ely, Ev=Eveleth, Gil=Gilbert, NYM=New York Mills, Sou=Soudan, Tow=Tower, N=Nashwauk, K=Keewatin, D=Duluth).

Column 4: Language (E=English, F=Finnish).

Column 5: Chronology code (year, month, day).

The index is organized chronologically, from the earliest to latest

Date/Source	Item	Loc	F/E	Date code
TM 6/11/1890 (Ishpeming)	"Toivontahti" Temperance Society hosts benefit Iltamat	Ch	F	1890/06/11
Ely Times 1/2/1891	New Year's Eve Play at Temperance Hall; dance after: Ely Cornet Band	E	E	1891/01/02
Ely Times 1/23/1891:5	Mattila Hall (and Cigars) ad	E	E	1891/01/23
Ely IRON HOME 6/30/ + 7/7/1891	Finnish American societies in full Uniform for July 4 (advertisement)	E	E	1891/06/30
Ely IRON HOME 9/15/1891	The Scandinavian procession through Ely including 150 from Tower (Ely Finn Band)	E	E	1891/09/15
Ely Times 12/24/1891:11	Finnish Activities in Ely (includes band)	E	E	1891/12/24

VA Enterprise, 12/7/1894:4	Iron Range train schedule	V	E	1894/12/07
VA Enterprise. 3/29/1895:1	Finnish Singing Society "Leivo" to give a concert at Crockett's opera	V	E	1895/03/29
Virginian. 5/2/1895:8	Finnish Hall is rapidly nearing completion (Temperance)	V	E	1895/05/02
Va Enterprise. 5/3/1895:1,4	Finnish Temperance Hall completed	V	E	1895/05/03
Hibbing Sentinel 6/22/1895	Tapio Temperance hall discussed	H	E	1895/06/22
Ely Miner 7/19/1895:1	Dedicated Finn temp Hall PROGRAM Finn Band	E	E	1895/07/12
Ely Miner 7/12/1895:1	Finn Band will play at new Hall	E	E	1895/07/19
Ely Miner, 7/21/1895:1	Finnish Temp band played in Austrian Catholic Picnic and Procession	E	E	1895/07/21
Ely Miner 7/24/1895	New Finnish Opera House dedicated (Temperance hall)	E	E	1895/07/24
Ely Miner, 7/31/1895	National Finnish Temperance Convention/ parade in Tower/ speeches at Temp Opera House	E	E	1895/07/31
Ely Times 8/2/1895 1+5	Finn Picnic /Finn Hall	E	E	1895/08/02
Ely Miner 8/ 14/1895	Ely Finnish temperance Band will visit Virginia on Aug 24 – will perform there	V	E	1895/08/14
Ely Miner 8/21/1895:5	Soudan Finnish Band directed by Oscar Castren (Ely)	E	E	1895/08/21
Ely Miner, 8/21/1895:5	Soudan Finnish Band organized by Prof. Oscar Castren of Ely, members' names, etc. (20)	Sou	E	1895/08/21
Va Enterprise, 09/20/1895	Mountain Iron Brass Band plays Finn dance at Crockett's Opera House	V	E	1895/09/20
Va Enterprise, 09/27/1895	Finnish Temperance Band grand ball at Crockett's Opera House	V	E	1895/09/27
Ely Miner, 10/2/1895:5	Virginia Finn Temp. band organized by Prof Oscar Castren of Ely (Ely Temp Band played in Virginia in streets, at Finn temperance Hall, dance at Crockett's Opera House)	V	E	1895/10/02
Va Enterprise, 10/18 1895	Finnish Temperance Band dance at Crockett's Opera House	V	E	1895/10/18
Va Enterprise, 11/01/1895 p1	"Finnish Temperance Band received their new instruments"	V	E	1895/11/01
Va Enterprise. 11/29/1895	Finnish couple gets married at Temperance hall, 25 pc Finnish temp band entertained (dance)	V	E	1895/11/29
Virginian. 12/26/1895:5	Temperance Entertainment at Finlander's (TEMPERANCE) Hall	V	E	1895/12/26
UK (NYM,MN) , 1/7/1896:5	Soudan Finnish organizations, Band, sewing circle	Sou	F	1896/01/07
Ely Miner, 2/12/1896	Wedding at Finn temperance hall (dancing afterwards, Finnish band played)	E	E	1896/02/12

Virginian. 4/2/1896:8	Regular Tuesday temperance meeting	V	E	1896/04/02
Virginian, 5/21/1896:8	Virginia Temperance Band get new uniforms	V	E	1896/05/21
Va Enterprise, 05/22/1896	Finnish temperance band received elegant new uniforms, and six fine new instruments	V	E	1896/05/22
UK (NYM) 6/4/1896 :2	Temperance hall, church, dance (Duluth)	D	F	1896/06/04
Va Enterprise, 06/19/1896	Finn band of Virginia—28 members—came to Biwabik and gave a dance at the Edna.	Biw	E	1896/06/19
Va Enterprise 7/1/1896:1	July 4th Parade; Finnish Temperance Band, Virginia City Band, Franklin band	V	E	1896/07/01
Ely Times 7/8/1896:5	Finnish Temperance hall (ad)	E	E	1896/07/08
Ely Times 7/8/1896:5	Annual Ely-Soudan Temperance Picnic at Sandy Point	E	E	1896/07/08
Virginian, 7/9/1896:1	Finnish Temperance Band in July 4th Parade	V	E	1896/07/09
Ely Times. 7/ 17, 1896:1	Temperance society Picnic	E	E	1896/07/17
Virginian, 7/30/1896:8	Virginia Temperance Society has meeting	V	E	1896/07/30
UK (NYM,MN , 8/27/1896:2	Soudan Finnish Temperance Society, Church, Band	Sou	F	1896/08/27
Virginian, 10/15/1896:1	Senator Knude Nelson met at RR station by Finnish Temperance Band	V	E	1896/10/15
Ely Miner, 1/27/1897	Public School in Ely-History (opened in 1895)	E	E	1897/01/27
Hibbing Sentinel -2/ 6 1897-	John Haapasaari-leader of first Hibbing band (from "Hibbing has its first band")	H	E	1897/02/06
Vermillion Iron Journal, Tower, 5/13/1897	O Castrén left Soudan to direct two Finnish bands in Ely, also includes notice from Marquette Mining Journal that Sound's band had recruited Alex Koivunen (from Negaunee MI) as the new director.	Sou	E	1897/05/13
Ely Miner 5/26/1897:5	Finn Temperance band to play at baseball games all summer	E	E	1897/05/26
Ely Miner 8/25/1897	"Mattila Hall" open for dancing and parties	E	E	1897/08/25
Virginia Enterprise 8/29/1897:1	New Finnish temperance society founded in Hibbing (Totuunen Etsia)	H	E	1897/8/29
Ely Miner 5/6,1898:5	Finn temp Society and its Hall announce program	E	E	1898/05/06
Ely Miner 6/29,1898:1	July 4 program: Tug of war: Austrians vs Finns (mention of music, too)	E	E	1898/06/29
Virginian 7/1/1898	July 4th Parade; Finnish Temperance Band and Virginia City Band	V	E	1898/07/01
Virginia Enterprise 7/1/1898:4	July 4th Parade; Finnish Temperance Band and Virginia City Band	V	E	1898/07/01
Ely Miner 7/5/1899: 1	Report on Ely July 4th celebrations	E	E	1899/07/05
Va Enterprise 7/ 27,1900:7	Your "Men of the City" sponsor dance at Finnish Hall tonight (Va City Orchestra)	V	E	1900/07/27
Ely Miner 12/28/1900	Mattila hall has a new hardwood floor	E	E	1900/12/28

Ely Miner 1/31/1902:8	Finnish Glee Club gives concert	E	E	1902/01/31
Am Suometar 2/19/1902:5	Ely Kaiku concert	E	F	1902/02/19
Ely Miner 4/25/1902:1	Finnish Singing Society of Ely at the temperance Opera House	E	E	1902/04/25
Ely Miner 6/6/1902:1	Everybody invited to Finn Temperance Picnic at Sandy Point	E	E	1902/06/06
Ely Miner 6/13/02:1	Finn Picnic at Sandy Point (Finns get bad press)	E	E	1902/06/13
Ely Miner 6/13/1902:1	Finn Temperance Picnic at Sandy Point report (parade, non Finns present)	E	E	1902/06/13
Amer Suometar 6/18/02:5	Finn Picnic at Sandy Point	E	F	1902/06/18
AmSuom. (H.Mi) 6/25/1902:5	Soudan Minn Temperance Society has own Hall	Sou	F	1902/06/25
Ely Miner 6/27/1902	Soudan Finnish Temperance Hall Dedicated	Sou	E	1902/06/27
Ely Miner 7/4/1902:4	Ely School Commencement held at Finnish Temperance Hall	E	E	1902/07/04
Ely Miner 6/16/05:5	Finns will celebrate (printed program)	E	E	1905/06/16
Ely Miner 6/30/05:1	Finnish celebration (Parades, bands, speeches, choirs)	E	E	1905/06/30
AmKaiku (Duluth) 7/30/07:8	Kaleva Ritarit/Naiset "Kenttajuhla" Aug 4th, Ely orchestra and "Ahti"	?	F	1907/07/30
HDT, 2/20/1908:1	Meeting of Finnish temperance and socialists in Tapio Hall	H	E	1908/02/20
Päivälehti (D Mn) 6/26/1908:27	1200 Finns at Juhannus	?	F	1908/06/26
Hibbing DT 6/2/1910:1	4th of July activities in Hibbing (Finns take a leading part)	H	E	1910/06/02
HibbingDT 7/25/1910:4	Ishpeming Finnish Band Grand Concert Sampo Hall Hibbing (program) 7/27 (also 7/29)	H	E	1910/07/25
HibbingDT 7/29/1910:4	Ishpeming Finnish Band Grand Concert "one of the best to visit range"	H	E	1910/07/29
HDT 3/11/1911:1	Mass meeting of temperance (Finns and others) in Tapio Hall	H	E	1911/03/11
Hibbing Daily Trib 6/2/11	Chisholm Finn Hall dedicated (largest on range)	Ch	E	1911/06/02
Siirtolainen 6/18/1912:7	Invitation to Juhannus	?	F	1912/06/18

Siirtolainen 7/30/1912:7	Laulujuhlat—Finnish Song Festival	?	F	1912/07/30
Siirtolainen 8/16/1912:1	Laulujuhlat—Finnish Song Festival	?	F	1912/08/16
Am Suometar 7/10/1913:7	Finnish Summer festival at Gilbert	Gil	F	1913/07/10
Am Suometar 7/10/1913:7	N Minn Finnish Festivities	?	F	1913/07/10
TM 10/11/13 :2 (Marquette)	Lauantai-iltana on tanssit, sosialistihaalilla, osaston soittokunta soittolla. Katsokaa lähemmin paikallisia ilmoituksia (Aurora, MN)	Au	F	1913/10/11
Työmies (H, Mn) 1/7/1914:3	Joulujuhla in Keewatin Socialist Hall	Kew	F	1914/01/07
Päivälehti 3/31/1914 pp	Hibbing Finnish History (several pages)	H	F	1914/03/31
Päivälehti (D, Mn) 6/25/1914	Virginia Socialist Opera ad	V	F	1914/06/25
DNT 7/27-31 1914	Duluth to Host Finnish Festival (several articles)	D	E	1914/07/31

BIBLIOGRAPHY

Detailed contact information about the most useful research sites used for this study are listed here. Much of the research material is not in general circulation; some of the items in this bibliography have therefore been coded with the following abbreviations that indicate where they may be found.

Abbreviation	Location
EW	Ely-Winton Historical Society, Vermilion Community College, 1900 E Camp St., Ely, MN 55731-1918, -, phone (218) 365-3226
F	Finnish-American Heritage Center and Historical Archives; Finlandia University, 601 Quincy St., Hancock, MI 49930 USA phone: 906-487-7302 Web page: www.finlandia.edu/fahc.html
HEL	Helsinki University Library, -The National Library of Finland, POB 15, Unioninkatu 36, Helsinki FI 00014, Phone (011)-358-9-191-23196 Web site: www.lib.helsinki.fi/english/
IHRC	Immigration History Research Center, University of Minnesota: 311 Elmer Anderson Library, 222-21st Avenue S. Minneapolis MN 55455-0439 Phone: (612) 625-4800, Fax:(612) 626-0018. Web page: http://www1.umn.edu/ihrc/
IRHC	Iron Range Historical Society, 19 South Broadway, P. O. Box 786, Gilbert, Minnesota 55741-0786. Phone (218) 749-3150, Web page; http//www.homestead.com/gilbertmn/files/ IronRangeHistorical Society.html
IRRC	Iron Range Research Center, Chisholm, MN: Ironworld, 801 SW Hwy. 169, Suite 1 Chisholm, MN 55719 phone 218-254-7965. Web page
MHC	Minnesota Historical Center, St. Paul: 345 Kellogg Blvd. West, St. Paul, Minnesota 55102-1906, Phone: 651-296-6126 or 1-800-657-3773; web page http://www.mnhs.org
NEMHC	Northeast Minnesota Historical Center, University of Minnesota- Duluth Library, Annex 202, 10 University Drive, Duluth, Minnesota 55812-2495,

Phone: (218) 726-8526;
Web page: mnhs.org d.umn.edu/lib/collections/nemn.html

P The author's personal library and archives.
<niemisto@stolaf.edu>

Sources

Aaltio, E. A. *Minnesotan suomalaisia* (Minnesota Finns). Vammala, I953- IHRC.

Alanen, Arnold. "The Locations: Company Communities in Minnesota's Iron Ranges."

Minnesota History, 48 (1982).

———. "Changes on the Iron Range." *Minnesota: A Century of Change: The State and its People Since 1900.* St. Paul: Minnesota Historical Society Press, 1989.

———. A Field Guide to Architecture and Landscapes of Northern Minnesota. Madison, WI: the author, 2000.

Airut, I. *Sibelius Seuran Julkaisu* (Sibelius Club Publication). Duluth: Sibelius Seura, 1917. IHRC, F.

Amerikan Albuumi. "Brooklyn: Kustantaja Suomalainen Kansaillis-kirjakauppa" ("Brooklyn: Pictures of Finnish-American Life"). *Kuvia Amerikan suomalaisten* asuinpaikoil*ta*, 1904. F, IHRC.

Anderson, Philip J., Dag Blanck and Peter Kivisto, eds. *Scandinavian immigrants and education in North America.* Chicago: Swedish-American Historical Society, 1995.

Beckman, Irja. *Echoes from the Past.* New York Mills, MN: Parta Printers, 1979.

Berman, Hyman. "Education for work and labor solidarity: the immigrant miners and radicalism on the Mesabi Range." Immigration History Research Center, University of Minnesota, 1963. IHRC.

Brownell, Lee, *Pioneer Life in Ely*: (Pictures collected by Lee Brownell, Marjorie Barton, ed.). Ely, MN: the authors, 1981. IRHC , EW.

Bryant, Carolyn. *And the Band Played On 1776-1976*. Washington, D.C.: Smithsonian Institution Press, 1975.

Burke, Peter. *Eyewitnessing: The Uses of Images as Historical Evidence*, Ithaca, NY: Cornell University Press, 2001.

Chambers, Clarke A. "Social Welfare Policies and Programs on the Minnesota Iron Range––1880–1930." Immigration History Research Center, University of Minnesota, 1963. IHRC.

Ciment, James, ed. *Encyclopedia of American Immigration*. Armonk, NY: M.E. Sharpe, 2000.

Clark Clifford E., Jr., ed., *Minnesota in a Century of Change: The State and its People since 1900.* St. Paul: Minnesota Historical Society Press, 1989.

Cuyuna Range, A History of a Minnesota Iron Mining District, prepared by theMinnesota Historical records survey project. Division of Professional and Service Projects, Work Projects Administration, Saint Paul, 1940.

DePaulis, Donald V. "Iron Range im[m]igrants and their music." Manuscript, Minnesota Historical Society, 1976.

Edwards, Elizabeth, ed. *Anthropology and Photography 1860–1920.* Yale University Press in association with the Royal Anthropological Institute, London, 1992.

Fransman, Holger. "Special Finland: Die Tradition der Blasmusiken (the Septet)" (in French, English and German), *Brass Bulletin* 53 (1986), 49–51.

Fritsch-Ripley, Karen. *Unlocking the Secrets in Old Photographs*, Salt Lake City: Ancestry, 1991.

Fry , A Ruth; *The Life of Emily Hobhouse.* London: J. Cape,1929.

Greene, Victor. *Passion for Polka: Old-Time Ethnic Music in America.* Berkeley: University of California Press, 1992.

Gronow, Pekka. "Ethnic Recordings–An Introduction." *Ethnic Recordings in America:A Neglected Heritage.* Washington, D.C.: Library of Congress, 1972.

———. *Studies in Scandinavian-American Discography I and II.* Helsinki: Suomen Äänitearkisto (Finnish Institute of Recorded Sound), 1977.

Hannikainen, Paivi Liisa. "Pommerista Pohjanmaalle—Saksalaissotilassoittaja ja urkurit suomessa 1700 Jualipuiskolla" (From Pomerania to Ostrobothnia—German Military Bandsmen and Organists in Finland in the 18th Century). *Tabulatura* (Sibelius Academy Church Music Department Journal) (1995), 62–78.

Hazen, Margaret and Robert. *The Music Men–An Illustrated History of Brass Bands in America.* Washington, Smithsonian Press, 1987.

Hillilä, Ruth Esther and Barbara Hong. *Biographical Encyclopedia of Finnish Music and Musicians.* Westport: Greenwood Press, 1998.

Hakala, Joyce E. *Memento of Finland: A Musical Legacy*. St. Paul: Pikebone Music, 1997.

Hannula, Reino. *An Album of Finnish Halls.* Van Hazinga, Toini Perko Laakso and Amy Wartiainen, eds. San Luis Obispo: Finn Heritage, 1991.

Heyde, Herbert. *Das Ventilblasinstrument* (The Brass Instrument), Leipzig: 1987.

History of the Sixty Years of Valontuote Temperance Society. Virginia, MN: 1953. IRRC.

Hodges, Leroy. "Report [on] the Vermilion and Mesabi iron ore ranges of

Northern Minnesota concerning immigrant life and institutions." Typescript. Special Agent, United States Immigration Commission, 1909.

Hoglund, William. "Union List of Finnish Newspapers Published by Finns in the United States and Canada 1876–1985," 1985. F, IHRC.

———. Finnish Immigrants in America 1880–1920. Salem, NH: Ayer Co., 1992. Holmio, Armas. *History of Finns in Michigan.* trans. Ellen M. Ryynänen. Detroit: Wayne State University Press, 2001.

———. *Michiganin suomalaisten historia.* Hancock, MI: Finnish-American Historical Society, 1967. F, IHRC.

Holmquist, June Drenning, ed. *They Chose Minnesota: A Survey of the State's Ethnic Groups.* St. Paul: Minnesota Historical Society Press, 1981.

Ilmonen, Salomon. *American suomalaisten historiaa.* Hancock, MI: 1919. F, IHRC.

———. *The History of Finnish-Americans–Volume III*: "The Finnish Settlements in United States and Canada,", trans. Timothy Laitala Vincent. Salt Lake City, UT: Family Sleuths, 1926, *R* 1998.

Jalkanen, Pekka: *Alaska, Bombay, ja Billy Boy Jazz kulturin murros Helsingissä 1920– luvulla* ("The rise of jazz music culture in Helsinki"). Helsinki: Jyväskylän yliopiston musiikkitieteen laitos, 1980.

Johnson, Judy. A Selected Bibliography of Primary and Secondary Sources about the Finnish Experience on the Iron Range. Chisholm, MN: Iron Range Research Center 11989. IRRC.

Jokinen, Walfrid. "The Finns in the United States, a Sociological Interpretation." Ph.D. diss., Louisiana State University, 1955. IHRC

Kanerva, Simo. Special Finland: ein kurzer Blick auf die gesichichte der finnische Blechblasmusik (in French, English, and German). Brass Bulletin 53 (1986), 52–55.

Karjalainen, Kauko. *The Brass Septet Tradition in Finland* (in French, English and German). *Brass Bulletin* 21 (1978).

———. Special Finland: Brass Achieves Respectability (in French, English, and German). Brass Bulletin 53 (1986), 36–38.

———. Suomalainen Torviseitsikko–Historia ja perinteen jatkuminen (The Finnish Brass Septet—History and Living Tradition). Tampere, Finland: Tampere University Press, 1995.

———. "The Brass Band Tradition in Finland." *Historic Brass Society Journal* 9 (1997). Kaups, Matti, Michael Karni and Douglas J. Ollila, Jr., eds. "The Finns in the Copper and Iron Ore Mines of the Western Great Lakes Region, 1864–1905: Some Preliminary Observations," *The Finnish Experience in the Great Lakes Region: New Perspectives.* Turku: Institute for Migration, 1975.

Kero, Reino. Migration from Finland to North American in the Years Between the United States Civil War and the First World War. Vammala: Vammalan Kirjapaino Oy, 1974.

——— Old Friends, Strong Ties: The Finnish Contribution to the Growth of the U.S.A. Turku: Institute of Migration, 1976.

Kivisto, Peter. *Pre-emigration Factors Contributing to the Development of Finnish- American Socialism*. New York Mills, MN: Finnish Americana Series, Parta Press Vol. 5, 1984.

Klinge, Matti. *A Brief History of Finland.* 10th ed. Helsinki: Otava Publishers, 1994.

Kolehmainen, John. "Finland's Agrarian Structure and Overseas Migration." *Agricultural History* 15 (1941). 44–48.

———. "Finnish Immigrants and a 'Frii Kontri." *Social Science* 22 (1947), 15–18.

———. "Finnish Temperance Societies in Minnesota." *Minnesota History*, 22 (1941), 391–403.

———. "Harmony Island: A Finnish Utopian Venture in British Columbia." *The British Columbia Historical Quarterly* 5 (1941).

———. *Sow the Golden Seed*. Fitchburg, 1955. F

———. Suomalaisten siirtolaisuus Norjasta Amerikaan. Fitchburg: 1946. F.

——— .The Finnish Immigrant." *Common Ground* 4 (1943), 105–6.

———. The Finns in America. A Bibliographical Guide to Their History. Hancock, 1947. F, IHRC.

———. "The Inimitable Marxists: The Finnish Immigrant Socialists," *Michigan* History 36 (1952), 395–405.

———. "Why We Came to America: The Finns." *Common Ground* 5 (1944), 77–79.

——— and George W Hill. Haven in the Woods: The Story of the Finns in Wisconsin. Madison, 1951

Koski, Ernest. "Tune of the First Festival." *Fifty Years of Progressive Cooperation, 1929–1979*. Superior, WI: Työmies Society, 1979. IHRC

Kurkela, Vesa, and Riitta Valkeila. Taistojen tiellä soiteltiin- ja soiton tahdin tanssittiin (History of the worker's band of the town of Varkaus). Jyväskylä: Harmonikka instituuti, 1983.

Laitinen, Kari. "Harmoniemusik in Finland: On Military Music in 18th Century Savo," *Balticum–A Coherent Musical Landscape in the 16th and 18th Centuries. Studia Musicologica* (1994), 104–116.

Lampi, Leona. At the Foot of the Beartooth Mountains: A History of the Finnish Communities of Red Lodge Montana. Coeur d'Alene, ID: Bookage Press, 1998. Landis, Paul H. Three Iron Mining Towns: A Study in Cultural

Change. Ann Arbor: Arno Press, 1938.

Lass, William E. *Minnesota: A Bicentennial History*. New York: Norton, 1977.

Ljungmark, Lars. *For Sale–Minnesota: Organized Promotion of Scandinavian Immigration, 1866–1873*. Chicago: Swedish Pioneer Historical Society, 1971.

Luntinen, Pertti. *The Imperial Russian Army and Navy in Finland 1808–1918.* Helsinki: Finnish Historical Society, 1997.

Malm, Paul. "The role of the Range Junior Colleges in the Acculturation of the Immigrant 1916–1941." Ph.D. diss., University of Minnesota, 1991.

Minnetti, Carlo and Vernon Malone. *The Golden Age of Music in Virginia, Minnesota*. Bloomington, MN: the authors, 1987.

Niemistö, Paul. "A Brief History of the Finnish Brass Septet." *Historic Brass Society Newsletter* 10 (1997), 13-16.

———. "Finland's Brass Band repertoire in the Autonomous Era." Kongressberichte Bad Waltersdorf / Steiermark 2000 Lana / Südtirol 2002. Alta Musica 24 (2003), 75-96.

———. "Finnish Brass Bands in Northern Minnesota," Kongressberichte Bad Waltersdorf / Steiermark 2000 Lana / Südtirol 2002. Alta Musica 24 (2003), 415-428.

———. "Music and Music Education in Finland" *Gopher Music Notes*, 52/3 (1996).

Nikander, Werner, ed. *Amerikan Suomalaisia* (Finnish-American Biographical Dictionary). Hancock MI: Finnish Lutheran Book Concern, 1927. F, P

O'Neill, Mary Daniel. "A Survey of and Interpretation of Slovenian Slovenian Folk Culture on the Minnesota Iron Range." MA thesis, University of Minnesota, 1952. MHS, IRRC

Pakkala, Alaine. "The Instrumental Music of the Finnish-American Community in the Great Lakes Region, 1880–1930." MA thesis, University of Michigan, 1982. IHRC

———. "The Finnish-American Bandsman." *Suomen Silta* 4 (1985).

Palonen Osmo. *Aspects of musical life and music education in Finland.* Helsinki: Sibelius Academy Education Series 8 (1993).

Polk, R. L. *Range Towns' Directory*. Duluth: R.L. Polk Company, published annually. NEMHC, IRHC

Porfir'yeva, A.L., and A. A Stepanov. *Musical St.Petersburg, a Musical-Encyclopedic Dictionary* St. Petersburg, 1998.

Puotinen, Arthur Edwin. *Finnish Radicals and Religion in Midwestern Mining Towns, 1865–1914*. New York: Arno Press, 1979.

Putnam, Robert D. Bowling Alone: The Collapse and Revival of American Community. New York: Simon and Schuster, 2000.

Rauanheimo, Akseli Järnefelt. *Suomalaiset Amerikassa* (*The Finns in America*). Helsinki: Otava, 1899.

Reed, David F. "Victor Ewald and the Russian Chamber Brass School (Viktor Vladimirovich eval'd Viktor 1860–1935). PhD diss., University of Rochester, 1979.

Ross, Carl. *The Finn Factor in American Labor, Culture and Society*. New York Mills, MN: Parta Printers, 1977.

Salmela, Chad. "The Ethnic Festival's Role in Finnish Ethnic Identity among Minnesota's Iron Range Finnish-Americans, 1999." Manuscript. IRRC

Salmenhaara, Erkki and Dahlstrom, Fabian. *Suomen Musiikki Historia* (*History of Finnish Music*) 4 vols. Helsinki: Werner Söderström, 1996.

Schulzenberge, Anthony C. "Life on the Vermilion Range before 1900." Typewritten manuscript, Minnesota History Center, 1963. MHC

Screen, J.E.O. *The Finnish Army 1881–1901 Training the Rifle Battalions*. Helsinki: Finnish Historical Society, 1996.

Sell, Vernon. "Musical Aptitude of Finnish Students: An Investigative Study in Comparative Music Education." PhD diss., University of Wisconsin, 1976.

Slobin, Mark. *Subcultural Sounds–Micromusics of the West*. Hanover: Wesleyan University Press, 1993.

———. "Icons of Ethnicity-Pictorial Themes in Commercial Euro-American Music." *Imago Musicae*, Bärenreiter, Basel, Switzerland, 1988.

Smeds ,Kerstin and Timo Mäkinen. *Kaiu Kaiu, lauluni*. Keuruu: Otava Publishing, 1984.

Smith, Timothy Lawrence. "Educational Beginnings, 1884-1910." Ms., Immigration History Research Center, University of Minnesota, 1963. IHRC

———. "Factors Affecting the Social Development of Iron Range Communities." Ms., Immigration History Research Center, University of Minnesota, 1963. IHRC

———. "Immigrant Social Aspirations and American Education, 1880–1930." Ms., University of Pennsylvania, 1969; Immigration History Research Center, University of Minnesota. IHRC

———. "School and Community: The Quest for Equal Opportunity, 1910–1921." Ms., Immigration History Research Center, University of Minnesota, 1963. IHRC

———. "The Progressive Movement Education, 1880–1900," *Harvard Educational Review*. Spring, 1961.

Swanson, Kenneth A. "Music of Two Finnish-Apostolic Lutheran Groups in Minnesota: The Heidemanians and the Pollarites." Thesis, University of Minnesota, 1971. IHRC, MHC

Syrjämäki, John. "Mesabi Communities—A Study in Their Development." PhD diss., Yale University, 1940. IHRC, IRRC, NEMHC

Talvio, Paavo. Kenttämusiikkia varuskuntasoittokuntiin (A History of Finnish Military Music). Helsinki: Topograffikunnan Kirjapaino, 1980.

Tiede, Clayton. "The Development of Minnesota Community Bands during the Nineteenth Century." PhD diss., University of Minnesota, 1970.

Tokoi, Oskari. *Sisu: The Autobiography of the First Premier of Finland.* New York: Robert Speller and Sons, 1957.

Vainio, Matti. *Music Education As a Part of Aesthetic Education in Finland and England.* London: University of London Institute of Education, 1981.

Van Cleef, Eugene. *The Finn in America.* Duluth, MN: Finnish Daily, 1918. MHC

Van Winkle, Mary Louise. "Education and Ethnicity in the1930's in a Minnesota Mining Community." PhD diss., Harvard University, 1982.

Vehmas, Jukka. Sytyttätvät Sävelet (Inspiring Tunes)–A Survey of Brass Bands in Laitila Parish Before World War II (English summary). Turku: University of Turku Folk Institute 11, 1983.

Virtamo, Keijo, ed. Otavan Musiikiktietosanakirja AÖ (Otava's Music Encyclopedia A- Z) Helsinki, 1987.

Walker, David Allan. *Iron Frontier: The Discovery and Early Development of Minnesota's Three Ranges.* St. Paul: Minnesota Historical Society Press, 1979.

Virtaranta, Pertti. *Amerikansuomalainen sanakirja (A Dictionary of American Finnish).*Turku: Institute of Migration, 1992.

Wasastjerna, Hans R., ed. "History of the Finns in Minnesota." trans. Toivo Rosvall.

Minnesotan suomalaisten historia. Duluth MN: Finnish-American Historical Society, 1959.

Waterhouse, William. The New Langwill Index: A Dictionary of Musical Wind Instrument Makers and Inventors. London: Tony Bingham, 1993.

Westerholm, Simo. "Suomalainen Seitsikko (The Finnish Brass Septet)." *Uusi Kansanmusiikki (New Folk Music).* Kaustinenä: Folk Music Institute, May, 1995 and June, 1995.

Who's Who Among Finnish-Americans. Fitchburg MA, Raivaaja Publishing, 1949.

Iron Range Community and Anniversary Books

Arranged alphabetically, by community:

Aurora

Diamond Jubilee Historical Souvenir Booklet. Aurora, MN: Diamond Jubilee, 1978.

IRRC

Engelhardt, Fred. *Survey Report. Aurora:* Aurora Public Schools, 1927. MHS

Automba

Reed, Daniel. *A Study of a Finnish Timber Boomtown*. Kettle River, MN: Automba Publications, 1990.

Biwabik

Coombe, Catherine, ed. *Diamond Jubilee—Historical Souvenir Booklet*. 1967. IRRC

Beckman, Irja. *Echoes from the Past* (About Bassett and Brimson). New York Mills, MN: Parta Printers, 1979.

Brimson

Brimson-Toimi Legacy Committee. *Brimson-Toimi Legac.*, Mountain Iron, MN: Glensco, 1995. IRRC

Buhl

Hecimovich, Steve. *Buhl—A Town is Born–Historical and Pictorial Review of Buhl*.

Buhl, MN. IRRC

Chisholm

Chisholm Minnesota: Presented to the state's fire departments by the people of the greatest, richest and most hospitable village of the great Mesaba Range. Duluth, MN: Christie Lithograph and Printing Co., 1915.

Cromwell

Beck, Bennett A. *Brief History of the Pioneers of the Cromwell, Minnesota Area*. 2nd ed.

Cloquet, MN: Carlton County Historical Society, 2001.

Ely

Ely since 1888. Centennial book. Ely, MN: Ely Echo, IRRC

Ely–Centennial Roaring Stoney Days–70th Anniversary Celebration, 1958. Ely, MN: Ely- Winton Historical Society. IRRC

Somrock, John A. *History of Incredible Ely*. Ely, MN: Cyko Art Printers, 1976.

Embarrass

Norha, Eino M., Vera Parin and Esther Norha. *History of Embarrass Township*. Minn

Historical Society: Toivo Waisanen, 1980.

Eveleth

Eveleth- A Century of Fame 1882-1992. Souvenir Booklet 1992. IRRC

More, Margaret E. *History of Eveleth, Minnesota*. Eveleth: News-Clarion, 1947. IRRC

History and Destiny of Eveleth : Its Inception and Evolution. Eveleth, MN: Eveleth Commercial Club, 1921. IRRC

Finland, (MN)

Tikkanen, Bonnie, Michelle Duhant and Suzan From. *How we Remember: Stories and Recollections of Finland, Minnesota's First Century, 1895–1995*. Finland, MN: Finland Historical Society, 1995.

Keeping our Heritage: Finland, Minnesota, 1895-1976. Finland Schools Reunion Committee, 1976, IRHC

Hay Creek

Banttari, Marlene and Marjorie Krohnfeldt. *The History of Hay Creek District 219, 1889–1958: Dedicated to the Parents, Students, and Teachers*. 1996. MHS

Hibbing

Higgins, Allen W. *Hibbing Minnesota 1893-1968–Diamond Jubilee Days Anniversary Booklet* (August 1968). IRRC

Fumia, Sylvester Michael. "A Brief History of Hibbing." IRRC manuscript, 1970. IRRC

DeMillo, Lorraine and Barbara E. Simons. *A Photo Essay of an Iron Mining Community, Seen Through the Eye of a Turn-of-the-Century Camera*. Hibbing, MN: Gilbert.

Maki, Heather-Jo, *Hibbing, Minnesota (Images of America)*. Charleston, SC: Arcadia Publishing, 2001.

Hibbing, Minnesota: On the Move Since 1893. Hibbing, MN: Hibbing Booklet Committee, 1991. IRRC

Iron Ore Capital, Hibbing, Minnesota: Here Is the Story of an Unusual Community that Grew from a Mining Camp to a Modern Metropolis. Hibbing, MN: Hibbing Bureau of Information, 1951. IRRC

Keewatin

Keewatin–From Pines to Pellets Keewatin 1906–1981, Diamond Jubilee. Northprint Co., 1981. IRRC

Manni, Edwin E. *Kettle River, Automba, Kalevala, and Surrounding Area History*. Also includes 1918 forest fire stories. 1978. IRHS

———.comp. *Kettle River, etc. History and Stories* (includes Cromwell–Eagle Lake). 1978. IRRC

Meadowlands

Palmer, Charles Victor. *The Immigrants*. Oklahoma City, OK: 1997. IRHC

Mountain Iron

Mountain Iron All-Class Reunion, 1915-1980: July 24, 25, 26, 1981. Mountain Iron, MN: 1981. MHS

Mountain Iron Golden Jubilee. *Historical Booklet of the Mesabi Iron Range, 1890–1940*. Virginia, MN: W. A. Fisher Co., 1940. IRRC

Messiah Lutheran Church (ELCA), Mountain Iron, Minnesota, 1894–1994. Centennial edition. Mountain Iron, MN: Messiah Lutheran Church, 1994.

Poropudas, Belinda, ed. *Mesaba Range Co-operative Park Association, 50 Years of Progressive Co-operation, 1929-1979*. Superior, WI: Tyomies Society, 1979.

Nashwauk

Nashwauk Seventy-Fifth Anniversary Committee. *Nashwauk—From Timber to Taconite*. Nashwauk, MN: Eastern Itascan, 1978. IRRC

New York Mills

Parta, Russell O. *New York Mills: 75 Years of Progress, 1884–1959*. New York Mills, MN: Northwestern Pub. Co., 1959.

Onnela

Koidahl, Ilona and Gertrude Bollrud. *Onnela, A Finnish Community, 1900–1950*. MHS, 1990.

Palo

Byrd, Mae S. *Iron Range Legacy: Recollections of a Homesteader in Palo, Minnesota*. Gilbert, MN: Iron Range Historical Society, 1982.

Mulari, Mary Koski. *Of Palo and Pot Lake: The Story of the Matti Perämäki Family*. 1982. IRHC

Sturgeon Lake

Nordlund, Sylvia, ed. *Sturgeon Reunion and Dedication 1907–1985*. 1985. IRRC

Toivola

Saralampi, Sorvari. *Echoing Footsteps*. Toivola: Little Swan, 1987.

Lee, Russell. *St. Louis County, MN Portraits and Places in and near Winton, Ely, Tower, Soudan*. Washington, D.C.: The Farm Security Administration, 1937. MHS

Virginia

Ellis, Charles E. *Iron Ranges of Minnesota Historical Souvenir of the Virginia Enterprise Virginia*. Virginia, MN: W.E. Hannaford, 1909. MHS, IRRC, NMHC

Turner, Ann Warren and Anna E. Laine. *The Story of Virginia Co-operative Society through 30 Years of Progress, 1909–1939*. Virginia, MN: Co-operative Print Association, 1980. VHS

Waasa Township and Argo Township

Eilola, Patricia. *A Finntown of the Heart*, (Saint Louis County, MN) St. Cloud, MN: North Star Press, 1998.

Murphy, Alice Niemi and Scott Murphy. *Se Tie: The Road.* Babbitt Weekly News, 1981.

Finnish Summary

Kornetteja & hakkuja tarkastelee vaskiyhtyeiden roolia suomalaisten siirtolaisten kulttuurielämässä Amerikassa. Maahanmuuton yleiskuvauksen lisäksi se keskittyy "Rautarenssi" (Iron Range) -alueeseen Pohjois-Minnesotassa lähellä Kanadan rajaa, jonne tuhansia suomalaisia siirtolaisia saapui töihin 1800-luvun lopulla nopeasti kasvaneiden rautakaivostoiminnan ja puutavarateollisuuden houkuttelemina. Suomalaiset toivat mukanaan kulttuuriperinteitään, uskontonsa, politiikan ja musiikin. Vaskiyhtyeet olivat uusi populaarimusiikin muoto Suomessa 1880-luvulla, ja ne tulivat maahanmuuttajien myötä Minnesotaan. Monissa tapauksissa suomalaiset vaskikokoonpanot olivat ensimmäisiä yhtyeitä Iron Range -yhteisöissä, ja niistä tuli kunnallisten ja kouluorkestereiden perusta.

Kirja kattaa vaskitradition syntyhetket Suomessa, sen saapumisen Minnesotaan ja muuttumisen osaksi paikallista (koulu)musiikkielämää. Lisäksi käsitellään myös vaskiaktiviteettia yhteiskunnallisesti, ohjelmistot, harjoituskäytänteet ja kapellimestarien elämänkertoja unohtamatta suomalaisten orkestereiden suhdetta sosialismiin ja raittiusliikkeeseen.

Maahanmuuttajien mukana oli aina pelimanneja ja kansanlaulajia, mutta todellinen kipinä amerikansuomalaiseen musiikkiin tuli 1890-luvun lopulla, kun Amerikkaan saapui huomattava määrä koulutettuja muusikoita: Bobrikovin kaudella lakkautettujen sotilassoittokuntien entisiä jäseniä. Näillä nuorilla miehillä oli utopistisia odotuksia uuden mantereen suhteen. He olivat kuulleet legendoja siitä, kuinka tässä maassa helppoa oli rikastua. He uskoivat, että tarvitsisi vain hankkia soittimet, aloittaa uusia orkestereita ja saada näin palkattua työtä. Heiltä vain unohtui silloinen amerikkalainen puhallinmusiikkimaku. Monet musikaaliset nuoret miehet pettyivätkin rikastumistoiveissaan ja vaihtoivat alaa. Jotkut, kuten Miettunen ja Taipale, olivat päättäväisiä ja pitivät kiinni unelmastaan.

Nämä entiset sotilasmuusikot olettivat perustavansa ja johtavansa paikallista orkesteria, vaikka heillä ei välttämättä edes ollut kokemusta kapellimestarin työstä. Harrastajaorkesterin saattaminen esiintymiskuntoon vaati paljon sekä kapellimestarilta että soittajilta. Tavallisesti piti aloittaa nuotinluvun opettamisesta, mutta usein päättäväisyyttä löytyi ja sinnikkäästi harjoiteltiin iltaisin ja sunnuntaisin, kun oli vapaata töistä. Toimintaa vaikeutti epävakaa taloudellinen tilanne, jonka takia työläiset joutuivat muuttamaan paljon. Ilmosen mukaan esimerkiksi "ohiolaisella Conneautin orkesterilla oli 30 toimintavuotensa aikana 20 eri johtajaa, ja soittajat vaihtuivat konsertista toiseen. Puhallinmusiikki edelsi yleensä muita musiikkityylejä, koska se oli suosittua myös Amerikassa ja suomalaisissa siirtolaisyhteisöissä oli niin vähän naisia, että oli hyvin vaikeaa perustaa vaikkapa sekakuoroja.

Muutos tuli kuitenkin nopeasti, ja kuorojen määrä lisääntyi. Palm on selittänyt tätä kehitystä: ”Epäilemättä suomalaiset ovat laulava kansa - jopa suomalaisessa tarustossa sankarit voittivat laulamalla eikä miekalla. Laulutraditio, sekä muut kansalliset perinteet tulivat siirtolaisten mukana ja luultavasti yhtään suomalaisten kokousta ei pidetty ilman laulua."

Vanhan maahanmuuttajaperinteen haihtuessa ei myöskään amerikansuomalainen vaskitraditio 1800- ja 1900-lukujen vaihteesta ole sellaisenaan voinut säilyä, vaikka sitä yrittävätkin ylläpitää uudet kokoonpanot kuten kirjoittajan johtama Ameriikan Poijat -vaskiseitsikko.

Translated by Jukka Viitasaari

The Author:

Paul Niemisto grew up in the Upper Peninsula Finnish farm town of Pelkie, Michigan, and graduated form Baraga High School. He received undergraduate and graduate degrees in music from the University of Michigan, and later a doctorate from the University of Minnesota, studying the material that is presented in this book.

From 1971 to 1978 he taught public school music in the Eastern Canadian province of Nova Scotia, where he also played with the CBC Halifax Orchestra. He joined music faculty at St. Olaf College in Northfield, Minnesota, in 1978, where he continues to teach today. At St. Olaf he is a wind band conductor, and teaches low brass instruments. He plays and teaches trombone and tuba, and especially the euphonium in Finnish brass music.

In 1979 he founded the Cannon Valley Regional Orchestra, which he still conducts. In 1990 he founded Boys of America (*Ameriikan Poijat*) a Finnish style brass septet made of American musicians, some with Finnish roots.

Niemisto has been interested in the history of wind music since his first summer trips to Finland in the early 1980's. The unique brass history of Finland fueled his many years of work, a Fulbright Research Grant in 1999, an American Scandinavian Foundation research grant, and a doctorate. He is an authority on Finnish brass and military band music, both from the origins and among the American immigrants, and has written some of the only published material in English on the subject. He received the Finnish Military Bands White Cross medal for outstanding service to Finnish military musical research and performance.

These interests also took him into the spheres of international research societies, where he shared his research. In 2006 he spearheaded the Inter- national Wind Music History Conference and the Vintage Band Music Festival held in Northfield, Minnesota. The VBF was repeated in 2010, and is happening again in August 2013. He and his harpist wife have three children, variously occupied as a reading specialist in the New Brunswick (Canada) public schools, curriculum director for Pete Seeger's "Clearwater" Hudson River environmental ship, and a media coordinator for Minnesota's public policy think tank "Minnesota 2020".

INDEX

I

R

S